Python: Practical Programming

Python: Practical Programming

Cooper Webb

STATES
ACADEMIC PRESS
www.statesacademicpress.com

Published by States Academic Press,
109 South 5th Street,
Brooklyn, NY 11249, USA

ISBN: 978-1-63989-454-3

Cataloging-in-Publication Data

Python : practical programming / Cooper Webb.
p. cm.
Includes bibliographical references and index.
ISBN 978-1-63989-454-3
1. Python (Computer program language). 2. Scripting languages (Computer science).
3. Computer programming. I. Webb, Cooper.
QA76.73.P98 P98 2022
005.133--dc23

For information on all States Academic Press publications
visit our website at www.statesacademicpress.com

Contents

Preface

Python is a general purpose high level language which focuses on code readability with its use of significant indentation. Python is an interpreted and multi-paradigm language. It fully supports structured programming, object oriented programming, functional programming and aspect-oriented programming. Due to its comprehensive standard library, it is often referred to as 'batteries included' language. For memory management, python uses dynamic typing and a combination of cycle detecting garbage collector and reference counting. It also offers support for functional programming in lisp tradition. Python is highly extensible. Due to its compact modularity, it has become popular as a means of adding programmable interfaces to existing applications. It also provides a simple and less cluttered syntax making it easy for beginners to understand. This book outlines the processes and applications of python programming in detail. It includes some of the vital pieces of work being conducted across the world, on various topics related to python programming. This book is a vital tool for all researching or studying python programming as it gives incredible insights into emerging trends and concepts.

The researches compiled throughout the book are authentic and of high quality, combining several disciplines and from very diverse regions from around the world. Drawing on the contributions of many researchers from diverse countries, the book's objective is to provide the readers with the latest achievements in the area of research. This book will surely be a source of knowledge to all interested and researching the field.

In the end, I would like to express my deep sense of gratitude to all the authors for meeting the set deadlines in completing and submitting their research chapters. I would also like to thank the publisher for the support offered to us throughout the course of the book. Finally, I extend my sincere thanks to my family for being a constant source of inspiration and encouragement.

Cooper Webb

1

Fundamentals of Python Program

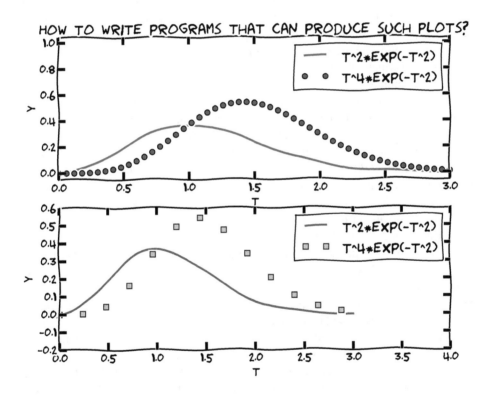

1.1 What Is a Program? And What Is Programming?

Today, most people are experienced with computer programs, typically programs such as Word, Excel, PowerPoint, Internet Explorer, and Photoshop. The interaction with such programs is usually quite simple and intuitive: you click on buttons, pull down menus and select operations, drag visual elements into locations, and so forth. The possible operations you can do in these programs can be combined in seemingly an infinite number of ways, only limited by your creativity and imagination.

Nevertheless, programs often make us frustrated when they cannot do what we wish. One typical situation might be the following. Say you have some measurements from a device, and the data are stored in a file with a specific format. You may want to analyze these data in Excel and make some graphics out of it. How-ever, assume there is no menu in Excel that allows you to import data in this specific format. Excel can work with many different data formats, but not this one. You start searching for alternatives to Excel that can do the same *and* read this type of data files. Maybe you cannot find any ready-made program directly applicable. You have reached the point where knowing how to write programs on your own would be of great help to you! With some programming skills, you may write your own little program which can translate one data format to another. With that little piece of tailored code, your data may be read and analyzed, perhaps in Excel, or perhaps by a new program tailored to the computations that the measurement data demand.

The real power of computers can only be utilized if you can program them. By programming you can get the computer to do (most often!) exactly what you want. Programming consists of writing a set of instructions in a very specialized language that has adopted words and expressions from English. Such languages are known as *programming* or *computer languages*. The set of instructions is given to a program which can translate the meaning of the instructions into real actions inside the computer.

The purpose of this book is to teach you to write such instructions dedicated to solve mathematical and engineering problems by fundamental numerical methods.

There are numerous computer languages for different purposes. Within the en-gineering area, the most widely used computer languages are Python, MATLAB, Octave, Fortran, C, C++, and to some extent Maple, and Mathematica. How you write the instructions (i.e. the *syntax*) differs between the languages. Let us use an analogy.

Assume you are an international kind of person, having friends abroad in Eng-land, Russia and China. They want to try your favorite cake. What can you do? Well, you may write down the recipe in those three languages and send them over. Now, if you have been able to think correctly when writing down the recipe, and you have written the explanations according to the rules in each language, each of your friends will produce the same cake. Your recipe is the "computer program", while English, Russian and Chinese represent the "computer languages" with their own rules of how to write things. The end product, though, is still the same cake. Note that you may unintentionally introduce errors in your "recipe". Depending on the error, this may cause "baking execution" to stop, or perhaps produce the wrong cake. In your computer program, the errors you introduce are called bugs (yes, small insects! ... for historical reasons), and the process of fixing them is called debugging. When you try to run your program that contains errors, you usually get warnings or error messages. However, the response you get depends on the er-ror and the programming language. You may even get no response, but simply the wrong "cake". Note that the rules of a programming language have to be followed very strictly. This differs from languages like English etc., where the meaning might be understood even with spelling errors and "slang" included.

This book comes in two versions, one that is based on Python, and one based on Matlab. Both Python and Matlab represent excellent programming environments for scientific and engineering tasks. The version you are reading now, is the Python version.

Some of Python's strong properties deserve mention here: Many global func-tions can be placed in only *one* file, functions are straightforwardly transferred as arguments to other functions, there is good support for interfacing C, C++ and Fortran code (i.e., a Python program may use code written in other languages), and functions explicitly written for scalar input often work fine (without modification) also with vector input. Another important thing, is that Python is available for *free*. It can be downloaded from the Internet and will run on most platforms.

Readers who want to expand their scientific programming skills beyond the introductory level of the present exposition, are encouraged to study the book *A Primer on Scientific Programming with Python* [13]. This comprehensive book is as suitable for beginners as for professional programmers, and teaches the art of programming through a huge collection of dedicated examples. This book is considered the primary reference, and a natural extension, of the programming matters in the present book.

Some computer science terms

Note that, quite often, the terms *script* and *scripting* are used as synonyms for program and programming, respectively.

The inventor of the Perl programming language, Larry Wall, tried to explain the difference between script and program in a humorous way (from perl.com[1]): *Suppose you went back to Ada Lovelace[2] and asked her the difference between a script and a program. She'd probably look at you funny, then say something like: Well, a script is what you give the actors, but a program is what you give the audience. That Ada was one sharp lady ... Since her time, we seem to have gotten a bit more confused about what we mean when we say scripting. It confuses even me, and I'm supposed to be one of the experts.*

There are many other widely used computer science terms to pick up. Writing a program (or script or code) is often expressed as *implementing* the program. *Executing* a program means running the program. An *algorithm* is a recipe for how to construct a program. A *bug* is an error in a program, and the art of tracking down and removing bugs is called *debugging*. *Simulating* or *simulation* refers to using a program to mimic processes in the real world, often through solving differential equations that govern the physics of the processes.

1.2 A Python Program with Variables

Our first example regards programming a mathematical model that predicts the position of a ball thrown up in the air. From Newton's 2nd law, and by assuming negligible air resistance, one can derive a mathematical model that predicts the vertical position y of the ball at time t. From the model one gets the formula

$$y = v_0 t - 0.5gt^2,$$

where v_0 is the initial upwards velocity and g is the acceleration of gravity, for which $9.81 \, \text{ms}^{-2}$ is a reasonable value (even if it depends on things like location on the earth). With this formula at hand, and when v_0 is known, you may plug in a value for time and get out the corresponding height.

---

[1] http://www.perl.com/pub/2007/12/06/soto-11.html
[2] http://en.wikipedia.org/wiki/Ada_Lovelace

1.2.1   The Program

Let us next look at a Python program for evaluating this simple formula. Assume the program is contained as text in a file named `ball.py`. The text looks as follows (file `ball.py`):

```
# Program for computing the height of a ball in vertical motion

v0 = 5              # Initial velocity
g = 9.81            # Acceleration of gravity
t = 0.6             # Time

y = v0*t - 0.5*g*t**2      # Vertical position

print y
```

Computer programs and parts of programs are typeset with a blue background in this book. A slightly darker top and bottom bar, as above, indicates that the code is a complete program that can be run as it stands. Without the bars, the code is just a *snippet* and will (normally) need additional lines to run properly.

1.2.2   Dissection of the Program

A computer program is plain text, as here in the file `ball.py`, which contains instructions to the computer. Humans can read the code and understand what the program is capable of doing, but the program itself does not trigger any actions on a computer before another program, the Python interpreter, reads the program text and translates this text into specific actions.

You must learn to play the role of a computer

Although Python is responsible for reading and understanding your program, it is of fundamental importance that you fully understand the program yourself. You have to know the implication of every instruction in the program and be able to figure out the consequences of the instructions. In other words, you must be able to play the role of a computer. The reason for this strong demand of knowledge is that errors unavoidably, and quite often, will be committed in the program text, and to track down these errors, you have to simulate what the computer does with the program. Next, we shall explain all the text in `ball.py` in full detail.

When you run your program in Python, it will interpret the text in your file line by line, from the top, reading each line from left to right. The first line it reads is

```
# Program for computing the height of a ball in vertical motion.
```

This line is what we call a *comment*. That is, the line is not meant for Python to read and execute, but rather for a human that reads the code and tries to understand what is going on. Therefore, one rule in Python says that whenever Python encounters the sign # it takes the rest of the line as a comment. Python then simply skips reading the rest of the line and jumps to the next line. In the code, you see several such comments and probably realize that they make it easier for you to understand (or guess) what is meant with the code. In simple cases, comments are probably not much needed, but will soon be justified as the level of complexity steps up.

The next line read by Python is

```
v0 = 5  # Initial velocity
```

In Python, a statement like v0 = 5 is known as an *assignment* statement (very different from a mathematical equation!). The result on the right-hand side, here the integer 5, becomes an *object* and the variable name on the left-hand side is a named reference for that object. Whenever we write v0, Python will replace it by an integer with value 5. Doing v1 = v0 creates a new name, v1, for the same integer object with value 5 and not a copy of an integer object with value 5. The next two lines

```
g = 9.81  # Acceleration of gravity
t = 0.6   # Time
```

are of the same kind, so having read them too, Python knows of three variables (v0, g, t) and their values. These variables are then used by Python when it reads the next line, the actual "formula",

```
y = v0*t - 0.5*g*t**2      # Vertical position
```

Again, according to its rules, Python interprets * as multiplication, - as minus and ** as exponent (let us also add here that, not surprisingly, + and / would have been understood as addition and division, if such signs had been present in the expression). Having read the line, Python performs the mathematics on the right-hand side, and then assigns the result (in this case the number 1.2342) to the variable name y. Finally, Python reads

```
print y
```

This makes Python print the value of y out in that window on the screen where you started the program. When ball.py is run, the number 1.2342 appears on the screen.

In the code above, you see several blank lines too. These are simply skipped by Python and you may use as many as you want to make a nice and readable layout of the code.

1.2.3 Why Not Just Use a Pocket Calculator?

Certainly, finding the answer as done by the program above could easily have been done with a pocket calculator. No objections to that and no programming would have been needed. However, what if you would like to have the position of the ball for every milli-second of the flight? All that punching on the calculator would have taken you something like four hours! If you know how to program, however, you could modify the code above slightly, using a minute or two of writing, and easily get all the positions computed in one go within a second. A much stronger argument, however, is that mathematical models from real life are often complicated and comprehensive. The pocket calculator cannot cope with such problems, even not the programmable ones, because their computational power and their programming tools are far too weak compared to what a real computer can offer.

1.2.4   Why You Must Use a Text Editor to Write Programs

When Python interprets some code in a file, it is concerned with every character in the file, exactly as it was typed in. This makes it troublesome to write the code into a file with word processors like, e.g., Microsoft Word, since such a program will insert extra characters, invisible to us, with information on how to format the text (e.g., the font size and type). Such extra information is necessary for the text to be nicely formatted for the human eye. Python, however, will be much annoyed by the extra characters in the file inserted by a word processor. Therefore, it is fundamental that you write your program in a *text editor* where what you type on the keyboard is *exactly* the characters that appear in the file and that Python will later read. There are many text editors around. Some are stand-alone programs like Emacs, Vim, Gedit, Notepad++, and TextWrangler. Others are integrated in graphical development environments for Python, such as Spyder. This book will primarily refer to Spyder and its text editor.

1.2.5   Installation of Python

You will need access to Python and several add-on packages for doing mathematical computations and display graphics. An obvious choice is to install a Python environment for scientific computing on your machine. Alternatively, you can use cloud services for running Python, or you can remote login on a computer system at a school or university. Available and recommended techniques for getting access to Python and the needed packages are documented in Appendix A.

The quickest way to get started with a Python installation for this book on your Windows, Mac, or Linux computer, is to install Anaconda[3].

1.2.6   Write and Run Your First Program

Reading *only* does not teach you computer programming: you have to program yourself and practice heavily before you master mathematical problem solving via programming. Therefore, it is crucial at this stage that you write and run a Python program. We just went through the program `ball.py` above, so let us next write and run that code.

---

[3] http://continuum.io/downloads

But first a warning: there are many things that must come together in the right way for `ball.py` to run correctly on your computer. There might be problems with your Python installation, with your writing of the program (it is very easy to introduce errors!), or with the location of the file, just to mention some of the most common difficulties for beginners. Fortunately, such problems are solvable, and if you do not understand how to fix the problem, ask somebody. Typically, once you are beyond these common start-up problems, you can move on to learn programming and how programs can do a lot of otherwise complicated mathematics for you.

We describe the first steps using the Spyder graphical user interface (GUI), but you can equally well use a standard text editor for writing the program and a terminal window (*Terminal* on Mac, *Power Shell* on Windows) for running the program. Start up Spyder and type in each line of the program `ball.py` shown earlier. Then run the program. More detailed descriptions of operating Spyder are found in Appendix A.3.

If you have had the necessary luck to get everything right, you should now get the number 1.2342 out in the rightmost lower window in the Spyder GUI. If so, congratulations! You have just executed your first self-written computer program in Python, and you are ready to go on studying this book! You may like to save the program before moving on (`File, save as`).

1.3   A Python Program with a Library Function

Imagine you stand on a distance, say 10 m away, watching someone throwing a ball upwards. A straight line from you to the ball will then make an angle with the horizontal that increases and decreases as the ball goes up and down. Let us consider the ball at a particular moment in time, at which it has a height of 10 m.

What is the angle of the line then? Again, this could easily be done with a calculator, but we continue to address gentle mathematical problems when learning to program. Before thinking of writing a program, one should always formulate the *algorithm*, i.e., the recipe for what kind of calculations that must be performed. Here, if the ball is x m away and y m up in the air, it makes an angle θ with the ground, where $\tan \theta = y/x$. The angle is then $\tan^{-1}(y/x)$.

Let us make a Python program for doing these calculations. We introduce names x and y for the position data x and y, and the descriptive name `angle` for the angle θ. The program is stored in a file `ball_angle_first_try.py`:

```
x = 10            # Horizontal position
y = 10            # Vertical position

angle = atan(y/x)

print (angle/pi)*180
```

Before we turn our attention to the running of this program, let us take a look at one new thing in the code. The line `angle = atan(y/x)`, illustrates how the *function* `atan`, corresponding to $\tan^{-1}$ in mathematics, is *called* with the ratio y/x as *input parameter* or *argument*. The atan function takes one argument, and the computed value is *returned* from atan. This means that where we see atan(y/x), a computation is performed ($\tan^{-1}(y/x)$) and the result "replaces" the text atan(y/x). This is actually no more magic than if we had written just y/x: then the computation of y/x would take place, and the result of that division would replace the text y/x. Thereafter, the result is assigned to the name angle on the left-hand side of =.

Note that the trigonometric functions, such as atan, work with angles in radians. The return value of atan must hence be converted to degrees, and that is why we perform the computation (angle/pi)*180. Two things happen in the print statement: first, the computation of (angle/pi)*180 is performed, resulting in a real number, and second, print prints that real number. Again, we may think that the arithmetic expression is replaced by its results and then print starts working with that result.

If we next execute ball_angle_first_try.py, we get an error message on the screen saying

```
NameError: name 'atan' is not defined
WARNING: Failure executing file: <ball_angle_first_try.py>
```

We have definitely run into trouble, but why? We are told that

```
name 'atan' is not defined
```

so apparently Python does not recognize this part of the code as anything familiar. On a pocket calculator the inverse tangent function is straightforward to use in a similar way as we have written in the code. In Python, however, this function has not yet been *imported* into the program. A lot of functionality is available to us in a program, but much more functionality exists in Python *libraries*, and to activate this functionality, we must explicitly import it. In Python, the atan function is grouped together with many other mathematical functions in the library called math. Such a library is referred to as a *module* in correct Python language. To get access to atan in our program we have to write

```
from math import atan
```

Inserting this statement at the top of the program and rerunning it, leads to a new problem: pi is not defined. The variable pi, representing π, is also available in the math module, but it has to be imported too:

```
from math import atan, pi
```

It is tedious if you need quite some math functions and variables in your program, e.g., also sin, cos, log, exp, and so on. A quick way of importing everything in math at once, is

```
from math import *
```

We will often use this import statement and then get access to all common mathematical functions. This latter statement is inserted in a program named `ball_angle.py`:

```
from math import *

x = 10              # Horizontal position
y = 10              # Vertical position

angle = atan(y/x)

print (angle/pi)*180
```

This program runs perfectly and produces 45.0 as output, as it should.

At first, it may seem cumbersome to have code in libraries, since you have to know which library to import to get the desired functionality. Having everything available anytime would be convenient, but this also means that you fill up the memory of your program with a lot of information that you rather would use for computations on big data. Python has so many libraries with so much functionality that one simply needs to import what is needed in a specific program.

1.4   A Python Program with Vectorization and Plotting

We return to the problem where a ball is thrown up in the air and we have a formula for the vertical position y of the ball. Say we are interested in y at every millisecond for the first second of the flight. This requires repeating the calculation of $y = v_0 t - 0.5gt^2$ one thousand times.

We will also draw a graph of y versus t for $t \in [0, 1]$. Drawing such graphs on a computer essentially means drawing straight lines between points on the curve, so we need many points to make the visual impression of a smooth curve. With one thousand points, as we aim to compute here, the curve looks indeed very smooth.

In Python, the calculations and the visualization of the curve may be done with the program `ball_plot.py`, reading

```
from numpy import linspace
import matplotlib.pyplot as plt

v0 = 5
g = 9.81
t = linspace(0, 1, 1001)

y = v0*t - 0.5*g*t**2

plt.plot(t, y)
plt.xlabel('t (s)')
plt.ylabel('y (m)')
plt.show()
```

This program produces a plot of the vertical position with time, as seen in Figure 1.1. As you notice, the code lines from the `ball.py` program in Chapter 1.2 have not changed much, but the height is now computed and plotted for a thousand points in time!

Let us take a look at the differences between the new program and our previous program. From the top, the first difference we notice are the lines

```
from numpy import *
from matplotlib.pyplot import *
```

You see the word `import` here, so you understand that numpy must be a library, or module in Python terminology. This library contains a lot of very useful functionality for mathematical computing, while the `matplotlib.pyplot` module contains functionality for plotting curves. The above import statement constitutes a quick way of populating your program with all necessary functionality for mathematical computing and plotting. However, we actually make use of only a few functions in the present program: `linspace`, `plot`, `xlabel`, and `ylabel`. Many computer scientists will therefore argue that we should explicitly import what we need and not everything (the star *):

```
from numpy import linspace
from matplotlib.pyplot import plot, xlabel, ylabel
```

Others will claim that we should do a slightly different import and prefix library functions by the library name:

```
import numpy as np
import matplotlib.pyplot as plt
...
t = np.linspace(0, 1, 1001)
...
plt.plot(t, y)
plt.xlabel('t (s)')
plt.ylabel('y (m)')
```

We will use all three techniques, and since all of them are in so widespread use, you should be familiar with them too. However, for the most part in this book we shall do

```
from numpy import *
from matplotlib.pyplot import *
```

for convenience and for making Python programs that look very similar to their Matlab counterparts.

The function `linspace` takes 3 parameters, and is generally called as

```
linspace(start, stop, n)
```

This is our first example of a Python function that takes multiple arguments. The `linspace` function generates n equally spaced coordinates, starting with `start`

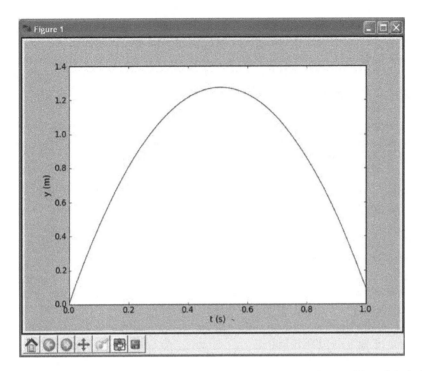

Fig. 1.1 Plot generated by the script `ball_plot.py` showing the vertical position of the ball at a thousand points in time

and ending with `stop`. The expression `linspace(0, 1, 1001)` creates 1001 co-ordinates between 0 and 1 (including both 0 and 1). The mathematically inclined reader will notice that 1001 coordinates correspond to 1000 equal-sized intervals in $[0, 1]$ and that the coordinates are then given by $t_i = i/1000$ ($i = 0, 1, \ldots, 1000$).

The value returned from `linspace` (being stored in `t`) is an *array*, i.e., a collection of numbers. When we start computing with this collection of numbers in the arithmetic expression `v0*t - 0.5*g*t**2`, the expression is calculated for every number in `t` (i.e., every t_i for $i = 0, 1, \ldots, 1000$), yielding a similar collection of 1001 numbers in the result `y`. That is, `y` is also an array.

This technique of computing all numbers "in one chunk" is referred to as *vectorization*. When it can be used, it is very handy, since both the amount of code and computation time is reduced compared to writing a corresponding `for` or `while` loop (Chapter 2) for doing the same thing.

The plotting commands are simple:

1. `plot(t, y)` means plotting all the y coordinates versus all the t coordinates
2. `xlabel('t (s)')` places the text t (s) on the *x* axis
3. `ylabel('y (m)')` places the text y (m) on the *y* axis

At this stage, you are strongly encouraged to do Exercise 1.4. It builds on the example above, but is much simpler both with respect to the mathematics and the amount of numbers involved.

1.5   More Basic Concepts

So far we have seen a few basic examples on how to apply Python programming to solve mathematical problems. Before we can go on with other and more realistic examples, we need to briefly treat some topics that will be frequently required in later chapters. These topics include computer science concepts like variables, objects, error messages, and warnings; more numerical concepts like rounding errors, arithmetic operator precedence, and integer division; in addition to more Python functionality when working with arrays, plotting, and printing.

1.5.1   Using Python Interactively

Python can also be used interactively. That is, we do not first write a program in a file and execute it, but we give statements and expressions to what is known as a Python *shell*. We recommend to use IPython as shell (because it is superior to alternative Python shells). With Spyder, Ipython is available at startup, appearing as the lower right window. Following the IPython prompt In [1]: (a *prompt* means a "ready sign", i.e. the program allows you to enter a command, and different programs often have different looking prompts), you may do calculations:

```
In  [1]: 2+2
Out [1]: 4

In  [2]: 2*3
Out [2]: 6

In  [3]: 10/2
Out [3]: 5

In  [4]: 2**3
Out [4]: 8
```

The response from IPython is preceded by Out [q]:, where q equals p when the response is to input "number" p.

Note that, as in a program, you may have to use import before using pi or functions like sin, cos, etc. That is, at the prompt, do the command from math import * before you use pi or sin, etc. Importing other modules than math may be relevant, depending on what your aim is with the computations.

You may also define variables and use formulas interactively as

```
In [1]: v0 = 5

In [2]: g = 9.81

In [3]: t = 0.6

In [4]: y = v0*t - 0.5*g*t**2

In [5]: print y
------> print(y)
1.2342
```

Sometimes you would like to repeat a command you have given earlier, or perhaps give a command that is almost the same as an earlier one. Then you can use the up-arrow key. Pressing this one time gives you the previous command, pressing two times gives you the command before that, and so on. With the down-arrow key you can go forward again. When you have the relevant command at the prompt, you may edit it before pressing enter (which lets Python read it and take action).

1.5.2   Arithmetics, Parentheses and Rounding Errors

When the arithmetic operators +, -, *, / and ** appear in an expression, Python gives them a certain precedence. Python interprets the expression from left to right, taking one term (part of expression between two successive + or -) at a time. Within each term, ** is done before * and /. Consider the expression x = 1*5**2 + 10*3 - 1.0/4. There are three terms here and interpreting this, Python starts from the left. In the first term, 1*5**2, it first does 5**2 which equals 25. This is then multiplied by 1 to give 25 again. The second term is 10*3, i.e., 30. So the first two terms add up to 55. The last term gives 0.25, so the final result is 54.75 which becomes the value of x.

Note that parentheses are often very important to group parts of expressions together in the intended way. Let us say x = 4 and that you want to divide 1.0 by x + 1. We know the answer is 0.2, but the way we present the task to Python is critical, as shown by the following example.

```
In [1]: x = 4

In [2]: 1.0/x+1
Out [2]: 1.25

In [3]: 1.0/(x+1)
Out [3]: 0.20000000000000001
```

In the first try, we see that 1.0 is divided by x (i.e., 4), giving 0.25, which is then added to 1. Python did not understand that our complete denominator was x+1. In our second try, we used parentheses to "group" the denominator, and we got what we wanted. That is, *almost* what we wanted! Since most numbers can be represented only approximately on the computer, this gives rise to what is called *rounding* errors. We should have got 0.2 as our answer, but the inexact number representation gave a small error. Usually, such errors are so small compared to the other numbers of the calculation, that we do not need to bother with them. Still, keep it in mind, since you will encounter this issue from time to time. More details regarding number representations on a computer is given in Section 3.4.3.

1.5.3   Variables and Objects

Variables in Python will be of a certain *type*. If you have an integer, say you have written x = 2 in some Python program, then x becomes an integer variable, i.e., a variable of type *int*. Similarly, with the statement x = 2.0, x becomes a *float* variable (the word float is just computer language for a real number). In any case, Python thinks of x as an *object*, of type int or float. Another common type of variable is *str*, i.e. a string, needed when you want to store text. When Python interprets x = "This is a string", it stores the text (in between the quotes) in the variable x. This variable is then an object of type str. You may convert between variable types if it makes sense. If, e.g., x is an int object, writing y = float(x) will make y a floating point representation of x. Similarly, you may write int(x) to produce an int if x is originally of type float. Type conversion may also occur automatically, as shown just below.

Names of variables should be chosen so that they are descriptive. When computing a mathematical quantity that has some standard symbol, e.g. α, this should be reflected in the name by letting the word alpha be part of the name for the corresponding variable in the program. If you, e.g., have a variable for counting the number of sheep, then one appropriate name could be no_of_sheep. Such naming makes it much easier for a human to understand the written code. Variable names may also contain any digit from 0 to 9, or underscores, but can not start with a digit. Letters may be lower or upper case, which to Python is different. Note that certain names in Python are *reserved*, meaning that you can not use these as names for variables. Some examples are for, while, if, else, global, return and elif. If you accidentally use a reserved word as a variable name you get an error message.

We have seen that, e.g., x = 2 will assign the value 2 to the variable x. But how do we write it if we want to increase x by 4? We may write an assignment like x = x + 4, or (giving a faster computation) x += 4. Now Python interprets this as: take whatever value that is in x, add 4, and let the result become the new value of x. In other words, the *old* value of x is used on the right hand side of =, no matter how messy the expression might be, and the result becomes the new value of x. In a similar way, x -= 4 reduces the value of x by 4, x *= 4 multiplies x by 4, and x /= 4 divides x by 4, updating the value of x accordingly.

What if x = 2, i.e., an object of type int, and we add 4.0, i.e., a float? Then *automatic type conversion* takes place, and the new x will have the value 6.0, i.e., an object of type float as seen here,

```
In  [1]: x = 2

In  [2]: x = x + 4.0

In  [3]: x
Out [3]: 6.0
```

Note that Python programmers, and Python (in printouts), often write, e.g., 2. which by definition is the integer 2 represented as a float.

1.5.4 Integer Division

Another issue that is important to be aware of is *integer division*. Let us look at a small example, assuming we want to divide one by four.

```
In  [1]: 1/4
Out [1]: 0

In  [2]: 1.0/4
Out [2]: 0.25
```

We see two alternative ways of writing it, but only the last way of writing it gave the correct (i.e., expected) result! Why?

With Python version 2, the first alternative gives what is called *integer division*, i.e., all decimals in the answer are disregarded, so the result is rounded down to the nearest integer. To avoid it, we may introduce an explicit decimal point in either the numerator, the denominator, or in both. If you are new to programming, this is certainly strange behavior. However, you will find the same feature in many programming languages, not only Python, but actually all languages with significant inheritance from C. If your numerator or denominator is a variable, say you have 1/x, you may write 1/float(x) to be on safe grounds.

Python version 3 implements mathematical real number division by / and requires the operator // for integer division (// is also available in Python version 2). Although Python version 3 eliminates the problems with unintended integer division, it is important to know about integer division when doing computing in most other languages.

1.5.5 Formatting Text and Numbers

Results from scientific computations are often to be reported as a mixture of text and numbers. Usually, we want to control how numbers are formatted. For example, we may want to write 1/3 as 0.33 or 3.3333e-01 ($3.3333 \cdot 10^{-1}$). The print command is the key tool to write out text and numbers with full control of the formatting. The first argument to print is a string with a particular syntax to specify the formatting, the so-called *printf syntax*. (The peculiar name stems from the printf function in the programming language C where the syntax was first introduced.)

Suppose we have a real number 12.89643, an integer 42, and a text 'some message' that we want to write out in the following two alternative ways:

```
real=12.896, integer=42, string=some message
real=1.290e+01, integer=   42, string=some message
```

The real number is first written in *decimal notation* with three decimals, as 12.896, but afterwards in *scientific notation* as 1.290e+01. The integer is first written as compactly as possible, while on the second line, 42 is formatted in a text field of width equal to five characters.

The following program, formatted_print.py, applies the printf syntax to control the formatting displayed above:

```
real = 12.89643
integer = 42
string = 'some message'
print 'real=%.3f, integer=%d, string=%s' % (real, integer, string)
print 'real=%9.3e, integer=%5d, string=%s' % (real, integer, string)
```

The output of `print` is a string, specified in terms of text and a set of variables to be inserted in the text. Variables are inserted in the text at places indicated by %. After % comes a specification of the formatting, e.g, %f (real number), %d (integer), or %s (string). The format %9.3f means a real number in decimal notation, with 3 decimals, written in a field of width equal to 9 characters. The variant %.3f means that the number is written as compactly as possible, in decimal notation, with three decimals. Switching f with e or E results in the scientific notation, here 1.290e+01 or 1.290E+01. Writing %5d means that an integer is to be written in a field of width equal to 5 characters. Real numbers can also be specified with %g, which is used to automatically choose between decimal or scientific notation, from what gives the most compact output (typically, scientific notation is appropriate for very small and very large numbers and decimal notation for the intermediate range).

A typical example of when printf formatting is required, arises when nicely aligned columns of numbers are to be printed. Suppose we want to print a column of t values together with associated function values $g(t) = t\sin(t)$ in a second column. The simplest approach would be

```
from math import sin

t0 = 2
dt = 0.55

# Unformatted print
t = t0 + 0*dt; g = t*sin(t)
print t, g

t = t0 + 1*dt; g = t*sin(t)
print t, g

t = t0 + 2*dt; g = t*sin(t)
print t, g
```

with output

```
2.0 1.81859485365
2.55 1.42209347935
3.1 0.128900053543
```

(Repeating the same set of statements multiple times, as done above, is not good programming practice - one should use a for loop, as explained later in Section 2.3.) Observe that the numbers in the columns are not nicely aligned. Using the printf syntax '%6.2f   %8.3f' % (t, g) for t and g, we can control the width of each column and also the number of decimals, such that the numbers in a column are aligned under each other and written with the same precision. The output then becomes

```
Formatting via printf syntax
   2.00     1.819
   2.55     1.422
   3.10     0.129
```

We shall frequently use the printf syntax throughout the book so there will be plenty of further examples.

The modern alternative to printf syntax

Modern Python favors the new *format string syntax* over printf:

```
print 'At t={t:g} s, y={y:.2f} m'.format(t=t, y=y)
```

which corresponds to the printf syntax

```
print 'At t=%g s, y=%.2f m' % (t, y)
```

The slots where variables are inserted are now recognized by curly braces, and in format we list the variable names inside curly braces and their equivalent variables in the program.

Since the printf syntax is so widely used in many programming languages, we stick to that in the present book, but Python programmers will frequently also meet the newer format string syntax, so it is important to be aware its existence.

1.5.6   Arrays

In the program ball_plot.py from Chapter 1.4 we saw how 1001 height computations were executed and stored in the variable y, and then displayed in a plot showing y versus t, i.e., height versus time. The collection of numbers in y (or t, respectively) was stored in what is called an *array*, a construction also found in most other programming languages. Such arrays are created and treated according to certain rules, and as a programmer, you may direct Python to compute and handle arrays as a whole, or as individual *array elements*. Let us briefly look at a smaller such collection of numbers.

Assume that the heights of four family members have been collected. These heights may be generated and stored in an array, e.g., named h, by writing

```
h = zeros(4)
h[0] = 1.60
h[1] = 1.85
h[2] = 1.75
h[3] = 1.80
```

where the array elements appear as h[0], h[1], etc. Generally, when we read or talk about the array elements of some array a, we refer to them by reading or saying "a of zero" (i.e., a[0]), "a of one" (i.e., a[1]), and so on. The very first line in the example above, i.e.

```
h = zeros(4)
```

instructs Python to reserve, or *allocate*, space in memory for an array h with four elements and initial values set to 0. The next four lines overwrite the zeros with the desired numbers (measured heights), one number for each element. Elements are, by rule, *indexed* (numbers within brackets) from 0 to the last element, in this case 3. We say that Python has *zero based indexing*. This differs from *one based indexing* (e.g., found in Matlab) where the array index starts with 1.

As illustrated in the code, you may refer to the array as a whole by the name h, but also to each individual element by use of the index. The array elements may enter in computations as individual variables, e.g., writing z = h[0] + h[1] + h[2] + h[3] will compute the sum of all the elements in h, while the result is assigned to the variable z. Note that this way of creating an array is a bit different from the one with linspace, where the filling in of numbers occurred automatically "behind the scene".

By the use of a colon, you may pick out a *slice* of an array. For example, to create a new array from the two elements h[1] and h[2], we could write slice_h = h[1:3]. Note that the index specification 1:3 means indices 1 and 2, i.e., the last index is not included. For the generated slice_h array, indices are as usual, i.e., 0 and 1 in this case. The very last entry in an array may be addressed as, e.g., h[-1].

Copying arrays requires some care since simply writing new_h = h will, when you afterwards change elements of new_h, also change the corresponding elements in h! That is, h[1] is also changed when writing

```
new_h = h
new_h[1] = 5.0
print h[1]
```

In this case we do not get 1.85 out on the screen, but 5.0. To really get a copy that is decoupled from the original array, you may write new_h = copy(h). However, copying a slice works straightforwardly (as shown above), i.e. an explicit use of copy is not required.

1.5.7 Plotting

Sometimes you would like to have two or more curves or *graphs* in the same plot. Assume we have h as above, and also an array H with the heights 0.50 m, 0.70 m, 1.90 m, and 1.75 m from a family next door. This may be done with the program plot_heights.py given as

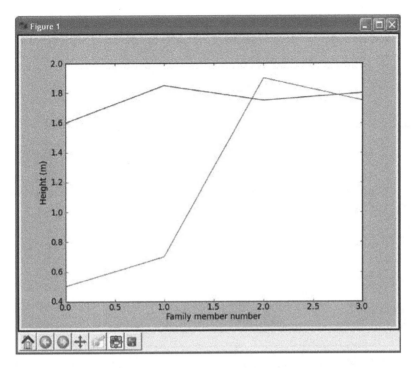

Fig. 1.2 Generated plot for the heights of family members from two families

```
from numpy import zeros
import matplotlib.pyplot as plt

h = zeros(4)
h[0] = 1.60; h[1] = 1.85; h[2] = 1.75; h[3] = 1.80
H = zeros(4)
H[0] = 0.50; H[1] = 0.70; H[2] = 1.90; H[3] = 1.75

family_member_no = zeros(4)
family_member_no[0] = 0; family_member_no[1] = 1
family_member_no[2] = 2; family_member_no[3] = 3

plt.plot(family_member_no, h, family_member_no, H)
plt.xlabel('Family member number')
plt.ylabel('Height (m)')
plt.show()
```

Running the program gives the plot shown in Figure 1.2.

Alternatively, the two curves could have been plotted in the same plot by use of two plot commands, which gives more freedom as to how the curves appear. To do this, you could plot the first curve by

```
plt.plot(family_member_no, h)
plt.hold('on')
```

Then you could (in principle) do a lot of other things in your code, before you plot the second curve by

```
plt.plot(family_member_no, H)
plt.hold('off')
```

Notice the use of hold here. hold('on') tells Python to plot also the following curve(s) in the same window. Python does so until it reads hold('off'). If you do not use the hold('on') or hold('off') command, the second plot command will overwrite the first one, i.e., you get only the second curve.

In case you would like the two curves plotted in two separate plots, you can do this by plotting the first curve straightforwardly with

```
plt.plot(family_member_no, h)
```

then do other things in your code, before you do

```
plt.figure()
plt.plot(family_member_no, H)
```

Note how the graphs are made continuous by Python, drawing straight lines between the four data points of each family. This is the standard way of doing it and was also done when plotting our 1001 height computations with ball_plot.py in Chapter 1.4. However, since there were so many data points then, the curve looked nice and smooth. If preferred, one may also plot only the data points. For example, writing

```
plt.plot(h, '*')
```

will mark only the data points with the star symbol. Other symbols like circles etc. may be used as well.

There are many possibilities in Python for adding information to a plot or for changing its appearance. For example, you may add a legend by the instruction

```
plt.legend('This is some legend')
```

or you may add a title by

```
plt.title('This is some title')
```

The command

```
plt.axis([xmin, xmax, ymin, ymax])
```

will define the plotting range for the x axis to stretch from xmin to xmax and, similarly, the plotting range for the y axis from ymin to ymax. Saving the figure to file is achieved by the command

```
plt.savefig('some_plot.png')     # PNG format
plt.savefig('some_plot.pdf')     # PDF format
plt.savefig('some_plot.jpg')     # JPG format
plt.savefig('some_plot.eps')     # Encanspulated PostScript format
```

For the reader who is into linear algebra, it may be useful to know that standard matrix/vector operations are straightforward with arrays, e.g., matrix-vector multiplication. What is needed though, is to create the right variable types (after having imported an appropriate module). For example, assume you would like to calculate the vector $\mathbf{y}$ (note that boldface is used for vectors and matrices) as $\mathbf{y} = \mathbf{Ax}$, where $\mathbf{A}$ is a 2×2 matrix and $\mathbf{x}$ is a vector. We may do this as illustrated by the program `matrix_vector_product.py` reading

```
from numpy import zeros, mat, transpose

x = zeros(2)
x = mat(x)
x = transpose(x)
x[0] = 3;    x[1] = 2    # Pick some values

A = zeros((2,2))
A = mat(A)
A[0,0] = 1;    A[0,1] = 0
A[1,0] = 0;    A[1,1] = 1

# The following gives y = x since A = I, the identity matrix
y = A*x
print y
```

Here, x is first created as an array, just as we did above. Then the variable type of x is changed to mat, i.e., matrix, by the line x = mat(x). This is followed by a transpose of x from dimension 1×2 (the default dimension) to 2×1 with the statement x = transpose(x), before some test values are plugged in. The matrix A is first created as a two dimensional array with A = zeros((2,2)) before conversion and filling in values take place. Finally, the multiplication is performed as y = A*x. Note the number of parentheses when creating the two dimensional array A. Running the program gives the following output on the screen:

```
[[3.]
 [2.]]
```

1.5.8   Error Messages and Warnings

All programmers experience error messages, and usually to a large extent during the early learning process. Sometimes error messages are understandable, sometimes they are not. Anyway, it is important to get used to them. One idea is to start with a program that initially is working, and then deliberately introduce errors in it, one by one. (But remember to take a copy of the original working code!) For each error, you try to run the program to see what Python's response is. Then you know what the problem is and understand what the error message is about. This will greatly help you when you get a similar error message or warning later.

Very often, you will experience that there are errors in the program you have written. This is normal, but frustrating in the beginning. You then have to find the problem, try to fix it, and then run the program again. Typically, you fix one error just to experience that another error is waiting around the corner. However, after some time you start to avoid the most common beginner's errors, and things run more smoothly. The process of finding and fixing errors, called *debugging*, is very important to learn. There are different ways of doing it too.

A special program (*debugger*) may be used to help you check (and do) different things in the program you need to fix. A simpler procedure, that often brings you a long way, is to print information to the screen from different places in the program. First of all, this is something you should do (several times) during program development anyway, so that things get checked as you go along. However, if the final program still ends up with error messages, you may save a copy of it, and do some testing on the copy. Useful testing may then be to remove, e.g., the latter half of the program (by inserting comment signs #), and insert print commands at clever places to see what is the case. When the first half looks ok, insert parts of what was removed and repeat the process with the new code. Using simple numbers and doing this in parallel with hand calculations on a piece of paper (for comparison) is often a very good idea.

Python also offers means to detect and handle errors by the program itself! The programmer must then foresee (when writing the code) that there is a potential for error at some particular point. If, for example, some user of the program is asked (by the running program) to provide a number, and intends to give the number 5, but instead writes the word *five*, the program could run into trouble. A `try-exception` construction may be used by the programmer to check for such errors and act appropriately (see Chapter 6.2 for an example), avoiding a program crash. This procedure of trying an action and then recovering from trouble, if necessary, is referred to as *exception handling* and is the modern way of dealing with errors in a program.

When a program finally runs without error messages, it might be tempting to think that *Ah..., I am finished!*. But no! Then comes program *testing*, you need to *verify* that the program does the computations as planned. This is almost an art and may take more time than to develop the program, but the program is useless unless you have much evidence showing that the computations are correct. Also, having a set of (automatic) tests saves huge amounts of time when you further develop the program.

Verification versus validation

Verification is important, but *validation* is equally important. It is great if your program can do the calculations according to the plan, *but* is it the right plan? Put otherwise, you need to check that the computations run correctly according to the *formula you have chosen/derived*. This is *verification*: doing the things right. Thereafter, you must also check whether the formula you have chosen/derived is *the right* formula for the case you are investigating. This is *validation*: doing the right things. In the present book, it is beyond scope to question how well the mathematical models describe a given phenomenon in nature or engineering,

as the answer usually involves extensive knowledge of the application area. We
will therefore limit our testing to the verification part.

1.5.9   Input Data

Computer programs need a set of input data and the purpose is to use these data to
compute output data, i.e., results. In the previous program we have specified input
data in terms of variables. However, one often wants to get the input through some
dialog with the user. Here is one example where the program asks a question, and
the user provides an answer by typing on the keyboard:

```
age = input('What is your age? ')
print "Ok, so you're half way to %d, wow!" % (age*2)
```

So, after having interpreted and run the first line, Python has established the variable
age and assigned your input to it. The second line combines the calculation of
twice the age with a message printed on the screen. Try these two lines in a little
test program to see for yourself how it works.

The input function is useful for numbers, lists (Chapter 2), and tuples (Chapter 2). For pure text, the user must either enclose the input in quotes, or the program
must use the raw_input function instead:

```
name = raw_input('What is your name? ')
```

There are other ways of providing input to a program as well, e.g., via a graphical
interface (as many readers will be used to) or at the command line (i.e., as parameters succeeding, on the same line, the command that starts the program). Reading
data from a file is yet another way. Logically, what the program produces when run,
e.g. a plot or printout to the screen or a file, is referred to as *program output*.

1.5.10   Symbolic Computations

Even though the main focus in this book is programming of *numerical* methods,
there are occasions where *symbolic* (also called *exact* or *analytical*) operations are
useful. Doing symbolic computations means, as the name suggests, that we do computations with the symbols themselves rather than with the numerical values they
could represent. Let us illustrate the difference between symbolic and numerical
computations with a little example. A numerical computation could be

```
x = 2
y = 3
z = x*y
print z
```

which will make the number 6 appear on the screen. A symbolic counterpart of this
code could be

```
from sympy import *
x, y = symbols('x y')
z = x*y
print z
```

which causes the *symbolic* result x*y to appear on the screen. Note that no numerical value was assigned to any of the variables in the symbolic computation. Only the symbols were used, as when you do symbolic mathematics by hand on a piece of paper.

Symbolic computations in Python make use of the *SymPy package*. Each symbol is represented by a standard variable, but the name of the symbol must be declared with Symbol(name) for a single symbol, or symbols(name1 name2 ...) for multiple symbols.. The following script example_symbolic.py is a quick demonstration of some of the basic symbolic operations that are supported in Python.

```
from sympy import *

x = Symbol('x')
y = Symbol('y')


print 2*x + 3*x - y               # Algebraic computation
print diff(x**2, x)               # Differentiates x**2 wrt. x
print integrate(cos(x), x)        # Integrates cos(x) wrt. x
print simplify((x**2 + x**3)/x**2) # Simplifies expression
print limit(sin(x)/x, x, 0)       # Finds limit of sin(x)/x as x->0
print solve(5*x - 15, x)          # Solves 5*x = 15
```

Other symbolic calculations like Taylor series expansion, linear algebra (with matrix and vector operations), and (some) differential equation solving are also possible.

Symbolic computations are also readily accessible through the (partly) free online tool WolframAlpha[4], which applies the very advanced Mathematica[5] package as symbolic engine. The disadvantage with WolframAlpha compared to the SymPy package is that the results cannot automatically be imported into your code and used for further analysis. On the other hand, WolframAlpha has the advantage that it displays many additional mathematical results related to the given problem. For example, if we type 2x + 3x - y in WolframAlpha, it not only simplifies the expression to 5x - y, but it also makes plots of the function $f(x, y) = 5x - y$, solves the equation $5x - y = 0$, and calculates the integral $\int \int (5x + y)dxdy$. The commercial Pro version can also show a step-by-step of the analytical computations in the problem. You are strongly encouraged to try out these commands in WolframAlpha:

- diff(x^2, x) or diff(x**2, x)
- integrate(cos(x), x)
- simplify((x**2 + x**3)/x**2)

---

[4] http://www.wolframalpha.com
[5] http://en.wikipedia.org/wiki/Mathematica

- `limit(sin(x)/x, x, 0)`
- `solve(5*x - 15, x)`

WolframAlpha is very flexible with respect to syntax.

Another impressive tool for symbolic computations is Sage[6], which is a very comprehensive package with the aim of "creating a viable free open source alternative to Magma, Maple, Mathematica and Matlab". Sage is implemented in Python. Projects with extensive symbolic computations will certainly benefit from exploring Sage.

1.5.11 Concluding Remarks

Programming demands you to be accurate!

In this chapter, you have seen some examples of how simple things may be done in Python. Hopefully, you have tried to do the examples on your own. If you have, most certainly you have discovered that what you write in the code has to be *very accurate*. For example, with our previous example of four heights collected in an array h, writing h(0) instead of h[0] gives an error, even if you and I know perfectly well what you mean! Remember that it is not a human that runs your code, it is a machine. Therefore, even if the meaning of your code looks fine to a human eye, it still has to comply in detail to the rules of the programming language. If not, you get warnings and error messages. This also goes for lower and upper case letters. If you do `from math import *` and give the command pi, you get 3.1415.... However, if you write Pi, you get an error message. Pay attention to such details also when they are given in later chapters.

Remember to insert comments to explain your code

When you write a computer program, you have two very different kinds of readers. One is Python, which will interpret and run your program according to the rules. The other is some human, for example, yourself or a peer. It is very important to organize and comment the code so that you can go back to your own code after, e.g., a year and still understand what clever constructions you put in there. This is relevant when you need to change or extend your code (which usually happens often in reality). Organized coding and good commenting is even more critical if other people are supposed to understand code that you have written.

Fast code versus readable and correct code

Numerical computing has a strong tradition in paying much attention to creating *fast code*. Real industrial applications of numerical computing often involves simulations that run for hours, days, and even weeks. Fast code is tremendously important in those cases. The problem with a strong focus on fast code, unfortunately, is sometimes that clear and easily understandable constructions are replaced by clever and less readable, but faster code. However, for beginners it is most important to learn to write readable and correct code. We will make some

---

[6] http://sagemath.org/

comments on constructions that are fast or slow, but the main focus of this book is to teach how to write correct programs, not the fastest possible programs.

Deleting data no longer in use

Python has *automatic garbage collection*, meaning that there is no need to delete variables (or objects) that are no longer in use. Python takes care of this by itself. This is opposed to, e.g., Matlab, where explicit deleting sometimes may be required.

Tip: how to deal with long lines

If a statement in a program gets too long, it may be continued on the next line by inserting a back-slash at the end of the line before proceeding on the next line. However, *no blanks* must occur after the back-slash!

The present introductory book just provides a tiny bit of all the functionality that Python has to offer. An important source of information is the official Python documentation website (http://docs.python.org/), which provides a Python tutorial, the *Python Library Reference*, a *Language Reference*, and more. Several excellent books are also available (http://wiki.python.org/moin/PythonBooks), but not so many with a scientific computing focus. One exception is Langtangen's comprehensive book *A Primer on Scientific Programming with Python*, Springer, 2016.

1.6 Exercises

Exercise 1.1: Error messages
Save a copy of the program `ball.py` and confirm that the copy runs as the original. You are now supposed to introduce errors in the code, one by one. For each error introduced, save and run the program, and comment how well Python's response corresponds to the actual error. When you are finished with one error, re-set the program to correct behavior (and check that it works!) before moving on to the next error.

a) Insert the word *hello* on the empty line above the assignment to v0.
b) Remove the # sign in front of the comment *initial velocity*.
c) Remove the = sign in the assignment to v0.
d) Change the reserved word `print` into `pint`.
e) Change the calculation of y to y = v0*t.
f) Change the line `print` y to `print` x.
g) Replace the statement

```
y = v0*t - 0.5*g*t**2
```

by

```
y = v0*t - (1/2)*g*t**2
```

Filename: `testing_ball.py`.

Exercise 1.2: Volume of a cube

Write a program that computes the volume V of a cube with sides of length $L = 4$ cm and prints the result to the screen. Both V and L should be defined as separate variables in the program. Run the program and confirm that the correct result is printed.

Hint See ball.py in the text.
Filename: cube_volume.py.

Exercise 1.3: Area and circumference of a circle

Write a program that computes both the circumference C and the area A of a circle with radius $r = 2$ cm. Let the results be printed to the screen on a single line with an appropriate text. The variables C, A and r should all be defined as a separate variables in the program. Run the program and confirm that the correct results are printed.
Filename: circumference_and_area.py.

Exercise 1.4: Volumes of three cubes

We are interested in the volume V of a cube with length L: $V = L^3$, computed for three different values of L.

a) Use the linspace function to compute three values of L, equally spaced on the interval $[1, 3]$.
b) Carry out by hand the computation $V = L^3$ if L is an array with three elements. That is, compute V for each value of L.
c) In a program, write out the result V of V = L**3 when L is an array with three elements as computed by linspace in a). Compare the resulting volumes with your hand calculations.
d) Make a plot of V versus L.

Filename: volume3cubes.py.

Exercise 1.5: Average of integers

Write a program that stores the sum $1 + 2 + 3 + 4 + 5$ in one variable and then creates another variable with the average of these five numbers. Print the average to the screen and check that the result is correct.
Filename: average_int.py.

Exercise 1.6: Interactive computing of volume and area

a) Compute the volume in Exercise 1.2 by using Python interactively, i.e., do the computations at the command prompt (in a Python shell as we also say). Compare with what you got previously from the written program.
b) Do the same also for Exercise 1.3.

Exercise 1.7: Peculiar results from division

Consider the following interactive Python session:

```
In [1]: x=2; y=4

In [2]: x/y
Out[2]: 0
```

What is the problem and how can you fix it?

Exercise 1.8: Update variable at command prompt

Invoke Python interactively and perform the following steps.

1. Initialize a variable x to 2.
2. Add 3 to x. Print out the result.
3. Print out the result of x + 1*2 and (x+1)*2. (Observe how parentheses make a difference).
4. What variable *type* is x?

Exercise 1.9: Formatted print to screen

Write a program that defines two variables as x = pi and y = 2. Then let the program compute the product z of these two variables and print the result to the screen as

```
Multiplying 3.14159 and 2 gives 6.283
```

Filename: `formatted_print.py`.

Exercise 1.10: Python documentation and random numbers

Write a program that prints four random numbers to the screen. The numbers should be drawn from a uniform distribution over the interval [0, 10) (0 inclusive, 10 exclusive). Find the information needed for the task, see for example http://docs.python.org.

Hint Python has a module random that contains a function by the name uniform. Filename: `drawing_random_numbers.py`.

2

Construction in Python

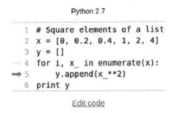

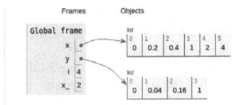

2.1   If Tests, Colon and Indentation

Very often in life, and in computer programs, the next action depends on the outcome of a question starting with "if". This gives the possibility to branch into
different types of action depending on some criterion. Let us as usual focus on
a specific example, which is the core of so-called random walk algorithms used in
a wide range of branches in science and engineering, including materials manufac-
turing and brain research. The action is to move randomly to the north (N), east (E),
south (S), or west (W) with the same probability. How can we implement such an
action in life and in a computer program?

We need to randomly draw one out of four numbers to select the direction in
which to move. A deck of cards can be used in practice for this purpose. Let the
four suits correspond to the four directions: clubs to N, diamonds to E, hearts to S,
and spades to W, for instance. We draw a card, perform the corresponding move,
and repeat the process a large number of times. The resulting path is a typical
realization of the path of a diffusing molecule.

In a computer program, we need to draw a random number, and depending on
the number, update the coordinates of the point to be moved. There are many ways
to draw random numbers and translate them into (e.g.) four random directions, but
the technical details usually depend on the programming language. Our technique
here is universal: we draw a random number in the interval $[0, 1)$ and let $[0, 0.25)$
correspond to N, $[0.25, 0.5)$ to E, $[0.5, 0.75)$ to S, and $[0.75, 1)$ to W. Let x and y

hold the coordinates of a point and let d be the length of the move. A pseudo code (i.e., not "real" code, just a "sketch of the logic") then goes like

```
r = random number in [0,1)
if 0 <= r < 0.25
    move north: y = y + d
else if 0.25 <= r < 0.5
    move east:  x = x + d
else if 0.5 <= r < 0.75
    move south:  y = y - d
else if 0.75 <= r < 1
    move west:  x = x - d
```

Note the need for first asking about the value of r and then performing an action. If the answer to the "if" question is positive (true), we are done and can skip the next else if questions. If the answer is negative (false), we proceed with the next question. The last test if $0.75 \le r < 1$ could also read just else, since we here cover all the remaining possible r values.

The exact code in Python reads

```
import random
r = random.random()        # random number in [0,1)
if 0 <= r < 0.25:
    # move north
    y = y + d
elif 0.25 <= r < 0.5:
    # move east
    x = x + d
elif 0.5 <= r < 0.75:
    # move south
    y = y - d
else:
    # move west
    x = x - d
```

We use else in the last test to cover the different types of syntax that is allowed. Python recognizes the reserved words if, elif (short for else if), and else and expects the code to be compatible with the rules of if tests:

- The test reads if condition:, elif condition:, or else:, where condition is a *boolean expression* that evaluates to True or False. Note the closing colon (easy to forget!).
- If condition is True, the following *indented* block of statements is executed and the remaining elif or else branches are skipped.
- If condition is False, the program flow jumps to the next elif or else branch.

The blocks after if, elif, or else may contain new if tests, if desired. Regarding colon and indent, you will see below that these are required in several other programming constructions as well.

Working with if tests requires mastering boolean expressions. Here are some basic boolean expressions involving the *logical operators* ==, !=, <, <=, >, and

>=. Given the assignment to `temp`, you should go through each boolean expression below and determine if it is true or false.

```
temp = 21        # assign value to a variable
temp == 20  # temp equal to 20
temp != 20  # temp not equal to 20
temp <  20  # temp less than 20
temp >  20  # temp greater than 20
temp <= 20  # temp less than or equal to 20
temp >= 20  # temp greater than or equal to 20
```

2.2 Functions

Functions are widely used in programming and is a concept that needs to be mastered. In the simplest case, a function in a program is much like a mathematical function: some input number x is transformed to some output number. One example is the $\tanh^{-1}(x)$ function, called `atan` in computer code: it takes one real number as input and returns another number. Functions in Python are more general and can take a series of variables as input and return one or more variables, or simply nothing. The purpose of functions is two-fold:

1. to *group statements* into separate units of code lines that naturally belong together (a strategy which may dramatically ease the problem solving process), and/or
2. to *parameterize* a set of statements such that they can be written only once and easily be re-executed with variations.

Examples will be given to illustrate how functions can be written in various contexts.

If we modify the program `ball.py` from Sect. 1.2 slightly, and include a function, we could let this be a new program `ball_function.py` as

```
def y(t):
    v0 = 5                    # Initial velocity
    g = 9.81                  # Acceleration of gravity
    return v0*t - 0.5*g*t**2

time = 0.6        # Just pick one point in time
print y(time)
time = 0.9        # Pick another point in time
print y(time)
```

When Python reads and interprets this program from the top, it takes the code from the line with `def`, to the line with `return`, to be the definition of a function with the name y (note colon and indentation). The *return statement* of the function y, i.e.

```
return v0*t - 0.5*g*t**2
```

will be understood by Python as *first compute the expression, then send the result back (i.e., return) to where the function was called from*. Both def and return are reserved words. The function depends on t, i.e., one variable (or we say that it takes one *argument* or *input parameter*), the value of which must be provided when the function is called.

What actually happens when Python meets this code? The def line just tells Python that here is a function with name y and it has one argument t. Python does not look into the function at this stage (except that it checks the code for syntax errors). When Python later on meets the statement print y(time), it recognizes a function call y(time) and recalls that there is a function y defined with one argument. The value of time is then transferred to the y(t) function such that t = time becomes the first action in the y function. Then Python executes one line at a time in the y function. In the final line, the arithmetic expression v0*t - 0.5*g*t**2 is computed, resulting in a number, and this number (or more precisely, the Python object representing the number) *replaces* the call y(time) in the calling code such that the word print now precedes a number rather than a function call.

Python proceeds with the next line and sets time to a new value. The next print statement triggers a new call to y(t), this time t is set to 0.9, the computations are done line by line in the y function, and the returned result replaces y(time). Instead of writing print y(time), we could alternatively have stored the returned result from the y function in a variable,

```
h = y(time)
print h
```

Note that when a function contains if-elif-else constructions, return may be done from within any of the branches. This may be illustrated by the following function containing three return statements:

```
def check_sign(x):
    if x > 0:
        return 'x is positive'
    elif x < 0:
        return 'x is negative'
    else:
        return 'x is zero'
```

Remember that only one of the branches is executed for a single call on check_sign, so depending on the number x, the return may take place from any of the three return alternatives.

To return at the end or not

Programmers disagree whether it is a good idea to use return inside a function where you want, or if there should only be one single return statement *at the end of the function*. The authors of this book emphasize readable code and think that return can be useful in branches as in the example above when the function is short. For longer or more complicated functions, it might be better to have one single `return` statement. Be prepared for critical comments if you return wherever you want...

An expression you will often encounter when dealing with programming, is *main program*, or that some code is *in main*. This is nothing particular to Python, and simply refers to that part of the program which is *outside* functions. However, note that the `def` line of functions is counted into main. So, in `ball_function.py` above, all statements outside the function y are in main, and also the line `def y(t):`.

A function may take no arguments, or many, in which case they are just listed within the parentheses (following the function name) and separated by a comma. Let us illustrate. Take a slight variation of the ball example and assume that the ball is not thrown straight up, but at an angle, so that two coordinates are needed to specify its position at any time. According to Newton's laws (when air resistance is negligible), the vertical position is given by $y(t) = v_{0y}t - 0.5gt^2$ and the horizontal position by $x(t) = v_{0x}t$. We can include both these expressions in a new version of our program that prints the position of the ball for chosen times. Assume we want to evaluate these expressions at two points in time, $t = 0.6s$ and $t = 0.9s$. We can pick some numbers for the initial velocity components v0y and v0x, name the program `ball_position_xy.py`, and write it for example as

```
def y(v0y, t):
    g = 9.81                    # Acceleration of gravity
    return v0y*t - 0.5*g*t**2

def x(v0x, t):
    return v0x*t

initial_velocity_x = 2.0
initial_velocity_y = 5.0

time = 0.6        # Just pick one point in time
print x(initial_velocity_x, time), y(initial_velocity_y, time)
time = 0.9        # ... Pick another point in time
print x(initial_velocity_x, time), y(initial_velocity_y, time)
```

Now we compute and print the two components for the position, for each of the two chosen points in time. Notice how each of the two functions now takes *two* arguments. Running the program gives the output

```
1.2   1.2342
1.8   0.52695
```

A function may also have no return value, in which case we simply drop the return statement, or it may return more than one value. For example, the two functions we just defined could alternatively have been written as one:

```
def xy(v0x, v0y, t):
    g = 9.81                    # acceleration of gravity
    return v0x*t, v0y*t - 0.5*g*t**2
```

Notice the two return values which are simply separated by a comma. When calling the function (and printing), arguments must appear in the same order as in the function definition. We would then write

```
print xy(initial_x_velocity, initial_y_velocity, time)
```

The two returned values from the function could alternatively have been assigned to variables, e.g., as

```
x_pos, y_pos = xy(initial_x_velocity, initial_y_velocity, time)
```

The variables x_pos and y_pos could then have been printed or used in other ways in the code.

There are possibilities for having a variable number of function input and output parameters (using *args and **kwargs constructions for the arguments). However, we do not go further into that topic here.

Variables that are defined inside a function, e.g., g in the last xy function, are *local variables*. This means they are only known inside the function. Therefore, if you had accidentally used g in some calculation outside the function, you would have got an error message. The variable time is defined outside the function and is therefore a *global variable*. It is known both outside and inside the function(s). If you define one global and one local variable, both with the same name, the function only sees the local one, so the global variable is not affected by what happens with the local variable of the same name.

The arguments named in the heading of a function definition are by rule local variables inside the function. If you want to change the value of a global variable inside a function, you need to declare the variable as global inside the function. That is, if the global variable was x, we would need to write global x inside the function definition before we let the function change it. After function execution, x would then have a changed value. One should strive to define variables mostly where they are needed and not everywhere.

Another very useful way of handling function parameters in Python, is by defining parameters as *keyword arguments*. This gives default values to parameters and allows more freedom in function calls, since the order and number of parameters may vary.

Let us illustrate the use of keyword arguments with the function xy. Assume we defined xy as

```
def xy(t, v0x=0, v0y=0):
    g = 9.81                        # acceleration of gravity
    return v0x*t, v0y*t - 0.5*g*t**2
```

Here, t is an *ordinary* or *positional argument*, whereas v0x and v0y are *keyword arguments* or *named arguments*. Generally, there can be many positional arguments and many keyword arguments, but the positional arguments must *always* be listed before the keyword arguments in function definition. Keyword arguments are given default values, as shown here with v0x and v0y, both having zero as default value. In a script, the function xy may now be called in many different ways. For example,

```
print xy(0.6)
```

would make xy perform the computations with $t = 0.6$ and the default values (i.e zero) of v0x and v0y. The two numbers returned from xy are printed to the screen. If we wanted to use another initial value for v0y, we could, e.g., write

```
print xy(0.6,v0y=4.0)
```

which would make xy perform the calculations with $t = 0.6$, $v0x = 0$ (i.e. the default value) and $v0y = 4.0$. When there are several positional arguments, they have to appear in the same order as defined in the function definition, unless we explicitly use the names of these also in the function call. With explicit name specification in the call, any order of parameters is acceptable. To illustrate, we could, e.g., call xy as

```
print xy(v0y=4.0, v0x=1.0, t=0.6)
```

In any programming language, it is a good habit to include a little explanation of what the function is doing, unless what is done by the function is obvious, e.g., when having only a few simple code lines. This explanation is called a *doc string*, which in Python should be placed just at the top of the function. This explanation is meant for a human who wants to understand the code, so it should say something about the purpose of the code and possibly explain the arguments and return values if needed. If we do that with our xy function from above, we may write the first lines of the function as

```
def xy(v0x, v0y, t):
    """Compute the x and y position of the ball at time t"""
```

Note that other functions may be called from within other functions, and function input parameters are not required to be numbers. Any object will do, e.g., string variables or other functions.

Functions are straightforwardly passed as arguments to other functions, as illustrated by the following script function_as_argument.py:

```
def sum_xy(x, y):
    return x + y

def prod_xy(x, y):
    return x*y

def treat_xy(f, x, y):
    return f(x, y)

x = 2;  y = 3
print treat_xy(sum_xy, x, y)
print treat_xy(prod_xy, x, y)
```

When run, this program first prints the sum of x and y (i.e., 5), and then it prints the product (i.e., 6). We see that `treat_xy` takes a function name as its first parameter. Inside `treat_xy`, that function is used to actually *call* the function that was given as input parameter. Therefore, as shown, we may call `treat_xy` with either `sum_xy` or `prod_xy`, depending on whether we want the sum or product of x and y to be calculated.

Functions may also be defined *within* other functions. It that case, they become *local functions*, or *nested functions*, known only to the function inside which they are defined. Functions defined in main are referred to as *global functions*. A nested function has full access to all variables in the *parent function*, i.e. the function within which it is defined.

Short functions can be defined in a compact way, using what is known as a *lambda function*:

```
f = lambda x, y: x + 2*y

# Equivalent
def f(x, y):
    return x + 2*y
```

The syntax consists of `lambda` followed by a series of arguments, colon, and some Python expression resulting in an object to be returned from the function. Lambda functions are particularly convenient as function arguments:

```
print treat_xy(lambda x, y: x*y, x, y)
```

Overhead of function calls

Function calls have the downside of slowing down program execution. Usually, it is a good thing to split a program into functions, but in very computing intensive parts, e.g., inside long loops, one must balance the convenience of calling a function and the computational efficiency of avoiding function calls. It is a good rule to develop a program using plenty of functions and then in a later optimization stage, when everything computes correctly, remove function calls that are quantified to slow down the code.

Here is a little example in IPython where we calculate the CPU time for doing array computations with and without a helper function:

```
In [1]: import numpy as np

In [2]: a = np.zeros(1000000)

In [3]: def add(a, b):
   ...:        return a + b
   ...:

In [4]: %timeit for i in range(len(a)): a[i] = add(i, i+1)
The slowest run took 16.01 times longer than the fastest.
This could mean that an intermediate result is being cached
1 loops, best of 3: 178 ms per loop

In [5]: %timeit for i in range(len(a)): a[i] = i + (i+1)
10 loops, best of 3: 109 ms per loop
```

We notice that there is some overhead in function calls. The impact of the overhead reduces quickly with the amount of computational work inside the function.

2.3   For Loops

Many computations are repetitive by nature and programming languages have certain *loop structures* to deal with this. Here we will present what is referred to as a *for loop* (another kind of loop is a *while* loop, to be presented afterwards). Assume you want to calculate the square of each integer from 3 to 7. This could be done with the following two-line program.

```
for i in [3, 4, 5, 6, 7]:
    print i**2
```

Note the colon and indentation again!

What happens when Python interprets your code here? First of all, the word for is a reserved word signalling to Python that a for loop is wanted. Python then sticks to the rules covering such constructions and understands that, in the present example, the loop should run 5 successive times (i.e., 5 *iterations* should be done), letting the variable i take on the numbers $3, 4, 5, 6, 7$ in turn. During each iteration, the statement inside the loop (i.e. print i**2) is carried out. After each iteration, i is automatically (behind the scene) updated. When the last number is reached, the last iteration is performed and the loop is finished. When executed, the program will therefore print out $9, 16, 25, 36$ and 49. The variable i is often referred to as a *loop index*, and its name (here i) is a choice of the programmer.

Note that, had there been several statements within the loop, they would all be executed with the same value of i (before i changed in the next iteration). Make sure you understand how program execution flows here, it is important.

In Python, integer values specified for the loop variable are often produced by the built-in function range. The function range may be called in different ways, that either explicitly, or implicitly, specify the start, stop and step (i.e., change) of the loop variable. Generally, a call to range reads

```
range(start, stop, step)
```

This call makes range return the integers from (and including) start, up to (but excluding!) stop, in steps of step. Note here that stop-1 is the last integer included. With range, the previous example would rather read

```
for i in range(3, 8, 1):
    print i**2
```

By default, if range is called with only two parameters, these are taken to be start and stop, in which case a step of 1 is understood. If only a single parameter is used in the call to range, this parameter is taken to be stop. The default step of

1 is then used (combined with the starting at 0). Thus, calling range, for example, as

```
range(6)
```

would return the integers 0, 1, 2, 3, 4, 5.

Note that decreasing integers may be produced by letting start > stop combined with a negative step. This makes it easy to, e.g., traverse arrays in either direction.

Let us modify ball_plot.py from Sect. 1.4 to illustrate how useful for loops are if you need to traverse arrays. In that example we computed the height of the ball at every milli-second during the first second of its (vertical) flight and plotted the height versus time.

Assume we want to find the maximum height during that time, how can we do it with a computer program? One alternative may be to compute all the thousand heights, store them in an array, and then run through the array to pick out the maximum. The program, named ball_max_height.py, may look as follows.

```
import matplotlib.pyplot as plt

v0 = 5                    # Initial velocity
g = 9.81                  # Acceleration of gravity
t = linspace(0, 1, 1000)  # 1000 points in time interval
y = v0*t - 0.5*g*t**2     # Generate all heights

# At this point, the array y with all the heights is ready.
# Now we need to find the largest value within y.

largest_height = y[0]           # Starting value for search
for i in range(1, 1000):
    if y[i] > largest_height:
        largest_height = y[i]

print "The largest height achieved was %f m" % (largest_height)

# We might also like to plot the path again just to compare
plt.plot(t,y)
plt.xlabel('Time (s)')
plt.ylabel('Height (m)')
plt.show()
```

There is nothing new here, except the for loop construction, so let us look at it in more detail. As explained above, Python understands that a for loop is desired when it sees the word for. The range() function will produce integers from, and including, 1, up to, and including, 999, i.e. 1000 − 1. The value in y[0] is used as the *preliminary* largest height, so that, e.g., the very first check that is made is testing whether y[1] is larger than this height. If so, y[1] is stored as the largest height. The for loop then updates i to 2, and continues to check y[2], and so on. Each time we find a larger number, we store it. When finished, largest_height will contain the largest number from the array y. When you run the program, you get

```
The largest height achieved was 1.274210 m
```

which compares favorably to the plot that pops up.

To implement the traversing of arrays with loops and indices, is sometimes challenging to get right. You need to understand the start, stop and step length choices for an index, and also how the index should enter expressions inside the loop. At the same time, however, it is something that programmers do often, so it is important to develop the right skills on these matters.

Having one loop inside another, referred to as a *double loop*, is sometimes useful, e.g., when doing linear algebra. Say we want to find the maximum among the numbers stored in a 4×4 matrix A. The code fragment could look like

```python
largest_number = A[0][0]

for i in range(4):
    for j in range(4):
        if A[i][j] > largest_number:
            largest_number = A[i][j]
```

Here, all the j indices (0 - 3) will be covered for *each* value of index i. First, i stays fixed at i = 0, while j runs over all its indices. Then, i stays fixed at i = 1 while j runs over all its indices again, and so on. Sketch A on a piece of paper and follow the first few loop iterations by hand, then you will realize how the double loop construction works. Using two loops is just a special case of using *multiple* or *nested loops*, and utilizing more than two loops is just a straightforward extension of what was shown here. Note, however, that the loop index *name* in multiple loops must be unique to each of the nested loops. Note also that each nested loop may have as many code lines as desired, both before and after the next inner loop.

The vectorized computation of heights that we did in ball_plot.py (Sect. 1.4) could alternatively have been done by traversing the time array (t) and, for each t element, computing the height according to the formula $y = v_0 t - \frac{1}{2}gt^2$. However, it is important to know that vectorization goes much quicker. So when speed is important, vectorization is valuable.

Use loops to compute sums

One important use of loops, is to calculate sums. As a simple example, assume some variable x given by the mathematical expression

$$x = \sum_{i=1}^{N} 2 \cdot i,$$

i.e., summing up the N first even numbers. For some given N, say $N = 5$, x would typically be computed in a computer program as:

```
N = 5
x = 0
for i in range(1, N+1):
    x += 2*i
print x
```

Executing this code will print the number 30 to the screen. Note in particular how the *accumulation variable* x is initialized to zero. The value of x then gets updated with each iteration of the loop, and not until the loop is finished will x have the correct value. This way of building up the value is very common in programming, so make sure you understand it by simulating the code segment above by hand. It is a technique used with loops in any programming language.

2.4 While Loops

Python also has another standard loop construction, the *while loop*, doing iterations with a loop index very much like the for loop. To illustrate what such a loop may look like, we consider another modification of `ball_plot.py` in Sect. 1.4. We will now change it so that it finds the time of flight for the ball. Assume the ball is thrown with a slightly lower initial velocity, say 4.5 ms^{-1}, while everything else is kept unchanged. Since we still look at the first second of the flight, the heights at the end of the flight become negative. However, this only means that the ball has fallen below its initial starting position, i.e., the height where it left the hand, so there is no problem with that. In our array y we will then have a series of heights which towards the end of y become negative. Let us, in a program named `ball_time.py` find the time when heights start to get negative, i.e., when the ball crosses $y = 0$. The program could look like this

```
from numpy import linspace

v0 = 4.5                 # Initial velocity
g = 9.81                 # Acceleration of gravity
t = linspace(0, 1, 1000) # 1000 points in time interval
y = v0*t - 0.5*g*t**2    # Generate all heights

# Find where the ball hits y=0
i = 0
while y[i] >= 0:
    i += 1

# Now, y[i-1]>0 and y[i]<0 so let's take the middle point
# in time as the approximation for when the ball hits h=0
print "y=0 at", 0.5*(t[i-1] + t[i])

# We plot the path again just for comparison
import matplotlib.pyplot as plt
plt.plot(t, y)
plt.plot(t, 0*t, 'g--')
plt.xlabel('Time (s)')
plt.ylabel('Height (m)')
plt.show()
```

If you type and run this program you should get

```
y=0 at 0.917417417417
```

The new thing here is the `while` loop only. The loop (note colon and indentation) will run as long as the boolean expression `y[i]` > 0 evaluates to True. Note that the programmer introduced a variable (the loop index) by the name i, initialized it (i = 0) before the loop, and updated it (i += 1) in the loop. So for each iteration, i is *explicitly* increased by 1, allowing a check of successive elements in the array y.

Compared to a `for` loop, the programmer does not have to specify the number of iterations when coding a `while` loop. It simply runs until the boolean expression becomes False. Thus, a loop index (as we have in a `for` loop) is not required. Furthermore, if a loop index is used in a `while` loop, it is not increased automatically; it must be done explicitly by the programmer. Of course, just as in `for` loops and `if` blocks, there might be (arbitrarily) many code lines in a `while` loop. Any `for` loop may also be implemented as a `while` loop, but `while` loops are more general so not all of them can be expressed as a `for` loop.

A problem to be aware of, is what is usually referred to as an *infinite loop*. In those unintentional (erroneous) cases, the boolean expression of the `while` test never evaluates to False, and the program can not escape the loop. This is one of the most frequent errors you will experience as a beginning programmer. If you accidentally enter an infinite loop and the program just hangs forever, press `Ctrl+c` to stop the program.

2.5   Lists and Tuples – Alternatives to Arrays

We have seen that a group of numbers may be stored in an array that we may treat as a whole, or element by element. In Python, there is another way of organizing data that actually is much used, at least in non-numerical contexts, and that is a construction called *list*.

A list is quite similar to an array in many ways, but there are pros and cons to consider. For example, the number of elements in a list is allowed to change, whereas arrays have a fixed length that must be known at the time of memory allocation. Elements in a list can be of different type, i.e you may mix integers, floats and strings, whereas elements in an array must be of the same type. In general, lists provide more flexibility than do arrays. On the other hand, arrays give faster computations than lists, making arrays the prime choice unless the flexibility of lists is needed. Arrays also require less memory use and there is a lot of ready-made code for various mathematical operations. Vectorization requires arrays to be used.

The `range()` function that we used above in our `for` loop actually returns a list. If you for example write `range(5)` at the prompt in ipython, you get [0, 1, 2, 3, 4] in return, i.e., a list with 5 numbers. In a for loop, the line `for i in range[5]` makes i take on each of the numbers $0, 1, 2, 3, 4$ in turn, as we saw above. Writing, e.g., x = range(5), gives a list by the name x, containing those five numbers. These numbers may now be accessed (e.g., as x[2], which contains the number 2) and used in computations just as we saw for array elements. As with arrays, indices run from 0 to $n - 1$, when n is the number of elements in a list. You may convert a list to an array by x = `array(L)`.

A list may also be created by simply writing, e.g.,

```
x = ['hello', 4, 3.14, 6]
```

giving a list where x[0] contains the string hello, x[1] contains the integer 4, etc. We may add and/or delete elements anywhere in the list as shown in the following example.

```
x = ['hello', 4, 3.14, 6]
x.insert(0, -2) # x then becomes [-2, 'hello', 4, 3.14, 6]
del x[3]        # x then becomes [-2, 'hello', 4, 6]
x.append(3.14)  # x then becomes [-2, 'hello', 4, 6, 3.14]
```

Note the ways of writing the different operations here. Using append() will always increase the list at the end. If you like, you may create an empty list as x = [] before you enter a loop which appends element by element. If you need to know the length of the list, you get the number of elements from len(x), which in our case is 5, after appending 3.14 above. This function is handy if you want to traverse all list elements by index, since range(len(x)) gives you all legal indices. Note that there are many more operations on lists possible than shown here.

Previously, we saw how a for loop may run over array elements. When we want to do the same with a list in Python, we may do it as this little example shows,

```
x = ['hello', 4, 3.14, 6]
for e in x:
    print 'x element: ', e
print 'This was all the elements in the list x'
```

This is how it usually is done in Python, and we see that e runs over the elements of x directly, avoiding the need for indexing. Be aware, however, that when loops are written like this, you can not change any element in x by "changing" e. That is, writing e += 2 will not change anything in x, since e can only be used to read (as opposed to overwrite) the list elements.

There is a special construct in Python that allows you to run through all elements of a list, do the same operation on each, and store the new elements in another list. It is referred to as *list comprehension* and may be demonstrated as follows.

```
List_1 = [1, 2, 3, 4]
List_2 = [e*10 for e in List_1]
```

This will produce a new list by the name List_2, containing the elements 10, 20, 30 and 40, in that order. Notice the syntax within the brackets for List_2, for e in List_1 signals that e is to successively be each of the list elements in List_1, and for each e, create the next element in List_2 by doing e*10. More generally, the syntax may be written as

```
List_2 = [E(e) for e in List_1]
```

where E(e) means some expression involving e.

In some cases, it is required to run through 2 (or more) lists at the same time. Python has a handy function called `zip` for this purpose. An example of how to use `zip` is provided in the code `file_handling.py` below.

We should also briefly mention about *tuples*, which are very much like lists, the main difference being that tuples cannot be changed. To a freshman, it may seem strange that such "constant lists" could ever be preferable over lists. However, the property of being constant is a good safeguard against unintentional changes. Also, it is quicker for Python to handle data in a tuple than in a list, which contributes to faster code. With the data from above, we may create a tuple and print the content by writing

```
x = ('hello', 4, 3.14, 6)
for e in x:
    print 'x element: ', e
print 'This was all the elements in the tuple x'
```

Trying `insert` or append for the tuple gives an error message (because it cannot be changed), stating that the tuple object has no such attribute.

2.6   Reading from and Writing to Files

Input data for a program often come from files and the results of the computations are often written to file. To illustrate basic file handling, we consider an example where we read x and y coordinates from two columns in a file, apply a function f to the y coordinates, and write the results to a new two-column data file. The first line of the input file is a heading that we can just skip:

```
# x and y coordinates
1.0   3.44
2.0   4.8
3.5   6.61
4.0   5.0
```

The relevant Python lines for reading the numbers and writing out a similar file are given in the file `file_handling.py`

```
filename = 'tmp.dat'
infile = open(filename, 'r')   # Open file for reading
line = infile.readline()       # Read first line
# Read x and y coordinates from the file and store in lists
x = []
y = []
for line in infile:
    words = line.split()       # Split line into words
    x.append(float(words[0]))
    y.append(float(words[1]))
infile.close()
```

```
# Transform y coordinates
from math import log

def f(y):
    return log(y)

for i in range(len(y)):
    y[i] = f(y[i])

# Write out x and y to a two-column file
filename = 'tmp_out.dat'
outfile = open(filename, 'w')   # Open file for writing
outfile.write('# x and y coordinates\n')
for xi, yi in zip(x, y):
    outfile.write('%10.5f %10.5f\n' % (xi, yi))
outfile.close()
```

Such a file with a comment line and numbers in tabular format is very common so numpy has functionality to ease reading and writing. Here is the same example using the loadtxt and savetxt functions in numpy for tabular data (file file_handling_numpy.py):

```
filename = 'tmp.dat'
import numpy
data = numpy.loadtxt(filename, comments='#')
x = data[:,0]
y = data[:,1]
data[:,1] = numpy.log(y)   # insert transformed y back in array
filename = 'tmp_out.dat'
filename = 'tmp_out.dat'
outfile = open(filename, 'w')   # open file for writing
outfile.write('# x and y coordinates\n')
numpy.savetxt(outfile, data, fmt='%10.5f')
```

2.7 Exercises

Exercise 2.1: Errors with colon, indent, etc.
Write the program ball_function.py as given in the text and confirm that the program runs correctly. Then save a copy of the program and use that program during the following error testing.

You are supposed to introduce errors in the code, one by one. For each error introduced, save and run the program, and comment how well Python's response corresponds to the actual error. When you are finished with one error, re-set the program to correct behavior (and check that it works!) before moving on to the next error.

a) Change the first line from def y(t): to def y(t), i.e., remove the colon.
b) Remove the indent in front of the statement v0 = 5 inside the function y, i.e., shift the text four spaces to the left.

c) Now let the statement v0 = 5 inside the function y have an indent of three spaces (while the remaining two lines of the function have four).

d) Remove the left parenthesis in the first statement def y(t):

e) Change the first line of the function definition from def y(t): to def y():, i.e., remove the parameter t.

f) Change the first occurrence of the statement print y(time) to print y().

Filename: errors_colon_indent_etc.py.

Exercise 2.2: Compare integers a and b

Explain briefly, in your own words, what the following program does.

```
a = input('Give an integer a: ')
b = input('Give an integer b: ')

if a < b:
    print "a is the smallest of the two numbers"
elif a == b:
    print "a and b are equal"
else:
    print "a is the largest of the two numbers"
```

Proceed by writing the program, and then run it a few times with different values for a and b to confirm that it works as intended. In particular, choose combinations for a and b so that all three branches of the if construction get tested.

Filename: compare_a_and_b.py.

Exercise 2.3: Functions for circumference and area of a circle

Write a program that takes a circle radius r as input from the user and then computes the circumference C and area A of the circle. Implement the computations of C and A as two separate functions that each takes r as input parameter. Print C and A to the screen along with an appropriate text. Run the program with $r = 1$ and confirm that you get the right answer.

Filename: functions_circumference_area.py.

Exercise 2.4: Function for area of a rectangle

Write a program that computes the area $A = bc$ of a rectangle. The values of b and c should be user input to the program. Also, write the area computation as a function that takes b and c as input parameters and returns the computed area. Let the program print the result to screen along with an appropriate text. Run the program with $b = 2$ and $c = 3$ to confirm correct program behavior.

Filename: function_area_rectangle.py.

Exercise 2.5: Area of a polygon

One of the most important mathematical problems through all times has been to find the area of a polygon, especially because real estate areas often had the shape of polygons, and it was necessary to pay tax for the area. We have a polygon as depicted below.

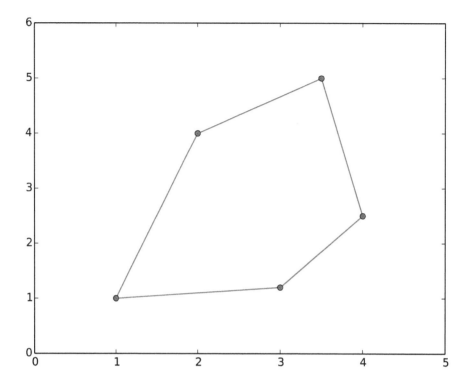

The vertices ("corners") of the polygon have coordinates (x_1, y_1), (x_2, y_2), ..., (x_n, y_n), numbered either in a clockwise or counter clockwise fashion. The area A of the polygon can amazingly be computed by just knowing the boundary coordinates:

$$A = \frac{1}{2} |(x_1 y_2 + x_2 y_3 + \cdots + x_{n-1} y_n + x_n y_1)$$

$$-(y_1 x_2 + y_2 x_3 + \cdots + y_{n-1} x_n + y_n x_1)| .$$

Write a function `polyarea(x, y)` that takes two coordinate arrays with the vertices as arguments and returns the area. Assume that x and y are either lists or arrays.

Test the function on a triangle, a quadrilateral, and a pentagon where you can calculate the area by alternative methods for comparison.

Hint Since Python lists and arrays has 0 as their first index, it is wise to rewrite the mathematical formula in terms of vertex coordinates numbered as $x_0, x_1, \ldots, x_{n-1}$ and $y_0, y_1, \ldots, y_{n-1}$.
Filename: `polyarea.py`.

Exercise 2.6: Average of integers
Write a program that gets an integer $N > 1$ from the user and computes the average of all integers $i = 1, \ldots, N$. The computation should be done in a function that takes N as input parameter. Print the result to the screen with an appropriate text. Run the program with $N = 5$ and confirm that you get the correct answer.
Filename: `average_1_to_N.py`.

Exercise 2.7: While loop with errors

Assume some program has been written for the task of adding all integers $i = 1, 2, \ldots, 10$:

```python
some_number = 0
i = 1
while i < 11
    some_number += 1
print some_number
```

a) Identify the errors in the program by just reading the code and simulating the program by hand.
b) Write a new version of the program with errors corrected. Run this program and confirm that it gives the correct output.

Filename: `while_loop_errors.py`.

Exercise 2.8: Area of rectangle versus circle

Consider one circle and one rectangle. The circle has a radius $r = 10.6$. The rectangle has sides a and b, but only a is known from the outset. Let $a = 1.3$ and write a program that uses a `while` loop to find the largest possible integer b that gives a rectangle area smaller than, but as close as possible to, the area of the circle. Run the program and confirm that it gives the right answer (which is $b = 271$).
Filename: `area_rectangle_vs_circle.py`.

Exercise 2.9: Find crossing points of two graphs

Consider two functions $f(x) = x$ and $g(x) = x^2$ on the interval $[-4, 4]$.

Write a program that, by trial and error, finds approximately for which values of x the two graphs cross, i.e., $f(x) = g(x)$. Do this by considering N equally distributed points on the interval, at each point checking whether $|f(x) - g(x)| < \epsilon$, where ϵ is some small number. Let N and ϵ be user input to the program and let the result be printed to screen. Run your program with $N = 400$ and $\epsilon = 0.01$. Explain the output from the program. Finally, try also other values of N, keeping the value of ϵ fixed. Explain your observations.
Filename: `crossing_2_graphs.py`.

Exercise 2.10: Sort array with numbers

The import statement `from random import *` will give access to a function `uniform` that may be used to draw (pseudo-)random numbers from a uniform distribution between two numbers a (inclusive) and b (inclusive). For example, writing `x = uniform(0,10)` makes x a float value larger than, or equal to, 0, and smaller than, or equal to, 10.

Write a script that generates an array of 6 random numbers between 0 and 10. The program should then sort the array so that numbers appear in increasing order. Let the program make a formatted print of the array to the screen both before and after sorting. The printouts should appear on the screen so that comparison is made easy. Confirm that the array has been sorted correctly.
Filename: `sort_numbers.py`.

Exercise 2.11: Compute π

Up through history, great minds have developed different computational schemes for the number π. We will here consider two such schemes, one by Leibniz (1646 − 1716), and one by Euler (1707 − 1783).

The scheme by Leibniz may be written

$$\pi = 8 \sum_{k=0}^{\infty} \frac{1}{(4k+1)(4k+3)},$$

while one form of the Euler scheme may appear as

$$\pi = \sqrt{6 \sum_{k=1}^{\infty} \frac{1}{k^2}}.$$

If only the first N terms of each sum are used as an approximation to π, each modified scheme will have computed π with some error.

Write a program that takes N as input from the user, and plots the error development with both schemes as the number of iterations approaches N. Your program should also print out the final error achieved with both schemes, i.e. when the number of terms is N. Run the program with $N = 100$ and explain briefly what the graphs show.

Filename: `compute_pi.py`.

Exercise 2.12: Compute combinations of sets

Consider an ID number consisting of two letters and three digits, e.g., RE198. How many different numbers can we have, and how can a program generate all these combinations?

If a collection of n things can have m_1 variations of the first thing, m_2 of the second and so on, the total number of variations of the collection equals $m_1 m_2 \cdots m_n$. In particular, the ID number exemplified above can have $26 \cdot 26 \cdot 10 \cdot 10 \cdot 10 = 676,000$ variations. To generate all the combinations, we must have five nested for loops. The first two run over all letters A, B, and so on to Z, while the next three run over all digits $0, 1, \ldots, 9$.

To convince yourself about this result, start out with an ID number on the form A3 where the first part can vary among A, B, and C, and the digit can be among 1, 2, or 3. We must start with A and combine it with 1, 2, and 3, then continue with B, combined with 1, 2, and 3, and finally combine C with 1, 2, and 3. A double for loop does the work.

a) In a deck of cards, each card is a combination of a rank and a suit. There are 13 ranks: ace (A), 2, 3, 4, 5, 6, 7, 8, 9, 10, jack (J), queen (Q), king (K), and four suits: clubs (C), diamonds (D), hearts (H), and spades (S). A typical card may be D3. Write statements that generate a deck of cards, i.e., all the combinations CA, C2, C3, and so on to SK.

b) A vehicle registration number is on the form DE562, where the letters vary from A to Z and the digits from 0 to 9. Write statements that compute all the possible registration numbers and stores them in a list.

c) Generate all the combinations of throwing two dice (the number of eyes can vary from 1 to 6). Count how many combinations where the sum of the eyes equals 7.

Filename: `combine_sets.py`.

Exercise 2.13: Frequency of random numbers

Write a program that takes a positive integer N as input and then draws N random integers in the interval $[1, 6]$ (both ends inclusive). In the program, count how many of the numbers, M, that equal 6 and write out the fraction M/N. Also, print all the random numbers to the screen so that you can check for yourself that the counting is correct. Run the program with a small value for N (e.g., N = 10) to confirm that it works as intended.

Hint Use `random.randint(1,6)` to draw a random integer between 1 and 6.
Filename: `count_random_numbers.py`.

Remarks For large N, this program computes the probability M/N of getting six eyes when throwing a die.

Exercise 2.14: Game 21

Consider some game where each participant draws a series of random integers evenly distributed from 0 and 10, with the aim of getting the sum as close as possible to 21, but *not larger* than 21. You are out of the game if the sum passes 21. After each draw, you are told the number and your total sum, and are asked whether you want another draw or not. The one coming closest to 21 is the winner.

Implement this game in a program.

Hint Use `random.randint(0,10)` to draw random integers in $[0, 10]$.
Filename: `game_21.py`.

Exercise 2.15: Linear interpolation

Some measurements y_i, $i = 0, 1, \ldots, N$ (given below), of a quantity y have been collected regularly, once every minute, at times $t_i = i$, $i = 0, 1, \ldots, N$. We want to find the value y *in between* the measurements, e.g., at $t = 3.2$ min. Computing such y values is called *interpolation*.

Let your program use *linear interpolation* to compute y between two consecutive measurements:

1. Find i such that $t_i \leq t \leq t_{i+1}$.
2. Find a mathematical expression for the straight line that goes through the points (i, y_i) and $(i + 1, y_{i+1})$.
3. Compute the y value by inserting the user's time value in the expression for the straight line.

a) Implement the linear interpolation technique in a function that takes an array with the y_i measurements as input, together with some time t, and returns the interpolated y value at time t.

b) Write another function with a loop where the user is asked for a time on the interval $[0, N]$ and the corresponding (interpolated) y value is written to the screen. The loop is terminated when the user gives a negative time.

c) Use the following measurements: $4.4, 2.0, 11.0, 21.5, 7.5$, corresponding to times $0, 1, \ldots, 4$ (min), and compute interpolated values at $t = 2.5$ and $t = 3.1$ min. Perform separate hand calculations to check that the output from the program is correct.

Filename: `linear_interpolation.py`.

Exercise 2.16: Test straight line requirement

Assume the straight line function $f(x) = 4x + 1$. Write a script that tests the "point-slope" form for this line as follows. Within a chosen interval on the x-axis (for example, for x between 0 and 10), randomly pick 100 points on the line and check if the following requirement is fulfilled for each point:

$$\frac{f(x_i) - f(c)}{x_i - c} = a, \qquad i = 1, 2, \ldots, 100,$$

where a is the slope of the line and c defines a fixed point $(c, f(c))$ on the line. Let $c = 2$ here.
Filename: `test_straight_line.py`.

Exercise 2.17: Fit straight line to data

Assume some measurements $y_i, i = 1, 2, \ldots, 5$ have been collected, once every second. Your task is to write a program that fits a straight line to those data.

a) Make a function that computes the error between the straight line $f(x) = ax + b$ and the measurements:

$$e = \sum_{i=1}^{5} (ax_i + b - y_i)^2 .$$

b) Make a function with a loop where you give a and b, the corresponding value of e is written to the screen, and a plot of the straight line $f(x) = ax + b$ together with the discrete measurements is shown.

Hint To make the plotting from the loop to work, you may have to insert `from matplotlib.pylab import *` at the top of the script and also add `show()` after the plot command in the loop.

c) Given the measurements $0.5, 2.0, 1.0, 1.5, 7.5$, at times $0, 1, 2, 3, 4$, use the function in b) to interactively search for a and b such that e is minimized.

Filename: `fit_straight_line.py`.

Remarks Fitting a straight line to measured data points is a very common task. The manual search procedure in c) can be automated by using a mathematical method called the *method of least squares*.

Exercise 2.18: Fit sines to straight line

A lot of technology, especially most types of digital audio devices for processing sound, is based on representing a signal of time as a sum of sine functions. Say the signal is some function $f(t)$ on the interval $[-\pi, \pi]$ (a more general interval $[a, b]$ can easily be treated, but leads to slightly more complicated formulas). Instead of working with $f(t)$ directly, we approximate f by the sum

$$S_N(t) = \sum_{n=1}^{N} b_n \sin(nt), \tag{2.1}$$

where the coefficients b_n must be adjusted such that $S_N(t)$ is a good approximation to $f(t)$. We shall in this exercise adjust b_n by a trial-and-error process.

a) Make a function `sinesum(t, b)` that returns $S_N(t)$, given the coefficients b_n in an array `b` and time coordinates in an array `t`. Note that if `t` is an array, the return value is also an array.

b) Write a function `test_sinesum()` that calls `sinesum(t, b)` in a) and determines if the function computes a test case correctly. As test case, let `t` be an array with values $-\pi/2$ and $\pi/4$, choose $N = 2$, and $b_1 = 4$ and $b_2 = -3$. Compute $S_N(t)$ by hand to get reference values.

c) Make a function `plot_compare(f, N, M)` that plots the original function $f(t)$ together with the sum of sines $S_N(t)$, so that the quality of the approximation $S_N(t)$ can be examined visually. The argument `f` is a Python function implementing $f(t)$, N is the number of terms in the sum $S_N(t)$, and M is the number of uniformly distributed t coordinates used to plot f and S_N.

d) Write a function `error(b, f, M)` that returns a mathematical measure of the error in $S_N(t)$ as an approximation to $f(t)$:

$$E = \sqrt{\sum_{i} (f(t_i) - S_N(t_i))^2},$$

where the t_i values are M uniformly distributed coordinates on $[-\pi, \pi]$. The array `b` holds the coefficients in S_N and `f` is a Python function implementing the mathematical function $f(t)$.

e) Make a function `trial(f, N)` for interactively giving b_n values and getting a plot on the screen where the resulting $S_N(t)$ is plotted together with $f(t)$. The error in the approximation should also be computed as indicated in d). The argument `f` is a Python function for $f(t)$ and N is the number of terms N in the sum $S_N(t)$. The `trial` function can run a loop where the user is asked for the b_n values in each pass of the loop and the corresponding plot is shown. You must find a way to terminate the loop when the experiments are over. Use M=500 in the calls to `plot_compare` and `error`.

Hint To make this part of your program work, you may have to insert `from matplotlib.pylab import *` at the top and also add `show()` after the plot command in the loop.

f) Choose $f(t)$ to be a straight line $f(t) = \frac{1}{\pi}t$ on $[-\pi, \pi]$. Call `trial(f, 3)` and try to find through experimentation some values b_1, b_2, and b_3 such that the sum of sines $S_N(t)$ is a good approximation to the straight line.

g) Now we shall try to automate the procedure in f). Write a function that has three nested loops over values of b_1, b_2, and b_3. Let each loop cover the interval $[-1, 1]$ in steps of 0.1. For each combination of b_1, b_2, and b_3, the error in the approximation S_N should be computed. Use this to find, and print, the smallest error and the corresponding values of b_1, b_2, and b_3. Let the program also plot f and the approximation S_N corresponding to the smallest error.

Filename: `fit_sines.py`.

Remarks

1. The function $S_N(x)$ is a special case of what is called a *Fourier series*. At the beginning of the 19th century, Joseph Fourier (1768-1830) showed that any function can be approximated analytically by a sum of cosines and sines. The approximation improves as the number of terms (N) is increased. Fourier series are very important throughout science and engineering today.

   (a) Finding the coefficients b_n is solved much more accurately in Exercise 3.12, by a procedure that also requires much less human and computer work!

   (b) In real applications, $f(t)$ is not known as a continuous function, but function values of $f(t)$ are provided. For example, in digital sound applications, music in a CD-quality WAV file is a signal with 44,100 samples of the corresponding analog signal $f(t)$ per second.

Exercise 2.19: Count occurrences of a string in a string

In the analysis of genes one encounters many problem settings involving searching for certain combinations of letters in a long string. For example, we may have a string like

```
gene = 'AGTCAATGGAATAGGCCAAGCGAATATTTGGGCTACCA'
```

We may traverse this string, letter by letter, by the for loop `for letter in gene`. The length of the string is given by `len(gene)`, so an alternative traversal over an index i is `for i in range(len(gene))`. Letter number i is reached through `gene[i]`, and a substring from index i up to, but not including j, is created by `gene[i:j]`.

a) Write a function `freq(letter, text)` that returns the frequency of the letter `letter` in the string `text`, i.e., the number of occurrences of `letter` divided by the length of `text`. Call the function to determine the frequency of C and G in the gene string above. Compute the frequency by hand too.

b) Write a function `pairs(letter, text)` that counts how many times a pair of the letter `letter` (e.g., GG) occurs within the string `text`. Use the function to determine how many times the pair AA appears in the string gene above. Perform a manual counting too to check the answer.

c) Write a function `mystruct(text)` that counts the number of a certain structure in the string `text`. The structure is defined as G followed by A or T until a double GG. Perform a manual search for the structure too to control the computations by `mystruct`.

Filename: `count_substrings.py`.

Remarks You are supposed to solve the tasks using simple programming with loops and variables. While a) and b) are quite straightforward, c) quickly involves demanding logic. However, there are powerful tools available in Python that can solve the tasks efficiently in very compact code: a) `text.count(letter)/float(len(text))`; b) `text.count(letter*2)`; c) `len(re.findall('G[AT]+?GG', text))`. That is, there is rich functionality for analysis of text in Python and this is particularly useful in analysis of gene sequences.

3

Computing Integrals Used in Python Programming

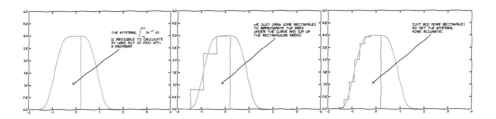

We now turn our attention to solving mathematical problems through computer programming. There are many reasons to choose integration as our first application. Integration is well known already from high school mathematics. Most integrals are not tractable by pen and paper, and a computerized solution approach is both very much simpler and much more powerful – you can essentially treat all integrals $\int_a^b f(x)dx$ in 10 lines of computer code (!). Integration also demonstrates the difference between exact mathematics by pen and paper and *numerical mathematics* on a computer. The latter approaches the result of the former without any worries about rounding errors due to finite precision arithmetics in computers (in contrast to differentiation, where such errors prevent us from getting a result as accurate as we desire on the computer). Finally, integration is thought of as a somewhat difficult mathematical concept to grasp, and programming integration should greatly help with the understanding of what integration is and how it works. Not only shall we understand how to use the computer to integrate, but we shall also learn a series of good habits to ensure your computer work is of the highest scientific quality. In particular, we have a strong focus on how to write Python code that is free of programming mistakes.

Calculating an integral is traditionally done by

$$\int_a^b f(x)\,dx = F(b) - F(a), \tag{3.1}$$

where

$$f(x) = \frac{dF}{dx}.$$

The major problem with this procedure is that we need to find the *anti-derivative* $F(x)$ corresponding to a given $f(x)$. For some relatively simple integrands $f(x)$, finding $F(x)$ is a doable task, but it can very quickly become challenging, even impossible!

The method (3.1) provides an *exact* or *analytical* value of the integral. If we relax the requirement of the integral being exact, and instead look for *approximate* values, produced by *numerical methods*, integration becomes a very straightforward task for any given $f(x)$ (!).

The downside of a numerical method is that it can only find an approximate answer. Leaving the exact for the approximate is a mental barrier in the beginning, but remember that most real applications of integration will involve an $f(x)$ function that contains physical parameters, which are measured with some error. That is, $f(x)$ is very seldom exact, and then it does not make sense to compute the integral with a smaller error than the one already present in $f(x)$.

Another advantage of numerical methods is that we can easily integrate a function $f(x)$ that is only known as *samples*, i.e., discrete values at some x points, and not as a continuous function of x expressed through a formula. This is highly relevant when f is measured in a physical experiment.

3.1 Basic Ideas of Numerical Integration

We consider the integral

$$\int_a^b f(x)dx .\tag{3.2}$$

Most numerical methods for computing this integral split up the original integral into a sum of several integrals, each covering a smaller part of the original integration interval $[a, b]$. This re-writing of the integral is based on a selection of *integration points* x_i, $i = 0, 1, \ldots, n$ that are distributed on the interval $[a, b]$. Integration points may, or may not, be evenly distributed. An even distribution simplifies expressions and is often sufficient, so we will mostly restrict ourselves to that choice. The integration points are then computed as

$$x_i = a + ih, \quad i = 0, 1, \ldots, n,\tag{3.3}$$

where

$$h = \frac{b - a}{n} .\tag{3.4}$$

Given the integration points, the original integral is re-written as a sum of integrals, each integral being computed over the sub-interval between two consecutive integration points. The integral in (3.2) is thus expressed as

$$\int_a^b f(x)dx = \int_{x_0}^{x_1} f(x)dx + \int_{x_1}^{x_2} f(x)dx + \ldots + \int_{x_{n-1}}^{x_n} f(x)dx .\tag{3.5}$$

Note that $x_0 = a$ and $x_n = b$.

Proceeding from (3.5), the different integration methods will differ in the way they approximate each integral on the right hand side. The fundamental idea is that each term is an integral over a small interval $[x_i, x_{i+1}]$, and over this small interval, it makes sense to approximate f by a simple shape, say a constant, a straight line, or a parabola, which we can easily integrate by hand. The details will become clear in the coming examples.

Computational example To understand and compare the numerical integration methods, it is advantageous to use a specific integral for computations and graphical illustrations. In particular, we want to use an integral that we can calculate by hand such that the accuracy of the approximation methods can easily be assessed. Our specific integral is taken from basic physics. Assume that you speed up your car from rest and wonder how far you go in T seconds. The distance is given by the integral $\int_0^T v(t)dt$, where $v(t)$ is the velocity as a function of time. A rapidly increasing velocity function might be

$$v(t) = 3t^2 e^{t^3}. \tag{3.6}$$

The distance after one second is

$$\int_0^1 v(t)dt, \tag{3.7}$$

which is the integral we aim to compute by numerical methods. Fortunately, the chosen expression of the velocity has a form that makes it easy to calculate the anti-derivative as

$$V(t) = e^{t^3} - 1. \tag{3.8}$$

We can therefore compute the exact value of the integral as $V(1) - V(0) \approx 1.718$ (rounded to 3 decimals for convenience).

3.2   The Composite Trapezoidal Rule

The integral $\int_a^b f(x)dx$ may be interpreted as the area between the x axis and the graph $y = f(x)$ of the integrand. Figure 3.1 illustrates this area for the choice (3.7). Computing the integral $\int_0^1 f(t)dt$ amounts to computing the area of the hatched region.

If we *replace* the true graph in Fig. 3.1 by a set of straight line segments, we may view the area rather as composed of trapezoids, the areas of which are easy to compute. This is illustrated in Fig. 3.2, where 4 straight line segments give rise to 4 trapezoids, covering the time intervals $[0, 0.2)$, $[0.2, 0.6)$, $[0.6, 0.8)$ and $[0.8, 1.0]$. Note that we have taken the opportunity here to demonstrate the computations with time intervals that differ in size.

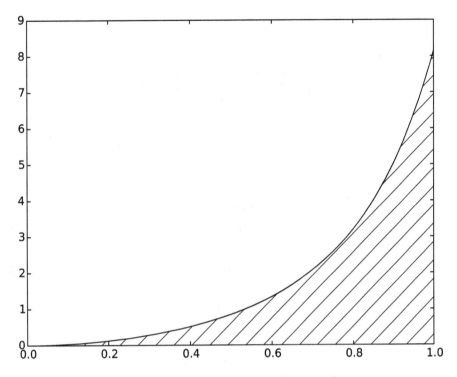

Fig. 3.1 The integral of $v(t)$ interpreted as the area under the graph of v

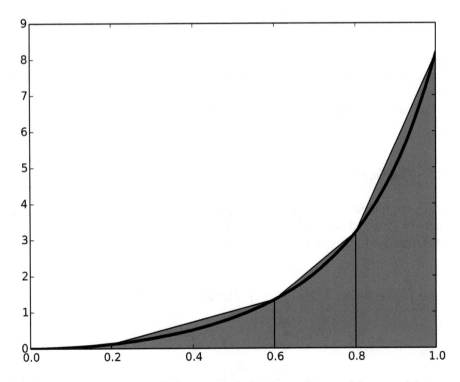

Fig. 3.2 Computing approximately the integral of a function as the sum of the areas of the trapezoids

The areas of the 4 trapezoids shown in Fig. 3.2 now constitute our approximation to the integral (3.7):

$$\int_0^1 v(t)dt \approx h_1 \left(\frac{v(0) + v(0.2)}{2} \right) + h_2 \left(\frac{v(0.2) + v(0.6)}{2} \right)$$

$$+ h_3 \left(\frac{v(0.6) + v(0.8)}{2} \right) + h_4 \left(\frac{v(0.8) + v(1.0)}{2} \right), \qquad (3.9)$$

where

$$h_1 = (0.2 - 0.0), \qquad\qquad\qquad (3.10)$$
$$h_2 = (0.6 - 0.2), \qquad\qquad\qquad (3.11)$$
$$h_3 = (0.8 - 0.6), \qquad\qquad\qquad (3.12)$$
$$h_4 = (1.0 - 0.8) \qquad\qquad\qquad (3.13)$$

With $v(t) = 3t^2 e^{t^3}$, each term in (3.9) is readily computed and our approximate computation gives

$$\int_0^1 v(t)dt \approx 1.895. \qquad\qquad\qquad (3.14)$$

Compared to the true answer of 1.718, this is off by about 10 %. However, note that we used just 4 trapezoids to approximate the area. With more trapezoids, the approximation would have become better, since the straight line segments in the upper trapezoid side then would follow the graph more closely. Doing another hand calculation with more trapezoids is not too tempting for a lazy human, though, but it is a perfect job for a computer! Let us therefore derive the expressions for approximating the integral by an arbitrary number of trapezoids.

3.2.1 The General Formula

For a given function $f(x)$, we want to approximate the integral $\int_a^b f(x)dx$ by n trapezoids (of equal width). We start out with (3.5) and approximate each integral on the right hand side with a single trapezoid. In detail,

$$\int_a^b f(x)\,dx = \int_{x_0}^{x_1} f(x)dx + \int_{x_1}^{x_2} f(x)dx + \ldots + \int_{x_{n-1}}^{x_n} f(x)dx,$$

$$\approx h\frac{f(x_0) + f(x_1)}{2} + h\frac{f(x_1) + f(x_2)}{2} + \ldots$$

$$+ h\frac{f(x_{n-1}) + f(x_n)}{2} \qquad\qquad (3.15)$$

By simplifying the right hand side of (3.15) we get

$$\int_a^b f(x)\,dx \approx \frac{h}{2}\left[f(x_0) + 2f(x_1) + 2f(x_2) + \ldots + 2f(x_{n-1}) + f(x_n)\right] \quad (3.16)$$

which is more compactly written as

$$\int_a^b f(x)\,dx \approx h\left[\frac{1}{2}f(x_0) + \sum_{i=1}^{n-1} f(x_i) + \frac{1}{2}f(x_n)\right]. \qquad (3.17)$$

Composite integration rules

The word *composite* is often used when a numerical integration method is applied with more than one sub-interval. Strictly speaking then, writing, e.g., "the trapezoidal method", should imply the use of only a single trapezoid, while "the composite trapezoidal method" is the most correct name when several trapezoids are used. However, this naming convention is not always followed, so saying just "the trapezoidal method" may point to a single trapezoid as well as the composite rule with many trapezoids.

3.2.2 Implementation

Specific or general implementation? Suppose our primary goal was to compute the specific integral $\int_0^1 v(t)\,dt$ with $v(t) = 3t^2 e^{t^3}$. First we played around with a simple hand calculation to see what the method was about, before we (as one often does in mathematics) developed a general formula (3.17) for the general or "abstract" integral $\int_a^b f(x)\,dx$. To solve our specific problem $\int_0^1 v(t)\,dt$ we must then apply the general formula (3.17) to the given data (function and integral limits) in our problem. Although simple in principle, the practical steps are confusing for many because the notation in the abstract problem in (3.17) differs from the notation in our special problem. Clearly, the f, x, and h in (3.17) correspond to v, t, and perhaps Δt for the trapezoid width in our special problem.

The programmer's dilemma

1. Should we write a special program for the special integral, using the ideas from the general rule (3.17), but replacing f by v, x by t, and h by Δt?
2. Should we implement the general method (3.17) as it stands in a general function `trapezoid(f, a, b, n)` and solve the specific problem at hand by a specialized call to this function?

Alternative 2 is always the best choice!

The first alternative in the box above sounds less abstract and therefore more attractive to many. Nevertheless, as we hope will be evident from the examples, the second alternative is actually the simplest *and* most reliable from both a mathematical and programming point of view. These authors will claim that the second alternative is the essence of the power of mathematics, while the first alternative is the source of much confusion about mathematics!

Implementation with functions For the integral $\int_a^b f(x)dx$ computed by the formula (3.17) we want the corresponding Python function `trapezoid` to take any f, a, b, and n as input and return the approximation to the integral.

We write a Python function `trapezoidal` in a file `trapezoidal.py` as close as possible to the formula (3.17), making sure variable names correspond to the mathematical notation:

```python
def trapezoidal(f, a, b, n):
    h = float(b-a)/n
    result = 0.5*f(a) + 0.5*f(b)
    for i in range(1, n):
        result += f(a + i*h)
    result *= h
    return result
```

Solving our specific problem in a session Just having the `trapezoidal` function as the only content of a file `trapezoidal.py` automatically makes that file a module that we can import and test in an interactive session:

```python
>>> from trapezoidal import trapezoidal
>>> from math import exp
>>> v = lambda t: 3*(t**2)*exp(t**3)
>>> n = 4
>>> numerical = trapezoidal(v, 0, 1, n)
>>> numerical
1.9227167504675762
```

Let us compute the exact expression and the error in the approximation:

```python
>>> V = lambda t: exp(t**3)
>>> exact = V(1) - V(0)
>>> exact - numerical
-0.20443492200853108
```

Is this error convincing? We can try a larger n:

```python
>>> numerical = trapezoidal(v, 0, 1, n=400)
>>> exact - numerical
-2.1236490512777095e-05
```

Fortunately, many more trapezoids give a much smaller error.

Solving our specific problem in a program Instead of computing our special problem in an interactive session, we can do it in a program. As always, a chunk of code doing a particular thing is best isolated as a function even if we do not see any future reason to call the function several times and even if we have no need for arguments to parameterize what goes on inside the function. In the present case, we just put the statements we otherwise would have put in a main program, inside a function:

```
def application():
    from math import exp
    v = lambda t: 3*(t**2)*exp(t**3)
    n = input('n: ')
    numerical = trapezoidal(v, 0, 1, n)

    # Compare with exact result
    V = lambda t: exp(t**3)
    exact = V(1) - V(0)
    error = exact - numerical
    print 'n=%d: %.16f, error: %g' % (n, numerical, error)
```

Now we compute our special problem by calling `application()` as the only statement in the main program. Both the `trapezoidal` and `application` functions reside in the file `trapezoidal.py`, which can be run as

--------------------------------- Terminal ---------------------------------

```
Terminal> python trapezoidal.py
n: 4
n=4: 1.9227167504675762, error: -0.204435
```

3.2.3 Making a Module

When we have the different pieces of our program as a collection of functions, it is very straightforward to create a *module* that can be imported in other programs. That is, having our code as a module, means that the `trapezoidal` function can easily be reused by other programs to solve other problems. The requirements of a module are simple: put everything inside functions and let function calls in the main program be in the so-called *test block*:

```
if __name__ == '__main__':
    application()
```

The `if` test is true if the module file, `trapezoidal.py`, is run as a program and false if the module is imported in another program. Consequently, when we do `from trapezoidal import trapezoidal` in some file, the test fails and `application()` is not called, i.e., our special problem is not solved and will not print anything on the screen. On the other hand, if we run `trapezoidal.py` in the terminal window, the test condition is positive, `application()` is called, and we get output in the window:

--------------------------------- Terminal ---------------------------------

```
Terminal> python trapezoidal.py
n: 400
n=400: 1.7183030649495579, error: -2.12365e-05
```

3.2.4   Alternative Flat Special-Purpose Implementation

Let us illustrate the implementation implied by alternative 1 in the *Programmer's dilemma* box in Sect. 3.2.2. That is, we make a special-purpose code where we adapt the general formula (3.17) to the specific problem $\int_0^1 3t^2 e^{t^3} dt$.

Basically, we use a for loop to compute the sum. Each term with $f(x)$ in the formula (3.17) is replaced by $3t^2 e^{t^3}$, x by t, and h by Δt [1]. A first try at writing a plain, flat program doing the special calculation is

```
from math import exp

a = 0.0;   b = 1.0
n = input('n: ')
dt = float(b - a)/n

# Integral by the trapezoidal method
numerical = 0.5*3*(a**2)*exp(a**3) + 0.5*3*(b**2)*exp(b**3)
for i in range(1, n):
    numerical += 3*((a + i*dt)**2)*exp((a + i*dt)**3)
numerical *= dt

exact_value = exp(1**3) - exp(0**3)
error = abs(exact_value - numerical)
rel_error = (error/exact_value)*100
print 'n=%d: %.16f, error: %g' % (n, numerical, error)
```

The problem with the above code is at least three-fold:

1. We need to reformulate (3.17) for our special problem with a different notation.
2. The integrand $3t^2 e^{t^3}$ is inserted many times in the code, which quickly leads to errors.
3. A lot of edits are necessary to use the code to compute a different integral – these edits are likely to introduce errors.

The potential errors involved in point 2 serve to illustrate how important it is to use Python functions as mathematical functions. Here we have chosen to use the lambda function to define the integrand as the variable v:

```
from math import exp

v = lambda t: 3*(t**2)*exp(t**3)   # Function to be integrated
a = 0.0;   b = 1.0
n = input('n: ')
dt = float(b - a)/n
```

---

[1] Replacing h by Δt is not strictly required as many use h as interval also along the time axis. Nevertheless, Δt is an even more popular notation for a small time interval, so we adopt that common notation.

```
# Integral by the trapezoidal method
numerical = 0.5*v(a) + 0.5*v(b)
for i in range(1, n):
    numerical += v(a + i*dt)
numerical *= dt

F = lambda t: exp(t**3)
exact_value = F(b) - F(a)
error = abs(exact_value - numerical)
rel_error = (error/exact_value)*100
print 'n=%d: %.16f, error: %g' % (n, numerical, error)
```

Unfortunately, the two other problems remain and they are fundamental.

Suppose you want to compute another integral, say $\int_{-1}^{1.1} e^{-x^2}\, dx$. How much do we need to change in the previous code to compute the new integral? Not so much:

- the formula for v must be replaced by a new formula
- the limits a and b
- the anti-derivative V is not easily known[2] and can be omitted, and therefore we cannot write out the error
- the notation should be changed to be aligned with the new problem, i.e., t and dt changed to x and h

These changes are straightforward to implement, but *they are scattered around in the program*, a fact that requires us to be very careful so we do not introduce new programming errors while we modify the code. It is also very easy to forget to make a required change.

With the previous code in `trapezoidal.py`, we can compute the new integral $\int_{-1}^{1.1} e^{-x^2}\, dx$ *without touching the mathematical algorithm*. In an interactive session (or in a program) we can just do

```
>>> from trapezoidal import trapezoidal
>>> from math import exp
>>> trapezoidal(lambda x: exp(-x**2), -1, 1.1, 400)
1.5268823686123285
```

When you now look back at the two solutions, the flat special-purpose program and the function-based program with the general-purpose function `trapezoidal`, you hopefully realize that *implementing a general mathematical algorithm in a general function* requires somewhat more abstract thinking, but the resulting code can be used over and over again. Essentially, if you apply the flat special-purpose style, you have to retest the implementation of the algorithm after every change of the program.

---

[2] You cannot integrate e^{-x^2} by hand, but this particular integral is appearing so often in so many contexts that the integral is a special function, called the Error function (http://en.wikipedia.org/wiki/Error_function) and written erf(x). In a code, you can call `erf(x)`. The erf function is found in the `math` module.

The present integral problems result in short code. In more challenging engineering problems the code quickly grows to hundreds and thousands of lines. Without abstractions in terms of general algorithms in general reusable functions, the complexity of the program grows so fast that it will be extremely difficult to make sure that the program works properly.

Another advantage of packaging mathematical algorithms in functions is that a function can be reused by anyone to solve a problem by just calling the function with a proper set of arguments. Understanding the function's inner details is not necessary to compute a new integral. Similarly, you can find libraries of functions on the Internet and use these functions to solve your problems without specific knowledge of every mathematical detail in the functions.

This desirable feature has its downside, of course: the user of a function may misuse it, and the function may contain programming errors and lead to wrong answers. Testing the output of downloaded functions is therefore extremely important before relying on the results.

3.3 The Composite Midpoint Method

The idea Rather than approximating the area under a curve by trapezoids, we can use plain rectangles (Fig. 3.3). It may sound less accurate to use horizontal lines and not skew lines following the function to be integrated, but an integration method based on rectangles (the *midpoint method*) is in fact slightly more accurate than the one based on trapezoids!

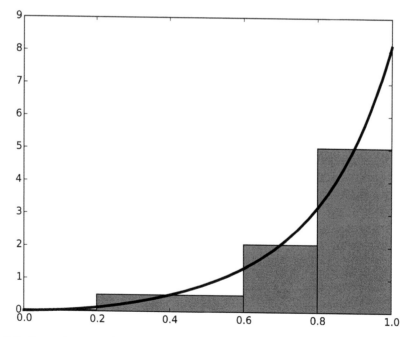

Fig. 3.3 Computing approximately the integral of a function as the sum of the areas of the rectangles

In the midpoint method, we construct a rectangle for every sub-interval where the height equals f at the midpoint of the sub-interval. Let us do this for four rectangles, using the same sub-intervals as we had for hand calculations with the trapezoidal method: $[0, 0.2)$, $[0.2, 0.6)$, $[0.6, 0.8)$, and $[0.8, 1.0]$. We get

$$\int_0^1 f(t)dt \approx h_1 f\left(\frac{0+0.2}{2}\right) + h_2 f\left(\frac{0.2+0.6}{2}\right)$$

$$+ h_3 f\left(\frac{0.6+0.8}{2}\right) + h_4 f\left(\frac{0.8+1.0}{2}\right),$$

(3.18)

where h_1, h_2, h_3, and h_4 are the widths of the sub-intervals, used previously with the trapezoidal method and defined in (3.10)–(3.13).

With $f(t) = 3t^2 e^{t^3}$, the approximation becomes 1.632. Compared with the true answer (1.718), this is about 5 % too small, but it is better than what we got with the trapezoidal method (10 %) with the same sub-intervals. More rectangles give a better approximation.

3.3.1   The General Formula

Let us derive a formula for the midpoint method based on n rectangles of equal width:

$$\int_a^b f(x)\,dx = \int_{x_0}^{x_1} f(x)dx + \int_{x_1}^{x_2} f(x)dx + \ldots + \int_{x_{n-1}}^{x_n} f(x)dx,$$

$$\approx hf\left(\frac{x_0+x_1}{2}\right) + hf\left(\frac{x_1+x_2}{2}\right) + \ldots + hf\left(\frac{x_{n-1}+x_n}{2}\right),$$

(3.19)

$$\approx h\left(f\left(\frac{x_0+x_1}{2}\right) + f\left(\frac{x_1+x_2}{2}\right) + \ldots + f\left(\frac{x_{n-1}+x_n}{2}\right)\right).$$

(3.20)

This sum may be written more compactly as

$$\int_a^b f(x)dx \approx h \sum_{i=0}^{n-1} f(x_i),$$

(3.21)

where $x_i = \left(a + \frac{h}{2}\right) + ih.$

3.3.2   Implementation

We follow the advice and lessons learned from the implementation of the trapezoidal method and make a function `midpoint(f, a, b, n)` (in a file `midpoint.py`) for implementing the general formula (3.21):

```
def midpoint(f, a, b, n):
    h = float(b-a)/n
    result = 0
    for i in range(n):
        result += f((a + h/2.0) + i*h)
    result *= h
    return result
```

We can test the function as we explained for the similar `trapezoidal` method. The error in our particular problem $\int_0^1 3t^2 e^{t^3} dt$ with four intervals is now about 0.1 in contrast to 0.2 for the trapezoidal rule. This is in fact not accidental: one can show mathematically that the error of the midpoint method is a bit smaller than for the trapezoidal method. The differences are seldom of any practical importance, and on a laptop we can easily use $n = 10^6$ and get the answer with an error of about 10^{-12} in a couple of seconds.

3.3.3   Comparing the Trapezoidal and the Midpoint Methods

The next example shows how easy we can combine the `trapezoidal` and `midpoint` functions to make a comparison of the two methods in the file `compare_integration_methods.py`:

```
from trapezoidal import trapezoidal
from midpoint import midpoint
from math import exp

g = lambda y: exp(-y**2)
a = 0
b = 2
print '    n          midpoint              trapezoidal'
for i in range(1, 21):
    n = 2**i
    m = midpoint(g, a, b, n)
    t = trapezoidal(g, a, b, n)
    print '%7d %.16f %.16f' % (n, m, t)
```

Note the efforts put into nice formatting – the output becomes

```
    n          midpoint              trapezoidal
    2 0.8842000076332692 0.8770372606158094
    4 0.8827889485397279 0.8806186341245393
    8 0.8822686991994210 0.8817037913321336
   16 0.8821288703366458 0.8819862452657772
```

```
      32 0.8820933014203766 0.8820575578012112
      64 0.8820843709743319 0.8820754296107942
     128 0.8820821359746071 0.8820799002925637
     256 0.8820815770754198 0.8820810181335849
     512 0.8820814373412922 0.8820812976045025
    1024 0.8820814024071774 0.8820813674728968
    2048 0.8820813936736116 0.8820813849400392
    4096 0.8820813914902204 0.8820813893068272
    8192 0.8820813909443684 0.8820813903985197
   16384 0.8820813908079066 0.8820813906714446
   32768 0.8820813907737911 0.8820813907396778
   65536 0.8820813907652575 0.8820813907567422
  131072 0.8820813907631487 0.8820813907610036
  262144 0.8820813907625702 0.8820813907620528
  524288 0.8820813907624605 0.8820813907623183
 1048576 0.8820813907624268 0.8820813907623890
```

A visual inspection of the numbers shows how fast the digits stabilize in both methods. It appears that 13 digits have stabilized in the last two rows.

Remark

The trapezoidal and midpoint methods are just two examples in a jungle of numerical integration rules. Other famous methods are Simpson's rule and Gauss quadrature. They all work in the same way:

$$\int_a^b f(x)dx \approx \sum_{i=0}^{n-1} w_i f(x_i).$$

That is, the integral is approximated by a sum of function evaluations, where each evaluation $f(x_i)$ is given a weight w_i. The different methods differ in the way they construct the evaluation points x_i and the weights w_i. We have used equally spaced points x_i, but higher accuracy can be obtained by optimizing the location of x_i.

3.4 Testing

3.4.1 Problems with Brief Testing Procedures

Testing of the programs for numerical integration has so far employed two strategies. If we have an exact answer, we compute the error and see that increasing n decreases the error. When the exact answer is not available, we can (as in the comparison example in the previous section) look at the integral values and see that they stabilize as n grows. Unfortunately, these are very weak test procedures and not at all satisfactory for claiming that the software we have produced is correctly implemented.

To see this, we can introduce a bug in the `application` function that calls `trapezoidal`: instead of integrating $3t^2 e^{t^3}$, we write "accidentally" $3t^3 e^{t^3}$, but keep the same anti-derivative $V(t)e^{t^3}$ for computing the error. With the bug and

$n = 4$, the error is 0.1, but without the bug the error is 0.2! It is of course completely impossible to tell if 0.1 is the right value of the error. Fortunately, increasing n shows that the error stays about 0.3 in the program with the bug, so the test procedure with increasing n and checking that the error decreases points to a problem in the code.

Let us look at another bug, this time in the mathematical algorithm: instead of computing $\frac{1}{2}(f(a) + f(b))$ as we should, we forget the second $\frac{1}{2}$ and write `0.5*f(a) + f(b)`. The error for $n = 4, 40, 400$ when computing $\int_{1.1}^{1.9} 3t^2 e^{t^3} dt$ goes like 1400, 107, 10, respectively, which looks promising. The problem is that the right errors should be 369, 4.08, and 0.04. That is, the error should be reduced faster in the correct than in the buggy code. The problem, however, is that it is reduced in both codes, and we may stop further testing and believe everything is correctly implemented.

Unit testing

A good habit is to test small pieces of a larger code individually, one at a time. This is known as *unit testing*. One identifies a (small) unit of the code, and then one makes a separate test for this unit. The unit test should be stand-alone in the sense that it can be run without the outcome of other tests. Typically, one algorithm in scientific programs is considered as a unit. The challenge with unit tests in numerical computing is to deal with numerical approximation errors. A fortunate side effect of unit testing is that the programmer is forced to use functions to modularize the code into smaller, logical pieces.

3.4.2 Proper Test Procedures

There are three serious ways to test the implementation of numerical methods via unit tests:

1. *Comparing with hand-computed results* in a problem with few arithmetic operations, i.e., small n.
2. *Solving a problem without numerical errors.* We know that the trapezoidal rule must be exact for linear functions. The error produced by the program must then be zero (to machine precision).
3. *Demonstrating correct convergence rates.* A strong test when we can compute exact errors, is to see how fast the error goes to zero as n grows. In the trapezoidal and midpoint rules it is known that the error depends on n as n^{-2} as $n \to \infty$.

Hand-computed results Let us use two trapezoids and compute the integral $\int_0^1 v(t)$, $v(t) = 3t^2 e^{t^3}$:

$$\frac{1}{2}h(v(0) + v(0.5)) + \frac{1}{2}h(v(0.5) + v(1)) = 2.463642041244344,$$

when $h = 0.5$ is the width of the two trapezoids. Running the program gives exactly the same result.

Solving a problem without numerical errors The best unit tests for numerical algorithms involve mathematical problems where we know the numerical result beforehand. Usually, numerical results contain unknown approximation errors, so knowing the numerical result implies that we have a problem where the approximation errors vanish. This feature may be present in very simple mathematical problems. For example, the trapezoidal method is exact for integration of linear functions $f(x) = ax + b$. We can therefore pick some linear function and construct a test function that checks equality between the exact analytical expression for the integral and the number computed by the implementation of the trapezoidal method.

A specific test case can be $\int_{1.2}^{4.4}(6x - 4)dx$. This integral involves an "arbitrary" interval $[1.2, 4.4]$ and an "arbitrary" linear function $f(x) = 6x - 4$. By "arbitrary" we mean expressions where we avoid the special numbers 0 and 1 since these have special properties in arithmetic operations (e.g., forgetting to multiply is equivalent to multiplying by 1, and forgetting to add is equivalent to adding 0).

Demonstrating correct convergence rates Normally, unit tests must be based on problems where the numerical approximation errors in our implementation remain unknown. However, we often know or may assume a certain *asymptotic* behavior of the error. We can do some experimental runs with the test problem $\int_0^1 3t^2 e^{t^3} dt$ where n is doubled in each run: $n = 4, 8, 16$. The corresponding errors are then 12 %, 3 % and 0.77 %, respectively. These numbers indicate that the error is roughly reduced by a factor of 4 when doubling n. Thus, the error converges to zero as n^{-2} and we say that the *convergence rate* is 2. In fact, this result can also be shown mathematically for the trapezoidal and midpoint method. Numerical integration methods usually have an error that converge to zero as n^{-p} for some p that depends on the method. With such a result, it does not matter if we do not know what the actual approximation error is: we know at what rate it is *reduced*, so running the implementation for two or more different n values will put us in a position to measure the expected rate and see if it is achieved.

The idea of a corresponding unit test is then to run the algorithm for some n values, compute the error (the absolute value of the difference between the exact analytical result and the one produced by the numerical method), and check that the error has *approximately* correct asymptotic behavior, i.e., that the error is proportional to n^{-2} in case of the trapezoidal and midpoint method.

Let us develop a more precise method for such unit tests based on convergence rates. We assume that the error E depends on n according to

$$E = Cn^r,$$

where C is an unknown constant and r is the convergence rate. Consider a set of experiments with various n: $n_0, n_1, n_2, \ldots, n_q$. We compute the corresponding errors $E_0, \ldots, E_q$. For two consecutive experiments, number i and $i - 1$, we have the error model

$$E_i = Cn_i^r, \tag{3.22}$$
$$E_{i-1} = Cn_{i-1}^r. \tag{3.23}$$

These are two equations for two unknowns C and r. We can easily eliminate C by dividing the equations by each other. Then solving for r gives

$$r_{i-1} = \frac{\ln(E_i/E_{i-1})}{\ln(n_i/n_{i-1})} \, . \tag{3.24}$$

We have introduced a subscript $i - 1$ in r since the estimated value for r varies with i. Hopefully, r_{i-1} approaches the correct convergence rate as the number of intervals increases and $i \to q$.

3.4.3   Finite Precision of Floating-Point Numbers

The test procedures above lead to comparison of numbers for checking that calculations were correct. Such comparison is more complicated than what a newcomer might think. Suppose we have a calculation a + b and want to check that the result is what we expect. We start with $1 + 2$:

```
>>> a = 1; b = 2; expected = 3
>>> a + b == expected
True
```

Then we proceed with $0.1 + 0.2$:

```
>>> a = 0.1; b = 0.2; expected = 0.3
>>> a + b == expected
False
```

So why is $0.1 + 0.2 \neq 0.3$? The reason is that real numbers cannot in general be exactly represented on a computer. They must instead be approximated by a floating-point number[3] that can only store a finite amount of information, usually about 17 digits of a real number. Let us print $0.1, 0.2, 0.1 + 0.2$, and 0.3 with 17 decimals:

```
>>> print '%.17f\n%.17f\n%.17f\n%.17f' % (0.1, 0.2, 0.1 + 0.2, 0.3)
0.10000000000000001
0.20000000000000001
0.30000000000000004
0.29999999999999999
```

We see that all of the numbers have an inaccurate digit in the 17th decimal place. Because $0.1 + 0.2$ evaluates to 0.30000000000000004 and 0.3 is represented as 0.29999999999999999, these two numbers are not equal. In general, real numbers in Python have (at most) 16 correct decimals.

When we compute with real numbers, these numbers are inaccurately represented on the computer, and arithmetic operations with inaccurate numbers lead to small rounding errors in the final results. Depending on the type of numerical algorithm, the rounding errors may or may not accumulate.

---

[3] https://en.wikipedia.org/wiki/Floating_point

If we cannot make tests like 0.1 + 0.2 == 0.3, what should we then do? The answer is that we must accept some small inaccuracy and make a test with a *tolerance*. Here is the recipe:

```
>>> a = 0.1; b = 0.2; expected = 0.3
>>> computed = a + b
>>> diff = abs(expected - computed)
>>> tol = 1E-15
>>> diff < tol
True
```

Here we have set the tolerance for comparison to 10^{-15}, but calculating 0.3 - (0.1 + 0.2) shows that it equals -5.55e-17, so a lower tolerance could be used in this particular example. However, in other calculations we have little idea about how accurate the answer is (there could be accumulation of rounding errors in more complicated algorithms), so 10^{-15} or 10^{-14} are robust values. As we demonstrate below, these tolerances depend on the magnitude of the numbers in the calculations.

Doing an experiment with $10^k + 0.3 - (10^k + 0.1 + 0.2)$ for $k = 1, \ldots, 10$ shows that the answer (which should be zero) is around 10^{16-k}. This means that the tolerance must be larger if we compute with larger numbers. Setting a proper tolerance therefore requires some experiments to see what level of accuracy one can expect. A way out of this difficulty is to work with *relative* instead of *absolute* differences. In a relative difference we divide by one of the operands, e.g.,

$$a = 10^k + 0.3, \quad b = (10^k + 0.1 + 0.2), \quad c = \frac{a - b}{a}.$$

Computing this c for various k shows a value around 10^{-16}. A safer procedure is thus to use *relative differences*.

3.4.4 Constructing Unit Tests and Writing Test Functions

Python has several frameworks for automatically running and checking a potentially very large number of tests for parts of your software by one command. This is an extremely useful feature during program development: whenever you have done some changes to one or more files, launch the test command and make sure nothing is broken because of your edits.

The test frameworks nose and py.test are particularly attractive as they are very easy to use. Tests are placed in special *test functions* that the frameworks can recognize and run for you. The requirements to a test function are simple:

- the name must start with test_
- the test function cannot have any arguments
- the tests inside test functions must be boolean expressions
- a boolean expression b must be tested with assert b, msg, where msg is an optional object (string or number) to be written out when b is false

Suppose we have written a function

```
def add(a, b):
    return a + b
```

A corresponding test function can then be

```
def test_add()
    expected = 1 + 1
    computed = add(1, 1)
    assert computed == expected, '1+1=%g' % computed
```

Test functions can be in any program file or in separate files, typically with names starting with test. You can also collect tests in subdirectories: running py.test -s -v will actually run all tests in all test*.py files in all subdirectories, while nosetests -s -v restricts the attention to subdirectories whose names start with test or end with _test or _tests.

As long as we add integers, the equality test in the test_add function is appropriate, but if we try to call add(0.1, 0.2) instead, we will face the rounding error problems explained in Sect. 3.4.3, and we must use a test with tolerance instead:

```
def test_add()
    expected = 0.3
    computed = add(0.1, 0.2)
    tol = 1E-14
    diff = abs(expected - computed)
    assert diff < tol, 'diff=%g' % diff
```

Below we shall write test functions for each of the three test procedures we suggested: comparison with hand calculations, checking problems that can be exactly solved, and checking convergence rates. We stick to testing the trapezoidal integration code and collect all test functions in one common file by the name test_trapezoidal.py.

Hand-computed numerical results Our previous hand calculations for two trapezoids can be checked against the trapezoidal function inside a test function (in a file test_trapezoidal.py):

```
from trapezoidal import trapezoidal

def test_trapezoidal_one_exact_result():
    """Compare one hand-computed result."""
    from math import exp
    v = lambda t: 3*(t**2)*exp(t**3)
    n = 2
    computed = trapezoidal(v, 0, 1, n)
    expected = 2.463642041244344
    error = abs(expected - computed)
    tol = 1E-14
    success = error < tol
    msg = 'error=%g > tol=%g' % (errror, tol)
    assert success, msg
```

Note the importance of checking err against exact with a tolerance: rounding errors from the arithmetics inside trapezoidal will not make the result exactly like the hand-computed one. The size of the tolerance is here set to 10^{-14}, which is a kind of all-round value for computations with numbers not deviating much from unity.

Solving a problem without numerical errors We know that the trapezoidal rule is exact for linear integrands. Choosing the integral $\int_{1.2}^{4.4}(6x-4)dx$ as test case, the corresponding test function for this unit test may look like

```python
def test_trapezoidal_linear():
    """Check that linear functions are integrated exactly."""
    f = lambda x: 6*x - 4
    F = lambda x: 3*x**2 - 4*x  # Anti-derivative
    a = 1.2; b = 4.4
    expected = F(b) - F(a)
    tol = 1E-14
    for n in 2, 20, 21:
        computed = trapezoidal(f, a, b, n)
        error = abs(expected - computed)
        success = error < tol
        msg = 'n=%d, err=%g' % (n, error)
        assert success, msg
```

Demonstrating correct convergence rates In the present example with integration, it is known that the approximation errors in the trapezoidal rule are proportional to n^{-2}, n being the number of subintervals used in the composite rule.

Computing convergence rates requires somewhat more tedious programming than the previous tests, but can be applied to more general integrands. The algorithm typically goes like

- for $i = 0, 1, 2, \ldots, q$
  - $n_i = 2^{i+1}$
  - Compute integral with n_i intervals
  - Compute the error E_i
  - Estimate r_i from (3.24) if $i > 0$

The corresponding code may look like

```python
def convergence_rates(f, F, a, b, num_experiments=14):
    from math import log
    from numpy import zeros
    expected = F(b) - F(a)
    n = zeros(num_experiments, dtype=int)
    E = zeros(num_experiments)
    r = zeros(num_experiments-1)
    for i in range(num_experiments):
        n[i] = 2**(i+1)
        computed = trapezoidal(f, a, b, n[i])
        E[i] = abs(expected - computed)
        if i > 0:
            r_im1 = log(E[i]/E[i-1])/log(float(n[i])/n[i-1])
            r[i-1] = float('%.2f' % r_im1) # Truncate to two decimals
    return r
```

Making a test function is a matter of choosing f, F, a, and b, and then checking the value of r_i for the largest i:

```
def test_trapezoidal_conv_rate():
    """Check empirical convergence rates against the expected -2."""
    from math import exp
    v = lambda t: 3*(t**2)*exp(t**3)
    V = lambda t: exp(t**3)
    a = 1.1; b = 1.9
    r = convergence_rates(v, V, a, b, 14)
    print r
    tol = 0.01
    msg = str(r[-4:])  # show last 4 estimated rates
    assert (abs(r[-1]) - 2) < tol, msg
```

Running the test shows that all r_i, except the first one, equal the target limit 2 within two decimals. This observation suggest a tolerance of 10^{-2}.

Remark about version control of files

Having a suite of test functions for automatically checking that your software works is considered as a fundamental requirement for reliable computing. Equally important is a system that can keep track of different versions of the files and the tests, known as a *version control system*. Today's most popular version control system is Git[4], which the authors strongly recommend the reader to use for programming and writing reports. The combination of Git and cloud storage such as GitHub is a very common way of organizing scientific or engineering work. We have a quick intro[5] to Git and GitHub that gets you up and running within minutes.

The typical workflow with Git goes as follows.

1. Before you start working with files, make sure you have the latest version of them by running `git pull`.
2. Edit files, remove or create files (new files must be registered by `git add`).
3. When a natural piece of work is done, *commit* your changes by the `git commit` command.
4. Implement your changes also in the cloud by doing `git push`.

A nice feature of Git is that people can edit the same file at the same time and very often Git will be able to automatically merge the changes (!). Therefore, version control is crucial when you work with others or when you do your work on different types of computers. Another key feature is that anyone can at any time view the history of a file, see who did what when, and roll back the entire file collection to a previous commit. This feature is, of course, fundamental for reliable work.

---

[4] https://en.wikipedia.org/wiki/Git_(software)
[5] http://hplgit.github.io/teamods/bitgit/Langtangen_bitgit-bootstrap.html

3.5 Vectorization

The functions `midpoint` and `trapezoid` usually run fast in Python and compute an integral to a satisfactory precision within a fraction of a second. However, long loops in Python may run slowly in more complicated implementations. To increase the speed, the loops can be replaced by vectorized code. The integration functions constitute a simple and good example to illustrate how to vectorize loops.

We have already seen simple examples on vectorization in Sect. 1.4 when we could evaluate a mathematical function $f(x)$ for a large number of x values stored in an array. Basically, we can write

```
def f(x):
    return exp(-x)*sin(x) + 5*x

from numpy import exp, sin, linspace
x = linspace(0, 4, 101)   # coordinates from 100 intervals on [0, 4]
y = f(x)                  # all points evaluated at once
```

The result `y` is the array that would be computed if we ran a `for` loop over the individual `x` values and called `f` for each value. Vectorization essentially eliminates this loop in Python (i.e., the looping over `x` and application of `f` to each `x` value are instead performed in a library with fast, compiled code).

Vectorizing the midpoint rule The aim of vectorizing the `midpoint` and `trapezoidal` functions is also to remove the explicit loop in Python. We start with vectorizing the `midpoint` function since `trapezoid` is not equally straightforward. The fundamental ideas of the vectorized algorithm are to

1. compute all the evaluation points in one array `x`
2. call `f(x)` to produce an array of corresponding function values
3. use the `sum` function to sum the `f(x)` values

The evaluation points in the midpoint method are $x_i = a + (i + \frac{1}{2})h, i = 0, \ldots, n - 1$. That is, n uniformly distributed coordinates between $a + h/2$ and $b - h/2$. Such coordinates can be calculated by `x = linspace(a+h/2, b-h/2, n)`. Given that the Python implementation `f` of the mathematical function f works with an array argument, which is very often the case in Python, `f(x)` will produce all the function values in an array. The array elements are then summed up by `sum`: `sum(f(x))`. This sum is to be multiplied by the rectangle width h to produce the integral value. The complete function is listed below.

```
from numpy import linspace, sum

def midpoint(f, a, b, n):
    h = float(b-a)/n
    x = linspace(a + h/2, b - h/2, n)
    return h*sum(f(x))
```

The code is found in the file `integration_methods_vec.py`.

Let us test the code interactively in a Python shell to compute $\int_0^1 3t^2 dt$. The file with the code above has the name `integration_methods_vec.py` and is a valid module from which we can import the vectorized function:

```
>>> from integration_methods_vec import midpoint
>>> from numpy import exp
>>> v = lambda t: 3*t**2*exp(t**3)
>>> midpoint(v, 0, 1, 10)
1.7014827690091872
```

Note the necessity to use `exp` from `numpy`: our v function will be called with x as an array, and the `exp` function must be capable of working with an array.

The vectorized code performs all loops very efficiently in compiled code, resulting in much faster execution. Moreover, many readers of the code will also say that the algorithm looks clearer than in the loop-based implementation.

Vectorizing the trapezoidal rule We can use the same approach to vectorize the `trapezoid` function. However, the trapezoidal rule performs a sum where the end points have different weight. If we do `sum(f(x))`, we get the end points `f(a)` and `f(b)` with weight unity instead of one half. A remedy is to subtract the error from `sum(f(x))`: `sum(f(x)) - 0.5*f(a) - 0.5*f(b)`. The vectorized version of the trapezoidal method then becomes

```
def trapezoidal(f, a, b, n):
    h = float(b-a)/n
    x = linspace(a, b, n+1)
    s = sum(f(x)) - 0.5*f(a) - 0.5*f(b)
    return h*s
```

3.6   Measuring Computational Speed

Now that we have created faster, vectorized versions of functions in the previous section, it is interesting to measure how much faster they are. The purpose of the present section is therefore to explain how we can record the CPU time consumed by a function so we can answer this question. There are many techniques for measuring the CPU time in Python, and here we shall just explain the simplest and most convenient one: the `%timeit` command in IPython. The following interactive session should illustrate a competition where the vectorized versions of the functions are supposed to win:

```
In [1]: from integration_methods_vec import midpoint as midpoint_vec

In [3]: from midpoint import midpoint

In [4]: from numpy import exp

In [5]: v = lambda t: 3*t**2*exp(t**3)
```

```
In [6]: %timeit midpoint_vec(v, 0, 1, 1000000)
1 loops, best of 3: 379 ms per loop

In [7]: %timeit midpoint(v, 0, 1, 1000000)
1 loops, best of 3: 8.17 s per loop

In [8]: 8.17/(379*0.001)      # efficiency factor
Out[8]: 21.556728232189972
```

We see that the vectorized version is about 20 times faster: 379 ms versus 8.17 s. The results for the trapezoidal method are very similar, and the factor of about 20 is independent of the number of intervals.

3.7 Double and Triple Integrals

3.7.1 The Midpoint Rule for a Double Integral

Given a double integral over a rectangular domain $[a, b] \times [c, d]$,

$$\int_a^b \int_c^d f(x, y) dy dx,$$

how can we approximate this integral by numerical methods?

Derivation via one-dimensional integrals Since we know how to deal with integrals in one variable, a fruitful approach is to view the double integral as two integrals, each in one variable, which can be approximated numerically by previous one-dimensional formulas. To this end, we introduce a help function $g(x)$ and write

$$\int_a^b \int_c^d f(x, y) dy dx = \int_a^b g(x) dx, \quad g(x) = \int_c^d f(x, y) dy.$$

Each of the integrals

$$\int_a^b g(x) dx, \quad g(x) = \int_c^d f(x, y) dy$$

can be discretized by any numerical integration rule for an integral in one variable. Let us use the midpoint method (3.21) and start with $g(x) = \int_c^d f(x, y) dy$. We introduce n_y intervals on $[c, d]$ with length h_y. The midpoint rule for this integral then becomes

$$g(x) = \int_c^d f(x, y) dy \approx h_y \sum_{j=0}^{n_y - 1} f(x, y_j), \quad y_j = c + \frac{1}{2} h_y + j h_y.$$

The expression looks somewhat different from (3.21), but that is because of the notation: since we integrate in the y direction and will have to work with both x and y as coordinates, we must use n_y for n, h_y for h, and the counter i is more naturally called j when integrating in y. Integrals in the x direction will use h_x and n_x for h and n, and i as counter.

The double integral is $\int_a^b g(x)dx$, which can be approximated by the midpoint method:

$$\int_a^b g(x)dx \approx h_x \sum_{i=0}^{n_x-1} g(x_i), \quad x_i = a + \frac{1}{2}h_x + ih_x .$$

Putting the formulas together, we arrive at the *composite midpoint method for a double integral*:

$$\int_a^b \int_c^d f(x,y)dydx \approx h_x \sum_{i=0}^{n_x-1} h_y \sum_{j=0}^{n_y-1} f(x_i, y_j)$$

$$= h_x h_y \sum_{i=0}^{n_x-1} \sum_{j=0}^{n_y-1} f\left(a + \frac{h_x}{2} + ih_x, c + \frac{h_y}{2} + jh_y\right).$$

$$(3.25)$$

Direct derivation The formula (3.25) can also be derived directly in the two-dimensional case by applying the idea of the midpoint method. We divide the rectangle $[a,b] \times [c,d]$ into $n_x \times n_y$ equal-sized cells. The idea of the midpoint method is to approximate f by a constant over each cell, and evaluate the constant at the midpoint. Cell (i,j) occupies the area

$$[a + ih_x, a + (i+1)h_x] \times [c + jh_y, c + (j+1)h_y],$$

and the midpoint is (x_i, y_j) with

$$x_i = a + ih_x + \frac{1}{2}h_x, \quad y_j = c + jh_y + \frac{1}{2}h_y .$$

The integral over the cell is therefore $h_x h_y f(x_i, y_j)$, and the total double integral is the sum over all cells, which is nothing but formula (3.25).

Programming a double sum The formula (3.25) involves a double sum, which is normally implemented as a double for loop. A Python function implementing (3.25) may look like

```
def midpoint_double1(f, a, b, c, d, nx, ny):
    hx = (b - a)/float(nx)
    hy = (d - c)/float(ny)
    I = 0
    for i in range(nx):
        for j in range(ny):
            xi = a + hx/2 + i*hx
            yj = c + hy/2 + j*hy
            I += hx*hy*f(xi, yj)
    return I
```

If this function is stored in a module file `midpoint_double.py`, we can compute some integral, e.g., $\int_2^3 \int_0^2 (2x + y) dx dy = 9$ in an interactive shell and demonstrate that the function computes the right number:

```
>>> from midpoint_double import midpoint_double1
>>> def f(x, y):
...     return 2*x + y
...
>>> midpoint_double1(f, 0, 2, 2, 3, 5, 5)
9.0
```

Reusing code for one-dimensional integrals It is very natural to write a two-dimensional midpoint method as we did in function `midpoint_double1` when we have the formula (3.25). However, we could alternatively ask, much as we did in the mathematics, can we reuse a well-tested implementation for one-dimensional integrals to compute double integrals? That is, can we use function `midpoint`

```
def midpoint(f, a, b, n):
    h = float(b-a)/n
    result = 0
    for i in range(n):
        result += f((a + h/2.0) + i*h)
    result *= h
    return result
```

from Sect. 3.3.2 "twice"? The answer is yes, if we think as we did in the mathematics: compute the double integral as a midpoint rule for integrating $g(x)$ and define $g(x_i)$ in terms of a midpoint rule over f in the y coordinate. The corresponding function has very short code:

```
def midpoint_double2(f, a, b, c, d, nx, ny):
    def g(x):
        return midpoint(lambda y: f(x, y), c, d, ny)

    return midpoint(g, a, b, nx)
```

The important advantage of this implementation is that we reuse a well-tested function for the standard one-dimensional midpoint rule and that we apply the one-dimensional rule exactly as in the mathematics.

Verification via test functions How can we test that our functions for the double integral work? The best unit test is to find a problem where the numerical approximation error vanishes because then we know exactly what the numerical answer should be. The midpoint rule is exact for linear functions, regardless of how many subinterval we use. Also, any linear two-dimensional function $f(x, y) = px + qy + r$ will be integrated exactly by the two-dimensional midpoint rule. We may pick $f(x, y) = 2x + y$ and create a proper *test function* that can automatically verify our two alternative implementations of the two-dimensional midpoint rule. To compute the integral of $f(x, y)$ we take advantage of SymPy to eliminate the possibility of errors in hand calculations. The test function becomes

```
def test_midpoint_double():
    """Test that a linear function is integrated exactly."""
    def f(x, y):
        return 2*x + y

    a = 0;  b = 2;  c = 2;  d = 3
    import sympy
    x, y = sympy.symbols('x  y')
    I_expected = sympy.integrate(f(x, y), (x, a, b), (y, c, d))
    # Test three cases: nx < ny, nx = ny, nx > ny
    for nx, ny in (3, 5), (4, 4), (5, 3):
        I_computed1 = midpoint_double1(f, a, b, c, d, nx, ny)
        I_computed2 = midpoint_double2(f, a, b, c, d, nx, ny)
        tol = 1E-14
        #print I_expected, I_computed1, I_computed2
        assert abs(I_computed1 - I_expected) < tol
        assert abs(I_computed2 - I_expected) < tol
```

Let test functions speak up?

If we call the above `test_midpoint_double` function and nothing happens, our implementations are correct. However, it is somewhat annoying to have a function that is completely silent when it works – are we sure all things are properly computed? During development it is therefore highly recommended to insert a print statement such that we can monitor the calculations and be convinced that the test function does what we want. Since a test function should not have any print statement, we simply comment it out as we have done in the function listed above.

The trapezoidal method can be used as alternative for the midpoint method. The derivation of a formula for the double integral and the implementations follow ex-actly the same ideas as we explained with the midpoint method, but there are more terms to write in the formulas.

Exercise 3.13 asks you to carry out the details. That exercise is a very good test on your understanding of the mathematical and programming ideas in the present section.

3.7.2   The Midpoint Rule for a Triple Integral

Theory Once a method that works for a one-dimensional problem is generalized to two dimensions, it is usually quite straightforward to extend the method to three dimensions. This will now be demonstrated for integrals. We have the triple integral

$$\int_a^b \int_c^d \int_e^f g(x, y, z)\,dz\,dy\,dx$$

and want to approximate the integral by a midpoint rule. Following the ideas for the double integral, we split this integral into one-dimensional integrals:

$$p(x, y) = \int_e^f g(x, y, z)dz$$

$$q(x) = \int_c^d p(x, y)dy$$

$$\int_a^b \int_c^d \int_e^f g(x, y, z)dzdydx = \int_a^b q(x)dx$$

For each of these one-dimensional integrals we apply the midpoint rule:

$$p(x, y) = \int_e^f g(x, y, z)dz \approx \sum_{k=0}^{n_z-1} g(x, y, z_k),$$

$$q(x) = \int_c^d p(x, y)dy \approx \sum_{j=0}^{n_y-1} p(x, y_j),$$

$$\int_a^b \int_c^d \int_e^f g(x, y, z)dzdydx = \int_a^b q(x)dx \approx \sum_{i=0}^{n_x-1} q(x_i),$$

where

$$z_k = e + \frac{1}{2}h_z + kh_z, \quad y_j = c + \frac{1}{2}h_y + jh_y \quad x_i = a + \frac{1}{2}h_x + ih_x.$$

Starting with the formula for $\int_a^b \int_c^d \int_e^f g(x, y, z)dzdydx$ and inserting the two previous formulas gives

$$\int_a^b \int_c^d \int_e^f g(x, y, z)\, dzdydx$$

$$\approx h_x h_y h_z \sum_{i=0}^{n_x-1} \sum_{j=0}^{n_y-1} \sum_{k=0}^{n_z-1} g\left(a + \frac{1}{2}h_x + ih_x, c + \frac{1}{2}h_y + jh_y, e + \frac{1}{2}h_z + kh_z\right).$$

(3.26)

Note that we may apply the ideas under *Direct derivation* at the end of Sect. 3.7.1 to arrive at (3.26) directly: divide the domain into $n_x \times n_y \times n_z$ cells of volumes $h_x h_y h_z$; approximate g by a constant, evaluated at the midpoint (x_i, y_j, z_k), in each cell; and sum the cell integrals $h_x h_y h_z g(x_i, y_j, z_k)$.

Implementation We follow the ideas for the implementations of the midpoint rule for a double integral. The corresponding functions are shown below and found in the file `midpoint_triple.py`.

```python
def midpoint_triple1(g, a, b, c, d, e, f, nx, ny, nz):
    hx = (b - a)/float(nx)
    hy = (d - c)/float(ny)
    hz = (f - e)/float(nz)
    I = 0
    for i in range(nx):
        for j in range(ny):
            for k in range(nz):
                xi = a + hx/2 + i*hx
                yj = c + hy/2 + j*hy
                zk = e + hz/2 + k*hz
                I += hx*hy*hz*g(xi, yj, zk)
    return I

def midpoint(f, a, b, n):
    h = float(b-a)/n
    result = 0
    for i in range(n):
        result += f((a + h/2.0) + i*h)
    result *= h
    return result

def midpoint_triple2(g, a, b, c, d, e, f, nx, ny, nz):
    def p(x, y):
        return midpoint(lambda z: g(x, y, z), e, f, nz)

    def q(x):
        return midpoint(lambda y: p(x, y), c, d, ny)

    return midpoint(q, a, b, nx)

def test_midpoint_triple():
    """Test that a linear function is integrated exactly."""
    def g(x, y, z):
        return 2*x + y - 4*z

    a = 0;  b = 2;  c = 2;  d = 3;  e = -1;  f = 2
    import sympy
    x, y, z = sympy.symbols('x y z')
    I_expected = sympy.integrate(
        g(x, y, z), (x, a, b), (y, c, d), (z, e, f))
    for nx, ny, nz in (3, 5, 2), (4, 4, 4), (5, 3, 6):
        I_computed1 = midpoint_triple1(
            g, a, b, c, d, e, f, nx, ny, nz)
        I_computed2 = midpoint_triple2(
            g, a, b, c, d, e, f, nx, ny, nz)
        tol = 1E-14
        print I_expected, I_computed1, I_computed2
        assert abs(I_computed1 - I_expected) < tol
        assert abs(I_computed2 - I_expected) < tol

if __name__ == '__main__':
    test_midpoint_triple()
```

3.7.3   Monte Carlo Integration for Complex-Shaped Domains

Repeated use of one-dimensional integration rules to handle double and triple integrals constitute a working strategy only if the integration domain is a rectangle or box. For any other shape of domain, completely different methods must be used. A common approach for two- and three-dimensional domains is to divide the domain into many small triangles or tetrahedra and use numerical integration methods for each triangle or tetrahedron. The overall algorithm and implementation is too complicated to be addressed in this book. Instead, we shall employ an alternative, very simple and general method, called Monte Carlo integration. It can be implemented in half a page of code, but requires orders of magnitude more function evaluations in double integrals compared to the midpoint rule.

However, Monte Carlo integration is much more computationally efficient than the midpoint rule when computing higher-dimensional integrals in more than three variables over hypercube domains. Our ideas for double and triple integrals can easily be generalized to handle an integral in m variables. A midpoint formula then involves m sums. With n cells in each coordinate direction, the formula requires n^m function evaluations. That is, the computational work explodes as an exponential function of the number of space dimensions. Monte Carlo integration, on the other hand, does not suffer from this explosion of computational work and is the preferred method for computing higher-dimensional integrals. So, it makes sense in a chapter on numerical integration to address Monte Carlo methods, both for handling complex domains and for handling integrals with many variables.

The Monte Carlo integration algorithm   The idea of Monte Carlo integration of $\int_a^b f(x)dx$ is to use the mean-value theorem from calculus, which states that the integral $\int_a^b f(x)dx$ equals the length of the integration domain, here $b-a$, times the *average* value of f, $\bar{f}$, in $[a, b]$. The average value can be computed by sampling f at a set of *random* points inside the domain and take the mean of the function values. In higher dimensions, an integral is estimated as the area/volume of the domain times the average value, and again one can evaluate the integrand at a set of random points in the domain and compute the mean value of those evaluations.

Let us introduce some quantities to help us make the specification of the integration algorithm more precise. Suppose we have some two-dimensional integral

$$\int_\Omega f(x, y)dxdx,$$

where Ω is a two-dimensional domain defined via a help function $g(x, y)$:

$$\Omega = \{(x, y) \,|\, g(x, y) \geq 0\}$$

That is, points (x, y) for which $g(x, y) \geq 0$ lie inside Ω, and points for which $g(x, y) < \Omega$ are outside Ω. The boundary of the domain $\partial\Omega$ is given by the implicit curve $g(x, y) = 0$. Such formulations of geometries have been very common during the last couple of decades, and one refers to g as a *level-set function* and the boundary $g = 0$ as the zero-level contour of the level-set function. For simple geometries one can easily construct g by hand, while in more complicated industrial applications one must resort to mathematical models for constructing g.

Let $A(\Omega)$ be the area of a domain Ω. We can estimate the integral by this Monte Carlo integration method:

1. embed the geometry Ω in a rectangular area R
2. draw a large number of *random* points (x, y) in R
3. count the fraction q of points that are inside Ω
4. approximate $A(\Omega)/A(R)$ by q, i.e., set $A(\Omega) = qA(R)$
5. evaluate the mean of f, $\bar{f}$, at the points inside Ω
6. estimate the integral as $A(\Omega)\bar{f}$

Note that $A(R)$ is trivial to compute since R is a rectangle, while $A(\Omega)$ is unknown. However, if we assume that the fraction of $A(R)$ occupied by $A(\Omega)$ is the same as the fraction of random points inside Ω, we get a simple estimate for $A(\Omega)$.

To get an idea of the method, consider a circular domain Ω embedded in a rectangle as shown below. A collection of random points is illustrated by black dots.

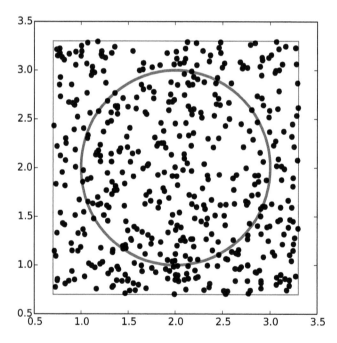

Implementation A Python function implementing $\int_\Omega f(x, y)\,dx\,dy$ can be written like this:

```
import numpy as np

def MonteCarlo_double(f, g, x0, x1, y0, y1, n):
    """
    Monte Carlo integration of f over a domain g>=0, embedded
    in a rectangle [x0,x1]x[y0,y1]. n^2 is the number of
    random points.
    """
```

```
# Draw n**2 random points in the rectangle
x = np.random.uniform(x0, x1, n)
y = np.random.uniform(y0, y1, n)
# Compute sum of f values inside the integration domain
f_mean = 0
num_inside = 0    # number of x,y points inside domain (g>=0)
for i in range(len(x)):
    for j in range(len(y)):
        if g(x[i], y[j]) >= 0:
            num_inside += 1
            f_mean += f(x[i], y[j])
f_mean = f_mean/float(num_inside)
area = num_inside/float(n**2)*(x1 - x0)*(y1 - y0)
return area*f_mean
```

(See the file MC_double.py.)

Verification A simple test case is to check the area of a rectangle $[0, 2] \times [3, 4.5]$ embedded in a rectangle $[0, 3] \times [2, 5]$. The right answer is 3, but Monte Carlo integration is, unfortunately, never exact so it is impossible to predict the output of the algorithm. All we know is that the estimated integral should approach 3 as the number of random points goes to infinity. Also, for a fixed number of points, we can run the algorithm several times and get different numbers that fluctuate around the exact value, since different sample points are used in different calls to the Monte Carlo integration algorithm.

The area of the rectangle can be computed by the integral $\int_0^2 \int_3^{4.5} dy\,dx$, so in this case we identify $f(x, y) = 1$, and the g function can be specified as (e.g.) 1 if (x, y) is inside $[0, 2] \times [3, 4.5]$ and -1 otherwise. Here is an example on how we can utilize the MonteCarlo_double function to compute the area for different number of samples:

```
>>> from MC_double import MonteCarlo_double
>>> def g(x, y):
...     return (1 if (0 <= x <= 2 and 3 <= y <= 4.5) else -1)
...
>>> MonteCarlo_double(lambda x, y: 1, g, 0, 3, 2, 5, 100)
2.9484
>>> MonteCarlo_double(lambda x, y: 1, g, 0, 3, 2, 5, 1000)
2.947032
>>> MonteCarlo_double(lambda x, y: 1, g, 0, 3, 2, 5, 1000)
3.0234600000000005
>>> MonteCarlo_double(lambda x, y: 1, g, 0, 3, 2, 5, 2000)
2.9984580000000003
>>> MonteCarlo_double(lambda x, y: 1, g, 0, 3, 2, 5, 2000)
3.1903469999999996
>>> MonteCarlo_double(lambda x, y: 1, g, 0, 3, 2, 5, 5000)
2.986515
```

We see that the values fluctuate around 3, a fact that supports a correct implementation, but in principle, bugs could be hidden behind the inaccurate answers.

It is mathematically known that the standard deviation of the Monte Carlo estimate of an integral converges as $n^{-1/2}$, where n is the number of samples. This kind of convergence rate estimate could be used to verify the implementation, but this topic is beyond the scope of this book.

Test function for function with random numbers To make a test function, we need a unit test that has identical behavior each time we run the test. This seems difficult when random numbers are involved, because these numbers are different every time we run the algorithm, and each run hence produces a (slightly) different result. A standard way to test algorithms involving random numbers is to *fix the seed* of the random number generator. Then the sequence of numbers is the same every time we run the algorithm. Assuming that the MonteCarlo_double function works, we fix the seed, observe a certain result, and take this result as the correct result. Provided the test function always uses this seed, we should get exactly this result every time the MonteCarlo_double function is called. Our test function can then be written as shown below.

```python
def test_MonteCarlo_double_rectangle_area():
    """Check the area of a rectangle."""
    def g(x, y):
        return (1 if (0 <= x <= 2 and 3 <= y <= 4.5) else -1)

    x0 = 0;  x1 = 3;  y0 = 2;  y1 = 5  # embedded rectangle
    n = 1000
    np.random.seed(8)        # must fix the seed!
    I_expected = 3.121092  # computed with this seed
    I_computed = MonteCarlo_double(
        lambda x, y: 1, g, x0, x1, y0, y1, n)
    assert abs(I_expected - I_computed) < 1E-14
```

(See the file MC_double.py.)

Integral over a circle The test above involves a trivial function $f(x, y) = 1$. We should also test a non-constant f function and a more complicated domain. Let Ω be a circle at the origin with radius 2, and let $f = \sqrt{x^2 + y^2}$. This choice makes it possible to compute an exact result: in polar coordinates, $\int_\Omega f(x, y)dxdy$ simplifies to $2\pi \int_0^2 r^2 dr = 16\pi/3$. We must be prepared for quite crude approximations that fluctuate around this exact result. As in the test case above, we experience better results with larger number of points. When we have such evidence for a working implementation, we can turn the test into a proper test function. Here is an example:

```python
def test_MonteCarlo_double_circle_r():
    """Check the integral of r over a circle with radius 2."""
    def g(x, y):
        xc, yc = 0, 0  # center
        R = 2          # radius
        return R**2 - ((x-xc)**2 + (y-yc)**2)

    # Exact: integral of r*r*dr over circle with radius R becomes
    # 2*pi*1/3*R**3
    import sympy
    r = sympy.symbols('r')
    I_exact = sympy.integrate(2*sympy.pi*r*r, (r, 0, 2))
```

```
print 'Exact integral:', I_exact.evalf()
x0 = -2;  x1 = 2;  y0 = -2;  y1 = 2
n = 1000
np.random.seed(6)
I_expected = 16.7970837117376384  # Computed with this seed
I_computed = MonteCarlo_double(
    lambda x, y: np.sqrt(x**2 + y**2),
    g, x0, x1, y0, y1, n)
print 'MC approximation %d samples): %.16f' % (n**2, I_computed)
assert abs(I_expected - I_computed) < 1E-15
```

(See the file MC_double.py.)

3.8 Exercises

Exercise 3.1: Hand calculations for the trapezoidal method
Compute by hand the area composed of two trapezoids (of equal width) that approximates the integral $\int_1^3 2x^3 dx$. Make a test function that calls the trapezoidal function in trapezoidal.py and compares the return value with the hand-calculated value.
Filename: trapezoidal_test_func.py.

Exercise 3.2: Hand calculations for the midpoint method
Compute by hand the area composed of two rectangles (of equal width) that approximates the integral $\int_1^3 2x^3 dx$. Make a test function that calls the midpoint function in midpoint.py and compares the return value with the hand-calculated value.
Filename: midpoint_test_func.py.

Exercise 3.3: Compute a simple integral
Apply the trapezoidal and midpoint functions to compute the integral $\int_2^6 x(x-1)dx$ with 2 and 100 subintervals. Compute the error too.
Filename: integrate_parabola.py.

Exercise 3.4: Hand-calculations with sine integrals
We consider integrating the sine function: $\int_0^b \sin(x)dx$.

a) Let $b = \pi$ and use two intervals in the trapezoidal and midpoint method. Compute the integral by hand and illustrate how the two numerical methods approximates the integral. Compare with the exact value.
b) Do a) when $b = 2\pi$.

Filename: integrate_sine.pdf.

Exercise 3.5: Make test functions for the midpoint method
Modify the file test_trapezoidal.py such that the three tests are applied to the function midpoint implementing the midpoint method for integration.
Filename: test_midpoint.py.

Exercise 3.6: Explore rounding errors with large numbers
The trapezoidal method integrates linear functions exactly, and this property was used in the test function `test_trapezoidal_linear` in the file `test_trapezoidal.py`. Change the function used in Sect. 3.4.2 to $f(x) = 6 \cdot 10^8 x - 4 \cdot 10^6$ and rerun the test. What happens? How must you change the test to make it useful? How does the convergence rate test behave? Any need for adjustment?
Filename: `test_trapezoidal2.py`.

Exercise 3.7: Write test functions for $\int_0^4 \sqrt{x}\,dx$
We want to test how the `trapezoidal` function works for the integral $\int_0^4 \sqrt{x}\,dx$. Two of the tests in `test_trapezoidal.py` are meaningful for this integral. Compute by hand the result of using 2 or 3 trapezoids and modify the `test_trapezoidal_one_exact_result` function accordingly. Then modify `test_trapezoidal_conv_rate` to handle the square root integral.
Filename: `test_trapezoidal3.py`.

Remarks The convergence rate test fails. Printing out r shows that the actual convergence rate for this integral is -1.5 and not -2. The reason is that the error in the trapezoidal method[6] is $-(b - a)^3 n^{-2} f''(\xi)$ for some (unknown) $\xi \in [a, b]$. With $f(x) = \sqrt{x}$, $f''(\xi) \rightarrow -\infty$ as $\xi \rightarrow 0$, pointing to a potential problem in the size of the error. Running a test with $a > 0$, say $\int_{0.1}^4 \sqrt{x}\,dx$ shows that the convergence rate is indeed restored to -2.

Exercise 3.8: Rectangle methods
The midpoint method divides the interval of integration into equal-sized subintervals and approximates the integral in each subinterval by a rectangle whose height equals the function value at the midpoint of the subinterval. Instead, one might use either the left or right end of the subinterval as illustrated in Fig. 3.4. This defines a *rectangle method* of integration. The height of the rectangle can be based on the left or right end or the midpoint.

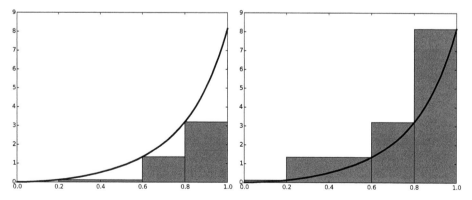

Fig. 3.4 Illustration of the rectangle method with evaluating the rectangle height by either the left or right point

---

[6] http://en.wikipedia.org/wiki/Trapezoidal_rule#Error_analysis

a) Write a function `rectangle(f, a, b, n, height='left')` for computing an integral $\int_a^b f(x)dx$ by the rectangle method with height computed based on the value of `height`, which is either `left`, `right`, or `mid`.

b) Write three test functions for the three unit test procedures described in Sect. 3.4.2. Make sure you test for `height` equal to `left`, `right`, and `mid`. You may call the `midpoint` function for checking the result when `height=mid`.

Hint Edit `test_trapezoidal.py`.
Filename: `rectangle_methods.py`.

Exercise 3.9: Adaptive integration

Suppose we want to use the trapezoidal or midpoint method to compute an integral $\int_a^b f(x)dx$ with an error less than a prescribed tolerance ϵ. What is the appropriate size of n?

To answer this question, we may enter an iterative procedure where we compare the results produced by n and $2n$ intervals, and if the difference is smaller than ϵ, the value corresponding to $2n$ is returned. Otherwise, we halve n and repeat the procedure.

Hint It may be a good idea to organize your code so that the function `adaptive_integration` can be used easily in future programs you write.

a) Write a function

```
adaptive_integration(f, a, b, eps, method=midpoint)
```

that implements the idea above (`eps` corresponds to the tolerance ϵ, and `method` can be `midpoint` or `trapezoidal`).

b) Test the method on $\int_0^2 x^2 dx$ and $\int_0^2 \sqrt{x}dx$ for $\epsilon = 10^{-1}, 10^{-10}$ and write out the exact error.

c) Make a plot of n versus $\epsilon \in [10^{-1}, 10^{-10}]$ for $\int_0^2 \sqrt{x}dx$. Use logarithmic scale for ϵ.

Filename: `adaptive_integration.py`.

Remarks The type of method explored in this exercise is called *adaptive*, because it tries to adapt the value of n to meet a given error criterion. The true error can very seldom be computed (since we do not know the exact answer to the computational problem), so one has to find other indicators of the error, such as the one here where the changes in the integral value, as the number of intervals is doubled, is taken to reflect the error.

Exercise 3.10: Integrating x raised to x

Consider the integral

$$I = \int_0^4 x^x \, dx.$$

The integrand x^x does not have an anti-derivative that can be expressed in terms of standard functions (visit http://wolframalpha.com and type `integral(x**x,x)` to convince yourself that our claim is right. Note that Wolfram alpha does give you an answer, but that answer is an approximation, it is *not* exact. This is because Wolfram alpha too uses numerical methods to arrive at the answer, just as you will in this exercise). Therefore, we are forced to compute the integral by numerical methods. Compute a result that is right to four digits.

Hint Use ideas from Exercise 3.9.
Filename: `integrate_x2x.py`.

Exercise 3.11: Integrate products of sine functions
In this exercise we shall integrate

$$I_{j,k} = \int\limits_{-\pi}^{\pi} \sin(jx)\sin(kx)dx,$$

where j and k are integers.

a) Plot $\sin(x)\sin(2x)$ and $\sin(2x)\sin(3x)$ for $x \in]-\pi, \pi]$ in separate plots. Explain why you expect $\int_{-\pi}^{\pi} \sin x \sin 2x \, dx = 0$ and $\int_{-\pi}^{\pi} \sin 2x \sin 3x \, dx = 0$.
b) Use the trapezoidal rule to compute $I_{j,k}$ for $j = 1, \ldots, 10$ and $k = 1, \ldots, 10$.

Filename: `products_sines.py`.

Exercise 3.12: Revisit fit of sines to a function
This is a continuation of Exercise 2.18. The task is to approximate a given function $f(t)$ on $[-\pi, \pi]$ by a sum of sines,

$$S_N(t) = \sum_{n=1}^{N} b_n \sin(nt) . \qquad (3.27)$$

We are now interested in computing the unknown coefficients b_n such that $S_N(t)$ is in some sense the *best approximation* to $f(t)$. One common way of doing this is to first set up a general expression for the *approximation error*, measured by "summing up" the squared deviation of S_N from f:

$$E = \int\limits_{-\pi}^{\pi} (S_N(t) - f(t))^2 dt .$$

We may view E as a function of $b_1, \ldots, b_N$. Minimizing E with respect to $b_1, \ldots, b_N$ will give us a *best approximation*, in the sense that we adjust $b_1, \ldots, b_N$ such that S_N deviates as little as possible from f.

Minimization of a function of N variables, $E(b_1, \ldots, b_N)$ is mathematically performed by requiring all the partial derivatives to be zero:

$$\frac{\partial E}{\partial b_1} = 0,$$

$$\frac{\partial E}{\partial b_2} = 0,$$

$$\vdots$$

$$\frac{\partial E}{\partial b_N} = 0.$$

a) Compute the partial derivative $\partial E/\partial b_1$ and generalize to the arbitrary case $\partial E/\partial b_n$, $1 \le n \le N$.
b) Show that

$$b_n = \frac{1}{\pi} \int\limits_{-\pi}^{\pi} f(t) \sin(nt) \, dt \, .$$

c) Write a function `integrate_coeffs(f, N, M)` that computes $b_1, \ldots, b_N$ by numerical integration, using M intervals in the trapezoidal rule.
d) A remarkable property of the trapezoidal rule is that it is exact for integrals $\int_{-\pi}^{\pi} \sin nt \, dt$ (when subintervals are of equal size). Use this property to create a function `test_integrate_coeff` to verify the implementation of `integrate_coeffs`.
e) Implement the choice $f(t) = \frac{1}{\pi} t$ as a Python function `f(t)` and call `integrate_coeffs(f, 3, 100)` to see what the optimal choice of b_1, b_2, b_3 is.
f) Make a function `plot_approx(f, N, M, filename)` where you plot `f(t)` together with the best approximation S_N as computed above, using M intervals for numerical integration. Save the plot to a file with name `filename`.
g) Run `plot_approx(f, N, M, filename)` for $f(t) = \frac{1}{\pi} t$ for $N = 3, 6, 12, 24$. Observe how the approximation improves.
h) Run `plot_approx` for $f(t) = e^{-(t-\pi)}$ and $N = 100$. Observe a fundamental problem: regardless of N, $S_N(-\pi) = 0$, not $e^{2\pi} \approx 535$. (There are ways to fix this issue.)

Filename: `autofit_sines.py`.

Exercise 3.13: Derive the trapezoidal rule for a double integral
Use ideas in Sect. 3.7.1 to derive a formula for computing a double integral $\int_a^b \int_c^d f(x, y) \, dy \, dx$ by the trapezoidal rule. Implement and test this rule.
Filename: `trapezoidal_double.py`.

Exercise 3.14: Compute the area of a triangle by Monte Carlo integration
Use the Monte Carlo method from Sect. 3.7.3 to compute the area of a triangle with vertices at $(-1, 0)$, $(1, 0)$, and $(3, 0)$.
Filename: `MC_triangle.py`.

4

Solutions to Ordinary Differential Equations

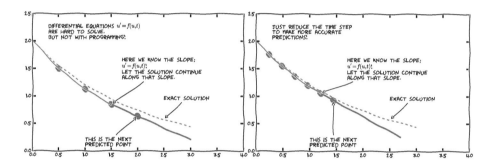

Differential equations constitute one of the most powerful mathematical tools to understand and predict the behavior of dynamical systems in nature, engineering, and society. A dynamical system is some system with some state, usually expressed by a set of variables, that evolves in time. For example, an oscillating pendulum, the spreading of a disease, and the weather are examples of dynamical systems. We can use basic laws of physics, or plain intuition, to express mathematical rules that govern the evolution of the system in time. These rules take the form of *differential equations*. You are probably well experienced with equations, at least equations like $ax + b = 0$ or $ax^2 + bx + c = 0$. Such equations are known as *algebraic equations*, and the unknown is a number. The unknown in a differential equation is a function, and a differential equation will almost always involve this function and one or more derivatives of the function. For example, $f'(x) = f(x)$ is a simple differential equation (asking if there is any function f such that it equals its derivative – you might remember that e^x is a candidate).

The present chapter starts with explaining how easy it is to solve both single (scalar) first-order ordinary differential equations and systems of first-order differential equations by the Forward Euler method. We demonstrate all the mathematical and programming details through two specific applications: population growth and spreading of diseases.

Then we turn to a physical application: oscillating mechanical systems, which arise in a wide range of engineering situations. The differential equation is now of second order, and the Forward Euler method does not perform well. This observation motivates the need for other solution methods, and we derive the Euler-Cromer scheme[1], the 2nd- and 4th-order Runge-Kutta schemes, as well as a finite difference scheme (the latter to handle the second-order differential equation directly without reformulating it as a first-order system). The presentation starts with undamped free oscillations and then treats general oscillatory systems with possibly nonlinear damping, nonlinear spring forces, and arbitrary external excitation. Besides developing programs from scratch, we also demonstrate how to access ready-made implementations of more advanced differential equation solvers in Python.

As we progress with more advanced methods, we develop more sophisticated and reusable programs, and in particular, we incorporate good testing strategies so that we bring solid evidence to correct computations. Consequently, the beginning with population growth and disease modeling examples has a very gentle learning curve, while that curve gets significantly steeper towards the end of the treatment of differential equations for oscillatory systems.

4.1 Population Growth

Our first taste of differential equations regards modeling the growth of some population, such as a cell culture, an animal population, or a human population. The ideas even extend trivially to growth of money in a bank. Let $N(t)$ be the number of individuals in the population at time t. How can we predict the evolution of $N(t)$ in time? Below we shall derive a differential equation whose solution is $N(t)$. The equation reads

$$N'(t) = rN(t), \tag{4.1}$$

where r is a number. Note that although N is an integer in real life, we model N as a real-valued function. We are forced to do this because the solution of differential equations are (normally continuous) real-valued functions. An integer-valued $N(t)$ in the model would lead to a lot of mathematical difficulties.

With a bit of guessing, you may realize that $N(t) = Ce^{rt}$, where C is any number. To make this solution unique, we need to fix C, done by prescribing the value of N at some time, usually $t = 0$. Say $N(0)$ is given as N_0. Then $N(t) = N_0 e^{rt}$.

In general, a differential equation model consists of a *differential equation*, such as (4.1) *and* an *initial condition*, such as $N(0) = N_0$. With a known initial condition, the differential equation can be solved for the unknown function and the solution is unique.

It is, of course, very seldom that we can find the solution of a differential equation as easy as in this example. Normally, one has to apply certain mathematical methods, but these can only handle some of the simplest differential equations. However, we can easily deal with almost any differential equation by applying numerical methods and a bit of programming. This is exactly the topic of the present chapter.

---

[1] The term *scheme* is used as synonym for method or computational recipe, especially in the context of numerical methods for differential equations.

4.1.1 Derivation of the Model

It can be instructive to show how an equation like (4.1) arises. Consider some population of (say) an animal species and let $N(t)$ be the number of individuals in a certain spatial region, e.g. an island. We are not concerned with the spatial distribution of the animals, just the number of them in some spatial area where there is no exchange of individuals with other spatial areas. During a time interval Δt, some animals will die and some new will be born. The number of deaths and births are expected to be proportional to N. For example, if there are twice as many individuals, we expect them to get twice as many newborns. In a time interval Δt, the net growth of the population will be

$$N(t + \Delta t) - N(t) = \bar{b}N(t) - \bar{d}N(t),$$

where $\bar{b}N(t)$ is the number of newborns and $\bar{d}N(t)$ is the number of deaths. If we double Δt, we expect the proportionality constants $\bar{b}$ and $\bar{d}$ to double too, so it makes sense to think of $\bar{b}$ and $\bar{d}$ as proportional to Δt and "factor out" Δt. That is, we introduce $b = \bar{b}/\Delta t$ and $d = \bar{d}/\Delta t$ to be proportionality constants for newborns and deaths independent of Δt. Also, we introduce $r = b - d$, which is the net rate of growth of the population per time unit. Our model then becomes

$$N(t + \Delta t) - N(t) = \Delta t \, rN(t). \tag{4.2}$$

Equation (4.2) is actually a computational model. Given $N(t)$, we can advance the population size by

$$N(t + \Delta t) = N(t) + \Delta t \, rN(t).$$

This is called a *difference equation*. If we know $N(t)$ for some t, e.g., $N(0) = N_0$, we can compute

$$N(\Delta t) = N_0 + \Delta t \, rN_0,$$
$$N(2\Delta t) = N(\Delta t) + \Delta t \, rN(\Delta t),$$
$$N(3\Delta t) = N(2\Delta t) + \Delta t \, rN(2\Delta t),$$
$$\vdots$$
$$N((k + 1)\Delta t) = N(k\Delta t) + \Delta t \, rN(k\Delta t),$$

where k is some arbitrary integer. A computer program can easily compute $N((k + 1)\Delta t)$ for us with the aid of a little loop.

Warning

Observe that the computational formula cannot be started unless we have an initial condition!

The solution of $N' = rN$ is $N = Ce^{rt}$ for any constant C, and the initial condition is needed to fix C so the solution becomes unique. However, from a mathematical point of view, knowing $N(t)$ at any point t is sufficient as initial condition. Numerically, we more literally need an initial condition: we need to know a starting value at the left end of the interval in order to get the computational formula going.

In fact, we do not need a computer since we see a repetitive pattern when doing hand calculations, which leads us to a mathematical formula for $N((k + 1)\Delta t)$, :

$$N((k + 1)\Delta t) = N(k\Delta t) + \Delta t \, rN(k\Delta t) = N(k\Delta t)(1 + \Delta t \, r)$$
$$= N((k - 1)\Delta t)(1 + \Delta t \, r)^2$$
$$\vdots$$
$$= N_0(1 + \Delta t \, r)^{k+1} \, .$$

Rather than using (4.2) as a computational model directly, there is a strong tradition for deriving a differential equation from this difference equation. The idea is to consider a very small time interval Δt and look at the instantaneous growth as this time interval is shrunk to an infinitesimally small size. In mathematical terms, it means that we let $\Delta t \to 0$. As (4.2) stands, letting $\Delta t \to 0$ will just produce an equation $0 = 0$, so we have to divide by Δt and then take the limit:

$$\lim_{\Delta t \to 0} \frac{N(t + \Delta t) - N(t)}{\Delta t} = rN(t) \, .$$

The term on the left-hand side is actually the definition of the derivative $N'(t)$, so we have

$$N'(t) = rN(t),$$

which is the corresponding differential equation.

There is nothing in our derivation that forces the parameter r to be constant – it can change with time due to, e.g., seasonal changes or more permanent environmental changes.

Detour: Exact mathematical solution

If you have taken a course on mathematical solution methods for differential equations, you may want to recap how an equation like $N' = rN$ or $N' = r(t)N$ is solved. The *method of separation of variables* is the most convenient solution strategy in this case:

$$N' = rN$$
$$\frac{dN}{dt} = rN$$
$$\frac{dN}{N} = rdt$$
$$\int_{N_0}^{N} \frac{dN}{N} = \int_0^t rdt$$

$$\ln N - \ln N_0 = \int_0^t r(t)dt$$

$$N = N_0 \exp\left(\int_0^t r(t)dt\right),$$

which for constant r results in $N = N_0 e^{rt}$. Note that $\exp(t)$ is the same as e^t.

As will be described later, r must in more realistic models depend on N. The method of separation of variables then requires to integrate $\int_{N_0}^N N/r(N)dN$, which quickly becomes non-trivial for many choices of $r(N)$. The only generally applicable solution approach is therefore a numerical method.

4.1.2 Numerical Solution

There is a huge collection of numerical methods for problems like (4.2), and in general any equation of the form $u' = f(u, t)$, where $u(t)$ is the unknown function in the problem, and f is some known formula of u and optionally t. For example, $f(u, t) = ru$ in (4.2). We will first present a simple *finite difference method* solving $u' = f(u, t)$. The idea is four-fold:

1. Introduce a mesh in time with $N_t + 1$ points $t_0, t_1, \ldots, t_{N_t}$. We seek the unknown u at the mesh points t_n, and introduce u^n as the numerical approximation to $u(t_n)$, see Fig. 4.1.
2. Assume that the differential equation is valid at the mesh points.
3. Approximate derivatives by finite differences, see Fig. 4.2.
4. Formulate a computational algorithm that can compute a new value u^n based on previously computed values u^i, $i < n$.

An example will illustrate the steps. First, we introduce the mesh, and very often the mesh is *uniform*, meaning that the spacing between points t_n and t_{n+1} is constant. This property implies that

$$t_n = n\Delta t, \quad n = 0, 1, \ldots, N_t.$$

Second, the differential equation is supposed to hold at the mesh points. Note that this is an approximation, because the differential equation is originally valid at all real values of t. We can express this property mathematically as

$$u'(t_n) = f(u^n, t_n), \quad n = 0, 1, \ldots, N_t.$$

For example, with our model equation $u' = ru$, we have the special case

$$u'(t_n) = ru^n, \quad n = 0, 1, \ldots, N_t,$$

or

$$u'(t_n) = r(t_n)u^n, \quad n = 0, 1, \ldots, N_t,$$

if r depends explicitly on t.

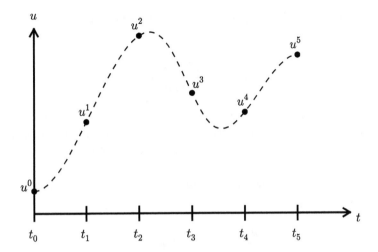

Fig. 4.1 Mesh in time with corresponding discrete values (unknowns)

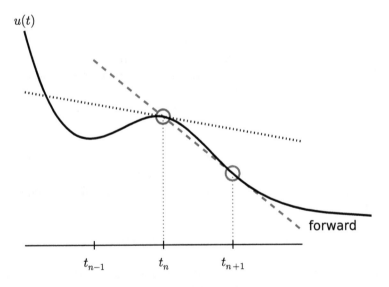

Fig. 4.2 Illustration of a forward difference approximation to the derivative

Third, derivatives are to be replaced by finite differences. To this end, we need to know specific formulas for how derivatives can be approximated by finite differences. One simple possibility is to use the definition of the derivative from any calculus book,

$$u'(t) = \lim_{\Delta t \to 0} \frac{u(t + \Delta t) - u(t)}{\Delta t}.$$

At an arbitrary mesh point t_n this definition can be written as

$$u'(t_n) = \lim_{\Delta t \to 0} \frac{u^{n+1} - u^n}{\Delta t}.$$

Instead of going to the limit $\Delta t \rightarrow 0$ we can use a small Δt, which yields a computable approximation to $u'(t_n)$:

$$u'(t_n) \approx \frac{u^{n+1} - u^n}{\Delta t}.$$

This is known as a *forward difference* since we go forward in time (u^{n+1}) to collect information in u to estimate the derivative. Figure 4.2 illustrates the idea. The error of the forward difference is proportional to Δt (often written as $\mathcal{O}(\Delta t)$, but we will not use this notation in the present book).

We can now plug in the forward difference in our differential equation sampled at the arbitrary mesh point t_n:

$$\frac{u^{n+1} - u^n}{\Delta t} = f(u^n, t_n), \tag{4.3}$$

or with $f(u, t) = ru$ in our special model problem for population growth,

$$\frac{u^{n+1} - u^n}{\Delta t} = ru^n. \tag{4.4}$$

If r depends on time, we insert $r(t_n) = r^n$ for r in this latter equation.

The fourth step is to derive a computational algorithm. Looking at (4.3), we realize that if u^n should be known, we can easily solve with respect to u^{n+1} to get a formula for u at the next time level t_{n+1}:

$$u^{n+1} = u^n + \Delta t f(u^n, t_n). \tag{4.5}$$

Provided we have a known starting value, $u^0 = U_0$, we can use (4.5) to advance the solution by first computing u^1 from u^0, then u^2 from u^1, u^3 from u^2, and so forth.

Such an algorithm is called a *numerical scheme* for the differential equation and often written compactly as

$$u^{n+1} = u^n + \Delta t f(u^n, t_n), \quad u^0 = U_0, \quad n = 0, 1, \ldots, N_t - 1. \tag{4.6}$$

This scheme is known as the *Forward Euler scheme*, also called *Euler's method*.

In our special population growth model, we have

$$u^{n+1} = u^n + \Delta t\, ru^n, \quad u^0 = U_0, \quad n = 0, 1, \ldots, N_t - 1. \tag{4.7}$$

We may also write this model using the problem-specific symbol N instead of the generic u function:

$$N^{n+1} = N^n + \Delta t\, rN^n, \quad N^0 = N_0, \quad n = 0, 1, \ldots, N_t - 1. \tag{4.8}$$

The observant reader will realize that (4.8) is nothing but the computational model (4.2) arising directly in the model derivation. The formula (4.8) arises, however, from a detour via a differential equation and a numerical method for the differential equation. This looks rather unnecessary! The reason why we bother to

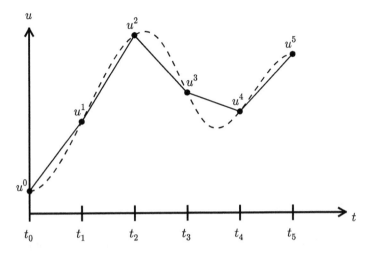

Fig. 4.3 The numerical solution at points can be extended by linear segments between the mesh points

derive the differential equation model and then discretize it by a numerical method is simply that the discretization can be done in many ways, and we can create (much) more accurate and more computationally efficient methods than (4.8) or (4.6). This can be useful in many problems! Nevertheless, the Forward Euler scheme is intuitive and widely applicable, at least when Δt is chosen to be small.

The numerical solution between the mesh points

Our numerical method computes the unknown function u at discrete mesh points $t_1, t_2, \ldots, t_{N_t}$. What if we want to evaluate the numerical solution between the mesh points? The most natural choice is to *assume* a linear variation between the mesh points, see Fig. 4.3. This is compatible with the fact that when we plot the array $u^0, u^1, \ldots$ versus $t_0, t_1, \ldots$, a straight line is drawn between the discrete points.

4.1.3 Programming the Forward Euler Scheme; the Special Case

Let us compute (4.8) in a program. The input variables are N_0, Δt, r, and N_t. Note that we need to compute $N_t + 1$ new values $N^1, \ldots, N^{N_t+1}$. A total of $N_t + 2$ values are needed in an array representation of N^n, $n = 0, \ldots, N_t + 1$.

Our first version of this program is as simple as possible:

```
N_0 = input('Give initial population size N_0: ')
r   = input('Give net growth rate r: ')
dt  = input('Give time step size: ')
N_t = input('Give number of steps: ')
from numpy import linspace, zeros
t = linspace(0, (N_t+1)*dt, N_t+2)
N = zeros(N_t+2)
```

```
N[0] = N_0
for n in range(N_t+1):
    N[n+1] = N[n] + r*dt*N[n]

import matplotlib.pyplot as plt
numerical_sol = 'bo' if N_t < 70 else 'b-'
plt.plot(t, N, numerical_sol, t, N_0*exp(r*t), 'r-')
plt.legend(['numerical', 'exact'], loc='upper left')
plt.xlabel('t'); plt.ylabel('N(t)')
filestem = 'growth1_%dsteps' % N_t
plt.savefig('%s.png' % filestem); plt.savefig('%s.pdf' % filestem)
```

The complete code above resides in the file growth1.py.

Let us demonstrate a simulation where we start with 100 animals, a net growth rate of 10 percent (0.1) per time unit, which can be one month, and $t \in [0, 20]$ months. We may first try Δt of half a month (0.5), which implies $N_t = 40$ (or to be absolutely precise, the last time point to be computed according to our set-up above is $t_{N_t+1} = 20.5$). Figure 4.4 shows the results. The solid line is the exact solution, while the circles are the computed numerical solution. The discrepancy is clearly visible. What if we make Δt 10 times smaller? The result is displayed in Fig. 4.5, where we now use a solid line also for the numerical solution (otherwise, 400 circles would look very cluttered, so the program has a test on how to display the numerical solution, either as circles or a solid line). We can hardly distinguish the exact and the numerical solution. The computing time is also a fraction of a second on a laptop, so it appears that the Forward Euler method is sufficiently accurate for practical purposes. (This is not always true for large, complicated simulation models in engineering, so more sophisticated methods may be needed.)

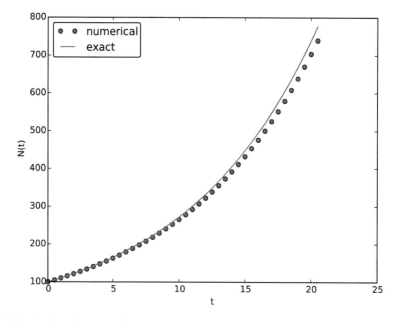

Fig. 4.4 Evolution of a population computed with time step 0.5 month

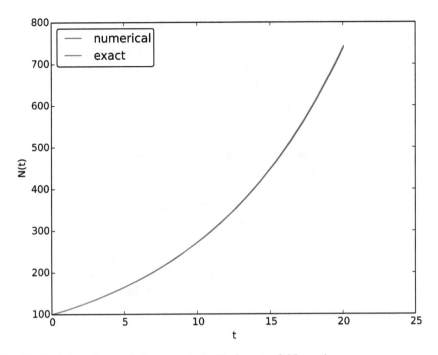

Fig. 4.5 Evolution of a population computed with time step 0.05 month

It is also of interest to see what happens if we increase Δt to 2 months. The results in Fig. 4.6 indicate that this is an inaccurate computation.

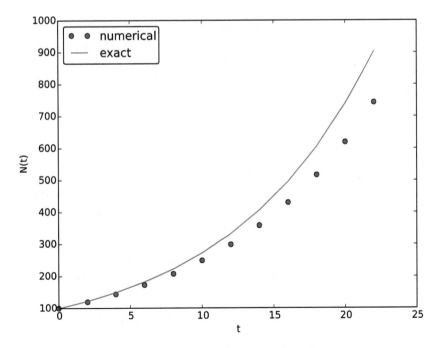

Fig. 4.6 Evolution of a population computed with time step 2 months

4.1.4   Understanding the Forward Euler Method

The good thing about the Forward Euler method is that it gives an understanding of what a differential equation is and a geometrical picture of how to construct the solution. The first idea is that we have already computed the solution up to some time point t_n. The second idea is that we want to progress the solution from t_n to t_{n+1} as a straight line.

We know that the line must go through the solution at t_n, i.e., the point (t_n, u^n). The differential equation tells us the slope of the line: $u'(t_n) = f(u^n, t_n) = ru^n$. That is, the differential equation gives a direct formula for the further *direction* of the solution curve. We can say that the differential equation expresses how the system (u) undergoes changes at a point.

There is a general formula for a straight line $y = ax + b$ with slope a that goes through the point (x_0, y_0): $y = a(x - x_0) + y_0$. Using this formula adapted to the present case, and evaluating the formula for t_{n+1}, results in

$$u^{n+1} = ru^n(t_{n+1} - t_n) + u^n = u^n + \Delta t\, ru^n,$$

which is nothing but the Forward Euler formula. You are now encouraged to do Exercise 4.1 to become more familiar with the geometric interpretation of the Forward Euler method.

4.1.5   Programming the Forward Euler Scheme; the General Case

Our previous program was just a flat main program tailored to a special differential equation. When programming mathematics, it is always good to consider a (large) class of problems and making a Python function to solve any problem that fits into the class. More specifically, we will make software for the class of differential equation problems of the form

$$u'(t) = f(u, t), \quad u = U_0,\ t \in [0, T],$$

for some given function f, and numbers U_0 and T. We also take the opportunity to illustrate what is commonly called a demo function. As the name implies, the purpose of such a function is solely to demonstrate how the function works (not to be confused with a test function, which does verification by use of `assert`). The Python function calculating the solution must take f, U_0, Δt, and T as input, find the corresponding N_t, compute the solution, and return an array with $u^0, u^1, \ldots, u^{N_t}$ and an array with $t_0, t_1, \ldots, t_{N_t}$. The Forward Euler scheme reads

$$u^{n+1} = u^n + \Delta t f(u^n, t_n), \quad n = 0, \ldots, N_t - 1.$$

The corresponding program may now take the form (file `ode_FE.py`):

```
from numpy import linspace, zeros, exp
import matplotlib.pyplot as plt

def ode_FE(f, U_0, dt, T):
    N_t = int(round(float(T)/dt))
    u = zeros(N_t+1)
    t = linspace(0, N_t*dt, len(u))
    u[0] = U_0
    for n in range(N_t):
        u[n+1] = u[n] + dt*f(u[n], t[n])
    return u, t

def demo_population_growth():
    """Test case: u'=r*u, u(0)=100."""
    def f(u, t):
        return 0.1*u

    u, t = ode_FE(f=f, U_0=100, dt=0.5, T=20)
    plt.plot(t, u, t, 100*exp(0.1*t))
    plt.show()

if __name__ == '__main__':
    demo_population_growth()
```

This program file, called ode_FE.py, is a reusable piece of code with a general ode_FE function that can solve any differential equation $u' = f(u, t)$ and a demo function for the special case $u' = 0.1u$, $u(0) = 100$. Observe that the call to the demo function is placed in a test block. This implies that the call is not active if ode_FE is imported as a module in another program, but active if ode_FE.py is run as a program.

The solution should be identical to what the growth1.py program produces with the same parameter settings ($r = 0.1$, $N_0 = 100$). This feature can easily be tested by inserting a print statement, but a much better, automated verification is suggested in Exercise 4.1. You are strongly encouraged to take a "break" and do that exercise now.

Remark on the use of u as variable

In the ode_FE program, the variable u is used in different contexts. Inside the ode_FE function, u is an array, but in the f(u,t) function, as exemplified in the demo_population_growth function, the argument u is a number. Typically, we call f (in ode_FE) with the u argument as one element of the array u in the ode_FE function: u[n].

4.1.6 Making the Population Growth Model More Realistic

Exponential growth of a population according the model $N' = rN$, with exponential solution $N = N_0 e^{rt}$, is unrealistic in the long run because the resources needed to feed the population are finite. At some point there will not be enough resources and the growth will decline. A common model taking this effect into account assumes that r depends on the size of the population, N:

$$N(t + \Delta t) - N(t) = r(N(t))N(t).$$

The corresponding differential equation becomes

$$N' = r(N)N.$$

The reader is strongly encouraged to repeat the steps in the derivation of the Forward Euler scheme and establish that we get

$$N^{n+1} = N^n + \Delta t\, r(N^n)N^n,$$

which computes as easy as for a constant r, since $r(N^n)$ is known when computing N^{n+1}. Alternatively, one can use the Forward Euler formula for the general problem $u' = f(u, t)$ and use $f(u, t) = r(u)u$ and replace u by N.

The simplest choice of $r(N)$ is a linear function, starting with some growth value $\bar{r}$ and declining until the population has reached its maximum, M, according to the available resources:

$$r(N) = \bar{r}(1 - N/M).$$

In the beginning, $N \ll M$ and we will have exponential growth $e^{\bar{r}t}$, but as N increases, $r(N)$ decreases, and when N reaches M, $r(N) = 0$ so there is now more growth and the population remains at $N(t) = M$. This linear choice of $r(N)$ gives rise to a model that is called the *logistic model*. The parameter M is known as the *carrying capacity* of the population.

Let us run the logistic model with aid of the `ode_FE` function in the `ode_FE` module. We choose $N(0) = 100$, $\Delta t = 0.5$ month, $T = 60$ months, $r = 0.1$, and $M = 500$. The complete program, called `logistic.py`, is basically a call to `ode_FE`:

```
from ode_FE import ode_FE
import matplotlib.pyplot as plt

for dt, T in zip((0.5, 20), (60, 100)):
    u, t = ode_FE(f=lambda u, t: 0.1*(1 - u/500.)*u, \
                      U_0=100, dt=dt, T=T)
    plt.figure()  # Make separate figures for each pass in the loop
    plt.plot(t, u, 'b-')
    plt.xlabel('t'); plt.ylabel('N(t)')
    plt.savefig('tmp_%g.png' % dt); plt.savefig('tmp_%g.pdf' % dt)
```

Figure 4.7 shows the resulting curve. We see that the population stabilizes around $M = 500$ individuals. A corresponding exponential growth would reach $N_0 e^{rt} = 100 e^{0.1 \cdot 60} \approx 40{,}300$ individuals!

It is always interesting to see what happens with large Δt values. We may set $\Delta t = 20$ and $T = 100$. Now the solution, seen in Fig. 4.8, oscillates and is hence qualitatively wrong, because one can prove that the exact solution of the differential equation is monotone. (However, there is a corresponding difference

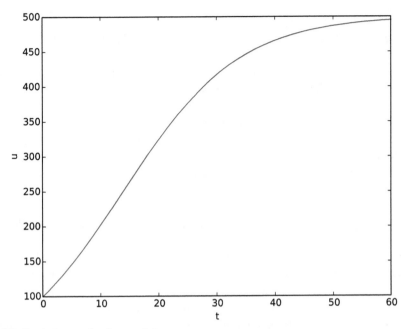

Fig. 4.7 Logistic growth of a population

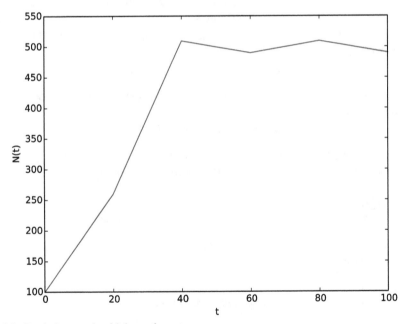

Fig. 4.8 Logistic growth with large time step

equation model, $N_{n+1} = rN_n(1 - N_n/M)$, which allows oscillatory solutions and those are observed in animal populations. The problem with large Δt is that it just leads to wrong mathematics – and two wrongs don't make a right in terms of a relevant model.)

Remark on the world population

The number of people on the planet[2] follows the model $N' = r(t)N$, where the net reproduction $r(t)$ varies with time and has decreased since its top in 1990. The current world value of r is 1.2%, and it is difficult to predict future values[3]. At the moment, the predictions of the world population point to a growth to 9.6 billion before declining.

This example shows the limitation of a differential equation model: we need to know all input parameters, including $r(t)$, in order to predict the future. It is seldom the case that we know all input parameters. Sometimes knowledge of the solution from measurements can help estimate missing input parameters.

4.1.7   Verification: Exact Linear Solution of the Discrete Equations

How can we verify that the programming of an ODE model is correct? The best method is to find a problem where there are no unknown numerical approximation errors, because we can then compare the exact solution of the problem with the result produced by our implementation and expect the difference to be within a very small tolerance. We shall base a unit test on this idea and implement a corresponding *test function* (see Sect. 3.4.4) for automatic verification of our implementation.

It appears that most numerical methods for ODEs will exactly reproduce a solution u that is linear in t. We may therefore set $u = at + b$ and choose any f whose derivative is a. The choice $f(u, t) = a$ is very simple, but we may add anything that is zero, e.g.,

$$f(u, t) = a + (u - (at + b))^m.$$

This is a valid $f(u, t)$ for any a, b, and m. The corresponding ODE looks highly non-trivial, however:

$$u' = a + (u - (at + b))^m.$$

Using the general ode_FE function in ode_FE.py, we may write a proper test function as follows (in file test_ode_FE_exact_linear.py):

```python
def test_ode_FE():
    """Test that a linear u(t)=a*t+b is exactly reproduced."""

    def exact_solution(t):
        return a*t + b

    def f(u, t):  # ODE
        return a + (u - exact_solution(t))**m

    a = 4
    b = -1
    m = 6
```

---

[2] http://en.wikipedia.org/wiki/Population_growth
[3] http://users.rcn.com/jkimball.ma.ultranet/BiologyPages/P/Populations.html

```
dt = 0.5
T = 20.0

u, t = ode_FE(f, exact_solution(0), dt, T)
diff = abs(exact_solution(t) - u).max()
tol = 1E-15            # Tolerance for float comparison
success = diff < tol
assert success
```

Recall that test functions should start with the name `test_`, have no arguments, and formulate the test as a boolean expression `success` that is `True` if the test passes and `False` if it fails. Test functions should make the test as `assert success` (here `success` can also be a boolean expression as in `assert diff < tol`).

Observe that we cannot compare `diff` to zero, which is what we mathematically expect, because `diff` is a floating-point variable that most likely contains small rounding errors. Therefore, we must compare `diff` to zero with a tolerance, here 10^{-15}.

You are encouraged to do Exercise 4.2 where the goal is to make a test function for a verification based on comparison with hand-calculated results for a few time steps.

4.2 Spreading of Diseases

Our aim with this section is to show in detail how one can apply mathematics and programming to investigate spreading of diseases. The mathematical model is now a system of three differential equations with three unknown functions. To derive such a model, we can use mainly intuition, so no specific background knowledge of diseases is required.

4.2.1 Spreading of a Flu

Imagine a boarding school out in the country side. This school is a small and closed society. Suddenly, one or more of the pupils get a flu. We expect that the flu may spread quite effectively or die out. The question is how many of the pupils and the school's staff will be affected. Some quite simple mathematics can help us to achieve insight into the dynamics of how the disease spreads.

Let the mathematical function $S(t)$ count how many individuals, at time t, that have the possibility to get infected. Here, t may count hours or days, for instance. These individuals make up a category called susceptibles, labeled as S. Another category, I, consists of the individuals that are infected. Let $I(t)$ count how many there are in category I at time t. An individual having recovered from the disease is assumed to gain immunity. There is also a small possibility that an infected will die. In either case, the individual is moved from the I category to a category we call the removed category, labeled with R. We let $R(t)$ count the number of individuals in the R category at time t. Those who enter the R category, cannot leave this category.

To summarize, the spreading of this disease is essentially the dynamics of moving individuals from the S to the I and then to the R category:

We can use mathematics to more precisely describe the exchange between the categories. The fundamental idea is to describe the changes that take place during a small time interval, denoted by Δt.

Our disease model is often referred to as a *compartment model*, where quantities are shuffled between compartments (here a synonym for categories) according to some rules. The rules express *changes* in a small time interval Δt, and from these changes we can let Δt go to zero and obtain derivatives. The resulting equations then go from difference equations (with finite Δt) to differential equations ($\Delta t \rightarrow 0$).

We introduce a uniform mesh in time, $t_n = n\Delta t$, $n = 0, \ldots, N_t$, and seek S at the mesh points. The numerical approximation to S at time t_n is denoted by S^n. Similarly, we seek the unknown values of $I(t)$ and $R(t)$ at the mesh points and introduce a similar notation I^n and R^n for the approximations to the exact values $I(t_n)$ and $R(t_n)$.

In the time interval Δt we know that some people will be infected, so S will decrease. We shall soon argue by mathematics that there will be $\beta \Delta t S I$ new infected individuals in this time interval, where β is a parameter reflecting how easy people get infected during a time interval of unit length. If the loss in S is $\beta \Delta t S I$, we have that the change in S is

$$S^{n+1} - S^n = -\beta \Delta t S^n I^n . \tag{4.9}$$

Dividing by Δt and letting $\Delta t \rightarrow 0$, makes the left-hand side approach $S'(t_n)$ such that we obtain a differential equation

$$S' = -\beta S I . \tag{4.10}$$

The reasoning in going from the difference equation (4.9) to the differential equation (4.10) follows exactly the steps explained in Sect. 4.1.1.

Before proceeding with how I and R develops in time, let us explain the formula $\beta \Delta t S I$. We have S susceptibles and I infected people. These can make up SI pairs. Now, suppose that during a time interval T we measure that m actual pairwise meetings do occur among n theoretically possible pairings of people from the S and I categories. The probability that people meet in pairs during a time T is (by the empirical frequency definition of probability) equal to m/n, i.e., the number of successes divided by the number of possible outcomes. From such statistics we normally derive quantities expressed per unit time, i.e., here we want the probability per unit time, μ, which is found from dividing by T: $\mu = m/(nT)$.

Given the probability μ, the expected number of meetings per time interval of SI possible pairs of people is (from basic statistics) $\mu S I$. During a time interval Δt, there will be $\mu S I \Delta t$ expected number of meetings between susceptibles and infected people such that the virus may spread. Only a fraction of the $\mu \Delta t S I$

meetings are effective in the sense that the susceptible actually becomes infected. Counting that m people get infected in n such pairwise meetings (say 5 are infected from 1000 meetings), we can estimate the probability of being infected as $p = m/n$. The expected number of individuals in the S category that in a time interval Δt catch the virus and get infected is then $p\mu\Delta t S I$. Introducing a new constant $\beta = p\mu$ to save some writing, we arrive at the formula $\beta\Delta t S I$.

The value of β must be known in order to predict the future with the disease model. One possibility is to estimate p and μ from their meanings in the derivation above. Alternatively, we can observe an "experiment" where there are S_0 susceptibles and I_0 infected at some point in time. During a time interval T we count that N susceptibles have become infected. Using (4.9) as a rough approximation of how S has developed during time T (and now T is not necessarily small, but we use (4.9) anyway), we get

$$N = \beta T S_0 I_0 \quad \Rightarrow \quad \beta = \frac{N}{T S_0 I_0}. \tag{4.11}$$

We need an additional equation to describe the evolution of $I(t)$. Such an equation is easy to establish by noting that the loss in the S category is a corresponding gain in the I category. More precisely,

$$I^{n+1} - I^n = \beta\Delta t S^n I^n. \tag{4.12}$$

However, there is also a loss in the I category because people recover from the disease. Suppose that we can measure that m out of n individuals recover in a time period T (say 10 of 40 sick people recover during a day: $m = 10, n = 40, T = 24\,\text{h}$). Now, $\gamma = m/(nT)$ is the probability that one individual recovers in a unit time interval. Then (on average) $\gamma\Delta t I$ infected will recover in a time interval Δt. This quantity represents a loss in the I category and a gain in the R category. We can therefore write the total change in the I category as

$$I^{n+1} - I^n = \beta\Delta t S^n I^n - \gamma\Delta t I^n. \tag{4.13}$$

The change in the R category is simple: there is always an increase from the I category:

$$R^{n+1} - R^n = \gamma\Delta t I^n. \tag{4.14}$$

Since there is no loss in the R category (people are either recovered and immune, or dead), we are done with the modeling of this category. In fact, we do not strictly need the equation (4.14) for R, but extensions of the model later will need an equation for R.

Dividing by Δt in (4.13) and (4.14) and letting $\Delta t \to 0$, results in the corresponding differential equations

$$I' = \beta S I - \gamma I, \tag{4.15}$$

and

$$R' = \gamma I. \tag{4.16}$$

To summarize, we have derived difference equations (4.9)–(4.14), and alternative differential equations (4.15)–(4.16). For reference, we list the complete set of the three difference equations:

$$S^{n+1} = S^n - \beta \Delta t S^n I^n, \tag{4.17}$$

$$I^{n+1} = I^n + \beta \Delta t S^n I^n - \gamma \Delta t I^n, \tag{4.18}$$

$$R^{n+1} = R^n + \gamma \Delta t I^n. \tag{4.19}$$

Note that we have isolated the new unknown quantities S^{n+1}, I^{n+1}, and R^{n+1} on the left-hand side, such that these can readily be computed if S^n, I^n, and R^n are known. To get such a procedure started, we need to know S^0, I^0, R^0. Obviously, we also need to have values for the parameters β and γ.

We also list the system of three differential equations:

$$S' = -\beta S I, \tag{4.20}$$

$$I' = \beta S I - \gamma I, \tag{4.21}$$

$$R' = \gamma I. \tag{4.22}$$

This differential equation model (and also its discrete counterpart above) is known as an *SIR model*. The input data to the differential equation model consist of the parameters β and γ as well as the initial conditions $S(0) = S_0$, $I(0) = I_0$, and $R(0) = R_0$.

4.2.2   A Forward Euler Method for the Differential Equation System

Let us apply the same principles as we did in Sect. 4.1.2 to discretize the differential equation system by the Forward Euler method. We already have a time mesh and time-discrete quantities S^n, I^n, R^n, $n = 0, \ldots, N_t$. The three differential equations are assumed to be valid at the mesh points. At the point t_n we then have

$$S'(t_n) = -\beta S(t_n) I(t_n), \tag{4.23}$$

$$I'(t_n) = \beta S(t_n) I(t_n) - \gamma I(t_n), \tag{4.24}$$

$$R'(t_n) = \gamma I(t_n), \tag{4.25}$$

for $n = 0, 1, \ldots, N_t$. This is an approximation since the differential equations are originally valid at all times t (usually in some finite interval $[0, T]$). Using forward finite differences for the derivatives results in an additional approximation,

$$\frac{S^{n+1} - S^n}{\Delta t} = -\beta S^n I^n, \tag{4.26}$$

$$\frac{I^{n+1} - I^n}{\Delta t} = \beta S^n I^n - \gamma I^n, \tag{4.27}$$

$$\frac{R^{n+1} - R^n}{\Delta t} = \gamma I^n. \tag{4.28}$$

As we see, these equations are identical to the difference equations that naturally arise in the derivation of the model. However, other numerical methods than the Forward Euler scheme will result in slightly different difference equations.

4.2.3   Programming the Numerical Method; the Special Case

The computation of (4.26)–(4.28) can be readily made in a computer program
SIR1.py:

```python
from numpy import zeros, linspace
import matplotlib.pyplot as plt

# Time unit: 1 h
beta = 10./(40*8*24)
gamma = 3./(15*24)
dt = 0.1                # 6 min
D = 30                  # Simulate for D days
N_t = int(D*24/dt)      # Corresponding no of hours

t = linspace(0, N_t*dt, N_t+1)
S = zeros(N_t+1)
I = zeros(N_t+1)
R = zeros(N_t+1)

# Initial condition
S[0] = 50
I[0] = 1
R[0] = 0

# Step equations forward in time
for n in range(N_t):
    S[n+1] = S[n] - dt*beta*S[n]*I[n]
    I[n+1] = I[n] + dt*beta*S[n]*I[n] - dt*gamma*I[n]
    R[n+1] = R[n] + dt*gamma*I[n]

fig = plt.figure()
l1, l2, l3 = plt.plot(t, S, t, I, t, R)
fig.legend((l1, l2, l3), ('S', 'I', 'R'), 'upper left')
plt.xlabel('hours')
plt.show()
plt.savefig('tmp.pdf'); plt.savefig('tmp.png')
```

This program was written to investigate the spreading of a flu at the mentioned
boarding school, and the reasoning for the specific choices β and γ goes as follows.
At some other school where the disease has already spread, it was observed that in
the beginning of a day there were 40 susceptibles and 8 infected, while the numbers
were 30 and 18, respectively, 24 hours later. Using 1 h as time unit, we then have
from (4.11) that $\beta = 10/(40 \cdot 8 \cdot 24)$. Among 15 infected, it was observed that
3 recovered during a day, giving $\gamma = 3/(15 \cdot 24)$. Applying these parameters to
a new case where there is one infected initially and 50 susceptibles, gives the graphs
in Fig. 4.9. These graphs are just straight lines between the values at times $t_i = i \Delta t$
as computed by the program. We observe that S reduces as I and R grows. After
about 30 days everyone has become ill and recovered again.

We can experiment with β and γ to see whether we get an outbreak of the disease
or not. Imagine that a "wash your hands" campaign was successful and that the
other school in this case experienced a reduction of β by a factor of 5. With this

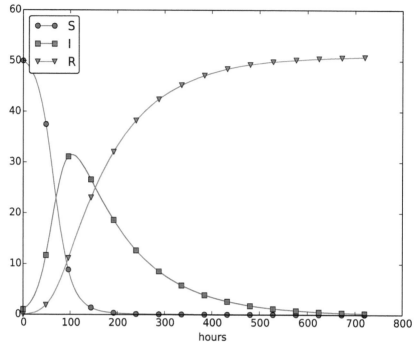

Fig. 4.9 Natural evolution of a flu at a boarding school

lower β the disease spreads very slowly so we simulate for 60 days. The curves appear in Fig. 4.10.

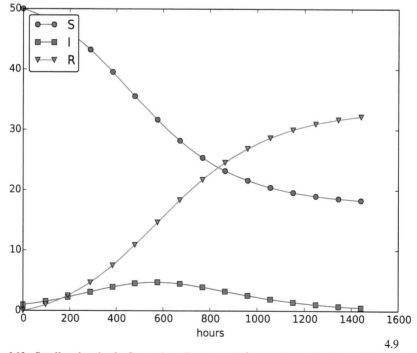

Fig. 4.10 Small outbreak of a flu at a boarding school (β is much smaller than in Fig. 4.9)

4.2.4 Outbreak or Not

Looking at the equation for I, it is clear that we must have $\beta SI - \gamma I > 0$ for I to increase. When we start the simulation it means that

$$\beta S(0)I(0) - \gamma I(0) > 0,$$

or simpler

$$\frac{\beta S(0)}{\gamma} > 1 \qquad\qquad (4.29)$$

to increase the number of infected people and accelerate the spreading of the disease. You can run the SIR1.py program with a smaller β such that (4.29) is violated and observe that there is no outbreak.

The power of mathematical modeling

The reader should notice our careful use of words in the previous paragraphs. We started out with modeling a very specific case, namely the spreading of a flu among pupils and staff at a boarding school. With purpose we exchanged words like pupils and flu with more neutral and general words like *individuals* and *disease*, respectively. Phrased equivalently, we raised the abstraction level by moving from a specific case (flu at a boarding school) to a more general case (disease in a closed society). Very often, when developing mathematical models, we start with a specific example and see, through the modeling, that what is going on of essence in this example also will take place in many similar problem settings. We try to incorporate this generalization in the model so that the model has a much wider application area than what we aimed at in the beginning. This is the very power of mathematical modeling: by solving one specific case we have often developed more generic tools that can readily be applied to solve seemingly different problems. The next sections will give substance to this assertion.

4.2.5 Abstract Problem and Notation

When we had a specific differential equation with one unknown, we quickly turned to an abstract differential equation written in the generic form $u' = f(u, t)$. We refer to such a problem as a *scalar ODE*. A specific equation corresponds to a specific choice of the formula $f(u, t)$ involving u and (optionally) t.

It is advantageous to also write a system of differential equations in the same abstract notation,

$$u' = f(u, t),$$

but this time it is understood that u is a vector of functions and f is also vector. We say that $u' = f(u, t)$ is a *vector ODE* or *system of ODEs* in this case. For the SIR model we introduce the two 3-vectors, one for the unknowns,

$$u = (S(t), I(t), R(t)),$$

and one for the right-hand side functions,

$$f(u, t) = (-\beta S I, \beta S I - \gamma I, \gamma I).$$

The equation $u' = f(u, t)$ means setting the two vectors equal, i.e., the components must be pairwise equal. Since $u' = (S', I', R')$, we get that $u' = f$ implies

$$S' = -\beta S I,$$
$$I' = \beta S I - \gamma I,$$
$$R' = \gamma I.$$

The generalized short notation $u' = f(u, t)$ is very handy since we can derive numerical methods and implement software for this abstract system and in a particular application just identify the formulas in the f vector, implement these, and call functionality that solves the differential equation system.

4.2.6 Programming the Numerical Method; the General Case

In Python code, the Forward Euler step

$$u^{n+1} = u^n + \Delta t f(u^n, t_n),$$

being a scalar or a vector equation, can be coded as

```
u[n+1] = u[n] + dt*f(u[n], t[n])
```

both in the scalar and vector case. In the vector case, u[n] is a one-dimensional numpy array of length $m + 1$ holding the mathematical quantity u^n, and the Python function f must return a numpy array of length $m + 1$. Then the expression u[n] + dt*f(u[n], t[n]) is an array plus a scalar times an array.

For all this to work, the complete numerical solution must be represented by a two-dimensional array, created by u = zeros((N_t+1, m+1)). The first index counts the time points and the second the components of the solution vector at one time point. That is, u[n,i] corresponds to the mathematical quantity u_i^n. When we use only one index, as in u[n], this is the same as u[n,:] and picks out all the components in the solution at the time point with index n. Then the assignment u[n+1] = ... becomes correct because it is actually an in-place assignment u[n+1, :] = ... The nice feature of these facts is that the same piece of Python code works for both a scalar ODE and a system of ODEs!

The ode_FE function for the vector ODE is placed in the file ode_system_FE.py and was written as follows:

```
from numpy import linspace, zeros, asarray
import matplotlib.pyplot as plt

def ode_FE(f, U_0, dt, T):
    N_t = int(round(float(T)/dt))
```

```
# Ensure that any list/tuple returned from f_ is wrapped as array
f_ = lambda u, t: asarray(f(u, t))
u = zeros((N_t+1, len(U_0)))
t = linspace(0, N_t*dt, len(u))
u[0] = U_0
for n in range(N_t):
    u[n+1] = u[n] + dt*f_(u[n], t[n])
return u, t
```

The line `f_ = lambda ...` needs an explanation. For a user, who just needs to define the f in the ODE system, it is convenient to insert the various mathematical expressions on the right-hand sides in a list and return that list. Obviously, we could demand the user to convert the list to a numpy array, but it is so easy to do a general such conversion in the `ode_FE` function as well. To make sure that the result from f is indeed an array that can be used for array computing in the formula `u[n] + dt*f(u[n], t[n])`, we introduce a new function `f_` that calls the user's f and sends the results through the numpy function `asarray`, which ensures that its argument is converted to a numpy array (if it is not already an array).

Note also the extra parenthesis required when calling `zeros` with two indices.

Let us show how the previous SIR model can be solved using the new general `ode_FE` that can solve *any* vector ODE. The user's `f(u, t)` function takes a vector u, with three components corresponding to S, I, and R as argument, along with the current time point `t[n]`, and must return the values of the formulas of the right-hand sides in the vector ODE. An appropriate implementation is

```
def f(u, t):
    S, I, R = u
    return [-beta*S*I, beta*S*I - gamma*I, gamma*I]
```

Note that the S, I, and R values correspond to S^n, I^n, and R^n. These values are then just inserted in the various formulas in the vector ODE. Here we collect the values in a list since the `ode_FE` function will anyway wrap this list in an array. We could, of course, returned an array instead:

```
def f(u, t):
    S, I, R = u
    return array([-beta*S*I, beta*S*I - gamma*I, gamma*I])
```

The list version looks a bit nicer, so that is why we prefer a list and rather introduce `f_ = lambda u, t: asarray(f(u,t))` in the general `ode_FE` function.

We can now show a function that runs the previous SIR example, while using the generic `ode_FE` function:

```
def demo_SIR():
    """Test case using a SIR model."""
    def f(u, t):
        S, I, R = u
        return [-beta*S*I, beta*S*I - gamma*I, gamma*I]
```

```
beta = 10./(40*8*24)
gamma = 3./(15*24)
dt = 0.1                 # 6 min
D = 30                   # Simulate for D days
N_t = int(D*24/dt)       # Corresponding no of hours
T = dt*N_t               # End time
U_0 = [50, 1, 0]

u, t = ode_FE(f, U_0, dt, T)

S = u[:,0]
I = u[:,1]
R = u[:,2]
fig = plt.figure()
l1, l2, l3 = plt.plot(t, S, t, I, t, R)
fig.legend((l1, l2, l3), ('S', 'I', 'R'), 'lower right')
plt.xlabel('hours')
plt.show()

# Consistency check:
N = S[0] + I[0] + R[0]
eps = 1E-12  # Tolerance for comparing real numbers
for n in range(len(S)):
    SIR_sum = S[n] + I[n] + R[n]
    if abs(SIR_sum - N) > eps:
        print '*** consistency check failed: S+I+R=%g != %g' %\
              (SIR_sum, N)

if __name__ == '__main__':
    demo_SIR()
```

Recall that the u returned from ode_FE contains all components (S, I, R) in the solution vector at all time points. We therefore need to extract the S, I, and R values in separate arrays for further analysis and easy plotting.

Another key feature of this higher-quality code is the consistency check. By adding the three differential equations in the SIR model, we realize that $S' + I' + R' = 0$, which means that $S + I + R = \text{const}$. We can check that this relation holds by comparing $S^n + I^n + R^n$ to the sum of the initial conditions. The check is not a full-fledged verification, but it is a much better than doing nothing and hoping that the computation is correct. Exercise 4.5 suggests another method for controlling the quality of the numerical solution.

4.2.7   Time-Restricted Immunity

Let us now assume that immunity after the disease only lasts for some certain time period. This means that there is transport from the R state to the S state:

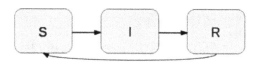

Modeling the loss of immunity is very similar to modeling recovery from the disease: the amount of people losing immunity is proportional to the amount of recovered patients and the length of the time interval Δt. We can therefore write the loss in the R category as $-\nu \Delta t R$ in time Δt, where ν^{-1} is the typical time it takes to lose immunity. The loss in $R(t)$ is a gain in $S(t)$. The "budgets" for the categories therefore become

$$S^{n+1} = S^n - \beta \Delta t S^n I^n + \nu \Delta t R^n, \tag{4.30}$$

$$I^{n+1} = I^n + \beta \Delta t S^n I^n - \gamma \Delta t I^n, \tag{4.31}$$

$$R^{n+1} = R^n + \gamma \Delta t I^n - \nu \Delta t R^n. \tag{4.32}$$

Dividing by Δt and letting $\Delta t \to 0$ gives the differential equation system

$$S' = -\beta S I + \nu R, \tag{4.33}$$

$$I' = \beta S I - \gamma I, \tag{4.34}$$

$$R' = \gamma I - \nu R. \tag{4.35}$$

This system can be solved by the same methods as we demonstrated for the original SIR model. Only one modification in the program is necessary: adding nu*R[n] to the S[n+1] update and subtracting the same quantity in the R[n+1] update:

```
for n in range(N_t):
    S[n+1] = S[n] - dt*beta*S[n]*I[n] + dt*nu*R[n]
    I[n+1] = I[n] + dt*beta*S[n]*I[n] - dt*gamma*I[n]
    R[n+1] = R[n] + dt*gamma*I[n] - dt*nu*R[n]
```

The modified code is found in the file SIR2.py.

Setting ν^{-1} to 50 days, reducing β by a factor of 4 compared to the previous example ($\beta = 0.00033$), and simulating for 300 days gives an oscillatory behavior in the categories, as depicted in Fig. 4.11. It is easy now to play around and study how the parameters affect the spreading of the disease. For example, making the disease slightly more effective (increase β to 0.00043) and increasing the average time to loss of immunity to 90 days lead to other oscillations, see Fig. 4.12.

4.2.8 Incorporating Vaccination

We can extend the model to also include vaccination. To this end, it can be useful to track those who are vaccinated and those who are not. So, we introduce a fourth category, V, for those who have taken a successful vaccination. Furthermore, we assume that in a time interval Δt, a fraction $p\Delta t$ of the S category is subject to a successful vaccination. This means that in the time Δt, $p\Delta t S$ people leave from the S to the V category. Since the vaccinated ones cannot get the disease, there is no impact on the I or R categories. We can visualize the categories, and the movement between them, as

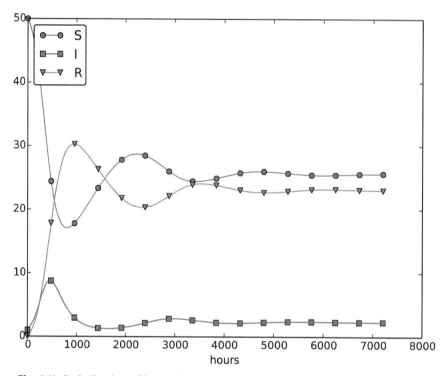

Fig. 4.11 Including loss of immunity

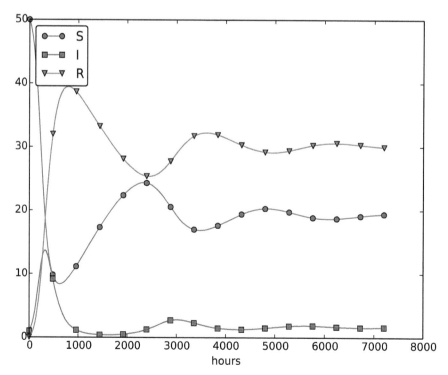

Fig. 4.12 Increasing β and reducing ν compared to Fig. 4.11

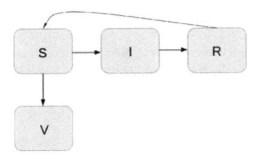

The new, extended differential equations with the V quantity become

$$S' = -\beta SI + vR - pS, \tag{4.36}$$
$$V' = pS, \tag{4.37}$$
$$I' = \beta SI - \gamma I, \tag{4.38}$$
$$R' = \gamma I - vR. \tag{4.39}$$

We shall refer to this model as the SIRV model.

The new equation for V' poses no difficulties when it comes to the numerical method. In a Forward Euler scheme we simply add an update

$$V^{n+1} = V^n + p\Delta t S^n.$$

The program needs to store $V(t)$ in an additional array V, and the plotting command must be extended with more arguments to plot V versus t as well. The complete code is found in the file SIRV1.py.

Using $p = 0.0005$ and $p = 0.0001$ as values for the vaccine efficiency parameter, the effect of vaccination is seen in Fig. 4.13 (other parameters are as in Fig. 4.11).

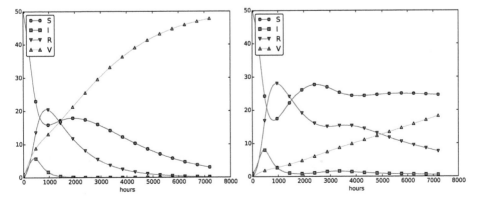

Fig. 4.13 The effect of vaccination: $p = 0.0005$ (*left*) and $p = 0.0001$ (*right*)

4.2.9 Discontinuous Coefficients: A Vaccination Campaign

What about modeling a vaccination campaign? Imagine that six days after the outbreak of the disease, the local health station launches a vaccination campaign. They reach out to many people, say 10 times as efficiently as in the previous (constant vaccination) case. If the campaign lasts for 10 days we can write

$$p(t) = \begin{cases} 0.005, & 6 \cdot 24 \leq t \leq 15 \cdot 24, \\ 0, & \text{otherwise} \end{cases}$$

Note that we must multiply the t value by 24 because t is measured in hours, not days. In the differential equation system, $pS(t)$ must be replaced by $p(t)S(t)$, and in this case we get a differential equation system with a term that is *discontinuous*. This is usually quite a challenge in mathematics, but as long as we solve the equations numerically in a program, a discontinuous coefficient is easy to treat.

There are two ways to implement the discontinuous coefficient $p(t)$: through a function and through an array. The function approach is perhaps the easiest:

```
def p(t):
    return 0.005 if (6*24 <= t <= 15*24) else 0
```

In the code for updating the arrays S and V we get a term p(t[n])*S[n].

We can also let $p(t)$ be an array filled with correct values prior to the simulation. Then we need to allocate an array p of length N_t+1 and find the indices corresponding to the time period between 6 and 15 days. These indices are found from the time point divided by Δt. That is,

```
p = zeros(N_t+1)
start_index = 6*24/dt
stop_index = 15*24/dt
p[start_index:stop_index] = 0.005
```

The $p(t)S(t)$ term in the updating formulas for S and V simply becomes p[n]*S[n]. The file SIRV2.py contains a program based on filling an array p.

The effect of a vaccination campaign is illustrated in Fig. 4.14. All the data are as in Fig. 4.13 (left), except that p is ten times stronger for a period of 10 days and $p = 0$ elsewhere.

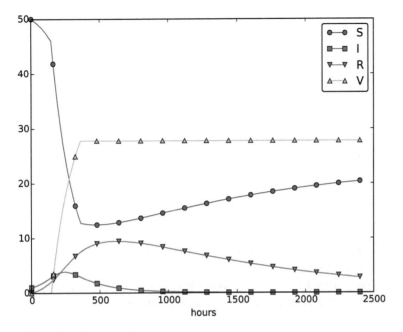

Fig. 4.14 The effect of a vaccination campaign

4.3 Oscillating One-Dimensional Systems

Numerous engineering constructions and devices contain materials that act like springs. Such springs give rise to oscillations, and controlling oscillations is a key engineering task. We shall now learn to simulate oscillating systems.

As always, we start with the simplest meaningful mathematical model, which for oscillations is a second-order differential equation:

$$u''(t) + \omega^2 u(t) = 0, \tag{4.40}$$

where ω is a given physical parameter. Equation (4.40) models a one-dimensional system oscillating without damping (i.e., with negligible damping). One-dimensional here means that some motion takes place along one dimension only in some coordinate system. Along with (4.40) we need the two *initial conditions* $u(0)$ and $u'(0)$.

4.3.1 Derivation of a Simple Model

Many engineering systems undergo oscillations, and differential equations constitute the key tool to understand, predict, and control the oscillations. We start with the simplest possible model that captures the essential dynamics of an oscillating system. Some body with mass m is attached to a spring and moves along a line without friction, see Fig. 4.15 for a sketch (rolling wheels indicate "no friction"). When the spring is stretched (or compressed), the spring force pulls (or pushes) the body back and work "against" the motion. More precisely, let $x(t)$ be the position

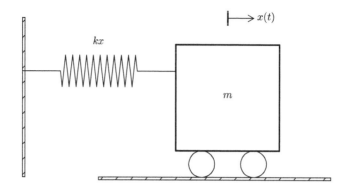

Fig. 4.15 Sketch of a one-dimensional, oscillating dynamic system (without friction)

of the body on the x axis, along which the body moves. The spring is not stretched when $x = 0$, so the force is zero, and $x = 0$ is hence the equilibrium position of the body. The spring force is $-kx$, where k is a constant to be measured. We assume that there are no other forces (e.g., no friction). Newton's 2nd law of motion $F = ma$ then has $F = -kx$ and $a = \ddot{x}$,

$$-kx = m\ddot{x}, \tag{4.41}$$

which can be rewritten as

$$\ddot{x} + \omega^2 x = 0, \tag{4.42}$$

by introducing $\omega = \sqrt{k/m}$ (which is very common).

Equation (4.42) is a *second-order* differential equation, and therefore we need *two* initial conditions, one on the position $x(0)$ and one on the velocity $x'(0)$. Here we choose the body to be at rest, but moved away from its equilibrium position:

$$x(0) = X_0, \quad x'(0) = 0.$$

The exact solution of (4.42) with these initial conditions is $x(t) = X_0 \cos \omega t$. This can easily be verified by substituting into (4.42) and checking the initial conditions. The solution tells that such a spring-mass system oscillates back and forth as described by a cosine curve.

The differential equation (4.42) appears in numerous other contexts. A classical example is a simple pendulum that oscillates back and forth. Physics books derive, from Newton's second law of motion, that

$$mL\theta'' + mg \sin \theta = 0,$$

where m is the mass of the body at the end of a pendulum with length L, g is the acceleration of gravity, and θ is the angle the pendulum makes with the vertical. Considering small angles θ, $\sin \theta \approx \theta$, and we get (4.42) with $x = \theta$, $\omega = \sqrt{g/L}$, $x(0) = \Theta$, and $x'(0) = 0$, if Θ is the initial angle and the pendulum is at rest at $t = 0$.

4.3.2 Numerical Solution

We have not looked at numerical methods for handling second-order derivatives, and such methods are an option, but we know how to solve first-order differential equations and even systems of first-order equations. With a little, yet very common, trick we can rewrite (4.42) as a first-order system of two differential equations. We introduce $u = x$ and $v = x' = u'$ as *two* new unknown functions. The two corresponding equations arise from the definition $v = u'$ and the original equation (4.42):

$$u' = v, \tag{4.43}$$
$$v' = -\omega^2 u. \tag{4.44}$$

(Notice that we can use $u'' = v'$ to remove the second-order derivative from Newton's 2nd law.)

We can now apply the Forward Euler method to (4.43)–(4.44), exactly as we did in Sect. 4.2.2:

$$\frac{u^{n+1} - u^n}{\Delta t} = v^n, \tag{4.45}$$
$$\frac{v^{n+1} - v^n}{\Delta t} = -\omega^2 u^n, \tag{4.46}$$

resulting in the computational scheme

$$u^{n+1} = u^n + \Delta t \, v^n, \tag{4.47}$$
$$v^{n+1} = v^n - \Delta t \, \omega^2 u^n. \tag{4.48}$$

4.3.3 Programming the Numerical Method; the Special Case

A simple program for (4.47)–(4.48) follows the same ideas as in Sect. 4.2.3:

```python
from numpy import zeros, linspace, pi, cos, array
import matplotlib.pyplot as plt

omega = 2
P = 2*pi/omega
dt = P/20
T = 3*P
N_t = int(round(T/dt))
t = linspace(0, N_t*dt, N_t+1)

u = zeros(N_t+1)
v = zeros(N_t+1)

# Initial condition
X_0 = 2
u[0] = X_0
v[0] = 0
```

```
# Step equations forward in time
for n in range(N_t):
    u[n+1] = u[n] + dt*v[n]
    v[n+1] = v[n] - dt*omega**2*u[n]

fig = plt.figure()
l1, l2 = plt.plot(t, u, 'b-', t, X_0*cos(omega*t), 'r--')
fig.legend((l1, l2), ('numerical', 'exact'), 'upper left')
plt.xlabel('t')
plt.show()
plt.savefig('tmp.pdf'); plt.savefig('tmp.png')
```

(See file osc_FE.py.)

Since we already know the exact solution as $u(t) = X_0 \cos \omega t$, we have reasoned as follows to find an appropriate simulation interval $[0, T]$ and also how many points we should choose. The solution has a period $P = 2\pi/\omega$. (The period P is the time difference between two peaks of the $u(t) \sim \cos \omega t$ curve.) Simulating for three periods of the cosine function, $T = 3P$, and choosing Δt such that there are 20 intervals per period gives $\Delta t = P/20$ and a total of $N_t = T/\Delta t$ intervals. The rest of the program is a straightforward coding of the Forward Euler scheme.

Figure 4.16 shows a comparison between the numerical solution and the exact solution of the differential equation. To our surprise, the numerical solution looks wrong. Is this discrepancy due to a programming error or a problem with the Forward Euler method?

First of all, even before trying to run the program, you should sit down and compute two steps in the time loop with a calculator so you have some intermediate results to compare with. Using $X_0 = 2$, $dt = 0.157079632679$, and $\omega = 2$, we

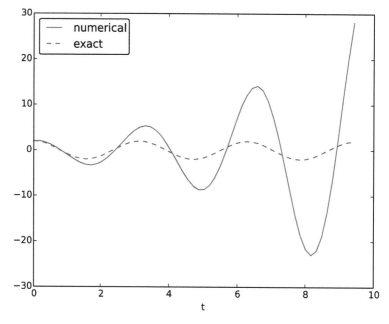

Fig. 4.16 Simulation of an oscillating system

get $u^1 = 2$, $v^1 = -1.25663706$, $u^2 = 1.80260791$, and $v^2 = -2.51327412$. Such calculations show that the program is seemingly correct. (Later, we can use such values to construct a unit test and a corresponding test function.)

The next step is to reduce the discretization parameter Δt and see if the results become more accurate. Figure 4.17 shows the numerical and exact solution for the cases $\Delta t = P/40, P/160, P/2000$. The results clearly become better, and the finest resolution gives graphs that cannot be visually distinguished. Nevertheless, the finest resolution involves 6000 computational intervals in total, which is considered quite much. This is no problem on a modern laptop, however, as the computations take just a fraction of a second.

Although 2000 intervals per oscillation period seem sufficient for an accurate numerical solution, the lower right graph in Fig. 4.17 shows that if we increase the simulation time, here to 20 periods, there is a little growth of the amplitude, which becomes significant over time. The conclusion is that the Forward Euler method has a fundamental problem with its growing amplitudes, and that a very small Δt is required to achieve satisfactory results. The longer the simulation is, the smaller Δt has to be. It is certainly time to look for more effective numerical methods!

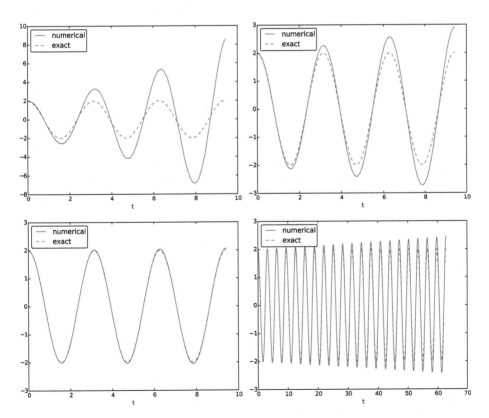

Fig. 4.17 Simulation of an oscillating system with different time steps. *Upper left*: 40 steps per oscillation period. *Upper right*: 160 steps per period. *Lower left*: 2000 steps per period. *Lower right*: 2000 steps per period, but longer simulation

4.3.4   A Magic Fix of the Numerical Method

In the Forward Euler scheme,

$$u^{n+1} = u^n + \Delta t\, v^n,$$
$$v^{n+1} = v^n - \Delta t\, \omega^2 u^n,$$

we can replace u^n in the last equation by the recently computed value u^{n+1} from the first equation:

$$u^{n+1} = u^n + \Delta t\, v^n, \tag{4.49}$$
$$v^{n+1} = v^n - \Delta t\, \omega^2 u^{n+1}. \tag{4.50}$$

Before justifying this fix more mathematically, let us try it on the previous example. The results appear in Fig. 4.18. We see that the amplitude *does not grow*, but the phase is not entirely correct. After 40 periods (Fig. 4.18 right) we see a significant difference between the numerical and the exact solution. Decreasing Δt decreases the error. For example, with 2000 intervals per period, we only see a small phase error even after 50,000 periods (!). We can safely conclude that the fix results in an excellent numerical method!

Let us interpret the adjusted scheme mathematically. First we order (4.49)–(4.50) such that the difference approximations to derivatives become transparent:

$$\frac{u^{n+1} - u^n}{\Delta t} = v^n, \tag{4.51}$$

$$\frac{v^{n+1} - v^n}{\Delta t} = -\omega^2 u^{n+1}. \tag{4.52}$$

We interpret (4.51) as the differential equation sampled at mesh point t_n, because we have v^n on the right-hand side. The left-hand side is then a *forward difference* or Forward Euler approximation to the derivative u', see Fig. 4.2. On the other hand, we interpret (4.52) as the differential equation sampled at mesh point t_{n+1}, since we

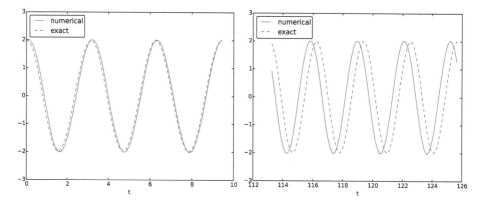

Fig. 4.18   Adjusted method: first three periods (*left*) and period 36–40 (*right*)

have u^{n+1} on the right-hand side. In this case, the difference approximation on the left-hand side is a *backward difference*,

$$v'(t_{n+1}) \approx \frac{v^{n+1} - v^n}{\Delta t} \quad \text{or} \quad v'(t_n) \approx \frac{v^n - v^{n-1}}{\Delta t}.$$

Figure 4.19 illustrates the backward difference. The error in the backward difference is proportional to Δt, the same as for the forward difference (but the proportionality constant in the error term has different sign). The resulting discretization method for (4.52) is often referred to as a Backward Euler scheme.

To summarize, using a forward difference for the first equation and a backward difference for the second equation results in a much better method than just using forward differences in both equations.

The standard way of expressing this scheme in physics is to change the order of the equations,

$$v' = -\omega^2 u, \tag{4.53}$$
$$u' = v, \tag{4.54}$$

and apply a forward difference to (4.53) and a backward difference to (4.54):

$$v^{n+1} = v^n - \Delta t\, \omega^2 u^n, \tag{4.55}$$
$$u^{n+1} = u^n + \Delta t\, v^{n+1}. \tag{4.56}$$

That is, first the velocity v is updated and then the position u, using the most recently computed velocity. There is no difference between (4.55)–(4.56) and (4.49)–(4.50) with respect to accuracy, so the order of the original differential equations does not matter. The scheme (4.55)–(4.56) goes under the names Semi-implicit Euler[4] or Euler-Cromer. The implementation of (4.55)–(4.56) is found in the file osc_EC.py. The core of the code goes like

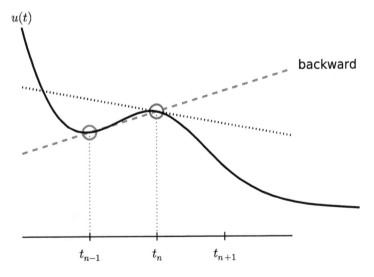

Fig. 4.19 Illustration of a backward difference approximation to the derivative

---

[4] http://en.wikipedia.org/wiki/Semi-implicit_Euler_method

```
u = zeros(N_t+1)
v = zeros(N_t+1)

# Initial condition
u[0] = 2
v[0] = 0

# Step equations forward in time
for n in range(N_t):
    v[n+1] = v[n] - dt*omega**2*u[n]
    u[n+1] = u[n] + dt*v[n+1]
```

4.3.5 The 2nd-Order Runge-Kutta Method (or Heun's Method)

A very popular method for solving scalar and vector ODEs of first order is the
2nd-order Runge-Kutta method (RK2), also known as Heun's method. The idea,
first thinking of a scalar ODE, is to form a *centered difference* approximation to the
derivative between two time points:

$$u'(t_n + \frac{1}{2}\Delta t) \approx \frac{u^{n+1} - u^n}{\Delta t}.$$

The centered difference formula is visualized in Fig. 4.20. The error in the centered
difference is proportional to Δt^2, one order higher than the forward and backward
differences, which means that if we halve Δt, the error is more effectively reduced
in the centered difference since it is reduced by a factor of four rather than two.

The problem with such a centered scheme for the general ODE $u' = f(u, t)$ is
that we get

$$\frac{u^{n+1} - u^n}{\Delta t} = f(u^{n+\frac{1}{2}}, t_{n+\frac{1}{2}}),$$

which leads to difficulties since we do not know what $u^{n+\frac{1}{2}}$ is. However, we can
approximate the value of f between two time levels by the arithmetic average of

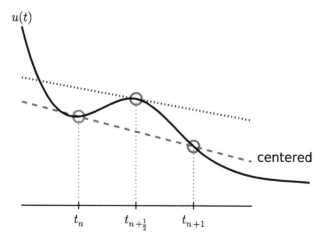

Fig. 4.20 Illustration of a centered difference approximation to the derivative

the values at t_n and t_{n+1}:

$$f(u^{n+\frac{1}{2}}, t_{n+\frac{1}{2}}) \approx \frac{1}{2}(f(u^n, t_n) + f(u^{n+1}, t_{n+1})).$$

This results in

$$\frac{u^{n+1} - u^n}{\Delta t} = \frac{1}{2}(f(u^n, t_n) + f(u^{n+1}, t_{n+1})),$$

which in general is a *nonlinear algebraic equation* for u^{n+1} if $f(u, t)$ is not a linear function of u. To deal with the unknown term $f(u^{n+1}, t_{n+1})$, without solving nonlinear equations, we can approximate or predict u^{n+1} using a Forward Euler step:

$$u^{n+1} = u^n + \Delta t f(u^n, t_n).$$

This reasoning gives rise to the method

$$u^* = u^n + \Delta t f(u^n, t_n), \tag{4.57}$$

$$u^{n+1} = u^n + \frac{\Delta t}{2}(f(u^n, t_n) + f(u^*, t_{n+1})). \tag{4.58}$$

The scheme applies to both scalar and vector ODEs.

For an oscillating system with $f = (v, -\omega^2 u)$ the file osc_Heun.py implements this method. The demo function in that file runs the simulation for 10 periods with 20 time steps per period. The corresponding numerical and exact solutions are shown in Fig. 4.21. We see that the amplitude grows, but not as much as for the Forward Euler method. However, the Euler-Cromer method is much better!

We should add that in problems where the Forward Euler method gives satisfactory approximations, such as growth/decay problems or the SIR model, the 2nd-order Runge-Kutta method or Heun's method, usually works considerably better and produces greater accuracy for the same computational cost. It is therefore a very valuable method to be aware of, although it cannot compete with the Euler-Cromer scheme for oscillation problems. The derivation of the RK2/Heun scheme is also good general training in "numerical thinking".

4.3.6   Software for Solving ODEs

There is a jungle of methods for solving ODEs, and it would be nice to have easy access to implementations of a wide range of methods, especially the sophisticated and complicated *adaptive* methods that adjust Δt automatically to obtain a prescribed accuracy. The Python package Odespy[5] gives easy access to a lot of numerical methods for ODEs.

The simplest possible example on using Odespy is to solve $u' = u$, $u(0) = 2$, for 100 time steps until $t = 4$:

---

[5] https://github.com/hplgit/odespy

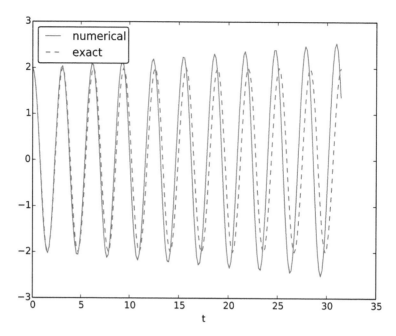

Fig. 4.21 Simulation of 10 periods of oscillations by Heun's method

```
import odespy

def f(u, t):
    return u

method = odespy.Heun    # or, e.g., odespy.ForwardEuler
solver = method(f)
solver.set_initial_condition(2)
time_points = np.linspace(0, 4, 101)
u, t = solver.solve(time_points)
```

In other words, you define your right-hand side function f(u, t), initialize an Odespy solver object, set the initial condition, compute a collection of time points where you want the solution, and ask for the solution. The returned arrays u and t can be plotted directly: plot(t, u).

A nice feature of Odespy is that problem parameters can be arguments to the user's f(u, t) function. For example, if our ODE problem is $u' = -au + b$, with two problem parameters a and b, we may write our f function as

```
def f(u, t, a, b):
    return -a*u + b
```

The extra, problem-dependent arguments a and b can be transferred to this function if we collect their values in a list or tuple when creating the Odespy solver and use the f_args argument:

```
a = 2
b = 1
solver = method(f, f_args=[a, b])
```

This is a good feature because problem parameters must otherwise be global variables – now they can be arguments in our right-hand side function in a natural way. Exercise 4.16 asks you to make a complete implementation of this problem and plot the solution.

Using Odespy to solve oscillation ODEs like $u'' + \omega^2 u = 0$, reformulated as a system $u' = v$ and $v' = -\omega^2 u$, is done as follows. We specify a given number of time steps per period and compute the associated time steps and end time of the simulation (T), given a number of periods to simulate:

```
import odespy

# Define the ODE system
# u' = v
# v' = -omega**2*u

def f(sol, t, omega=2):
    u, v = sol
    return [v, -omega**2*u]

# Set and compute problem dependent parameters
omega = 2
X_0 = 1
number_of_periods = 40
time_intervals_per_period = 20
from numpy import pi, linspace, cos
P = 2*pi/omega                      # length of one period
dt = P/time_intervals_per_period    # time step
T = number_of_periods*P             # final simulation time

# Create Odespy solver object
odespy_method = odespy.RK2
solver = odespy_method(f, f_args=[omega])

# The initial condition for the system is collected in a list
solver.set_initial_condition([X_0, 0])

# Compute the desired time points where we want the solution
N_t = int(round(T/dt))              # no of time intervals
time_points = linspace(0, T, N_t+1)

# Solve the ODE problem
sol, t = solver.solve(time_points)

# Note: sol contains both displacement and velocity
# Extract original variables
u = sol[:,0]
v = sol[:,1]
```

The last two statements are important since our two functions u and v in the ODE system are packed together in one array inside the Odespy solver. The solution of the ODE system is returned as a two-dimensional array where the first column (sol[:,0]) stores u and the second (sol[:,1]) stores v. Plotting u and v is a matter of running plot(t, u, t, v).

Remark

In the right-hand side function we write f(sol, t, omega) instead of f(u, t, omega) to indicate that the solution sent to f is a solution at time t where the values of u and v are packed together: sol = [u, v]. We might well use u as argument:

```
def f(u, t, omega=2):
    u, v = u
    return [v, -omega**2*u]
```

This just means that we redefine the name u inside the function to mean the solution at time t for the first component of the ODE system.

To switch to another numerical method, just substitute RK2 by the proper name of the desired method. Typing pydoc odespy in the terminal window brings up a list of all the implemented methods. This very simple way of choosing a method suggests an obvious extension of the code above: we can define a list of methods, run all methods, and compare their u curves in a plot. As Odespy also contains the Euler-Cromer scheme, we rewrite the system with $v' = -\omega^2 u$ as the first ODE and $u' = v$ as the second ODE, because this is the standard choice when using the Euler-Cromer method (also in Odespy):

```
def f(u, t, omega=2):
    v, u = u
    return [-omega**2*u, v]
```

This change of equations also affects the initial condition: the first component is zero and second is X_0 so we need to pass the list [0, X_0] to solver.set_ initial_condition.

The code osc_odespy.py contains the details:

```
def compare(odespy_methods,
            omega,
            X_0,
            number_of_periods,
            time_intervals_per_period=20):

    from numpy import pi, linspace, cos
    P = 2*pi/omega                      # length of one period
    dt = P/time_intervals_per_period
    T = number_of_periods*P
```

```
# If odespy_methods is not a list, but just the name of
# a single Odespy solver, we wrap that name in a list
# so we always have odespy_methods as a list
if type(odespy_methods) != type([]):
    odespy_methods = [odespy_methods]

# Make a list of solver objects
solvers = [method(f, f_args=[omega]) for method in
           odespy_methods]
for solver in solvers:
    solver.set_initial_condition([0, X_0])

# Compute the time points where we want the solution
dt = float(dt)  # avoid integer division
N_t = int(round(T/dt))
time_points = linspace(0, N_t*dt, N_t+1)

legends = []
for solver in solvers:
    sol, t = solver.solve(time_points)
    v = sol[:,0]
    u = sol[:,1]

    # Plot only the last p periods
    p = 6
    m = p*time_intervals_per_period  # no time steps to plot
    plot(t[-m:], u[-m:])
    hold('on')
    legends.append(solver.name())
    xlabel('t')
# Plot exact solution too
plot(t[-m:], X_0*cos(omega*t)[-m:], 'k--')
legends.append('exact')
legend(legends, loc='lower left')
axis([t[-m], t[-1], -2*X_0, 2*X_0])
title('Simulation of %d periods with %d intervals per period'
      % (number_of_periods, time_intervals_per_period))
savefig('tmp.pdf'); savefig('tmp.png')
show()
```

A new feature in this code is the ability to plot only the last p periods, which allows us to perform long time simulations and watch the end results without a cluttered plot with too many periods. The syntax t[-m:] plots the last m elements in t (a negative index in Python arrays/lists counts from the end).

We may compare Heun's method (or equivalently the RK2 method) with the Euler-Cromer scheme:

```
compare(odespy_methods=[odespy.Heun, odespy.EulerCromer],
        omega=2, X_0=2, number_of_periods=20,
        time_intervals_per_period=20)
```

Figure 4.22 shows how Heun's method (the blue line with small disks) has considerable error in both amplitude and phase already after 14–20 periods (upper left), but using three times as many time steps makes the curves almost equal (upper

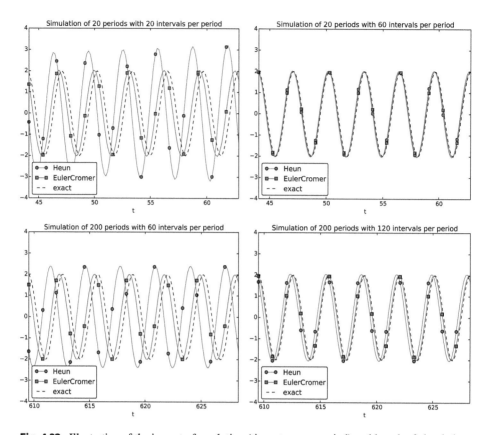

Fig. 4.22 Illustration of the impact of resolution (time steps per period) and length of simulation

right). However, after 194–200 periods the errors have grown (lower left), but can be sufficiently reduced by halving the time step (lower right).

With all the methods in Odespy at hand, it is now easy to start exploring other methods, such as backward differences instead of the forward differences used in the Forward Euler scheme. Exercise 4.17 addresses that problem.

Odespy contains quite sophisticated adaptive methods where the user is "guaranteed" to get a solution with prescribed accuracy. There is no mathematical guarantee, but the error will for most cases not deviate significantly from the user's tolerance that reflects the accuracy. A very popular method of this type is the Runge-Kutta-Fehlberg method, which runs a 4th-order Runge-Kutta method and uses a 5th-order Runge-Kutta method to estimate the error so that Δt can be adjusted to keep the error below a tolerance. This method is also widely known as ode45, because that is the name of the function implementing the method in Matlab. We can easily test the Runge-Kutta-Fehlberg method as soon as we know the corresponding Odespy name, which is RKFehlberg:

```
compare(odespy_methods=[odespy.EulerCromer, odespy.RKFehlberg],
        omega=2, X_0=2, number_of_periods=200,
        time_intervals_per_period=40)
```

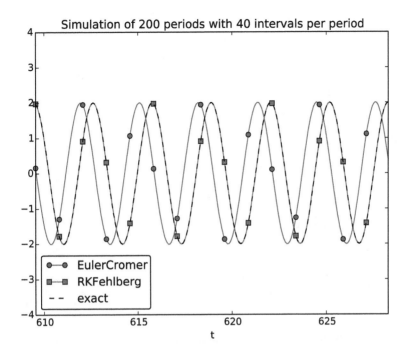

Fig. 4.23 Comparison of the Runge-Kutta-Fehlberg adaptive method against the Euler-Cromer scheme for a long time simulation (200 periods)

Note that the `time_intervals_per_period` argument refers to the time points where we want the solution. These points are also the ones used for numerical computations in the `odespy.EulerCromer` solver, while the `odespy.RKFehlberg` solver will use an unknown set of time points since the time intervals are adjusted as the method runs. One can easily look at the points actually used by the method as these are available as an array `solver.t_all` (but plotting or examining the points requires modifications inside the `compare` method).

Figure 4.23 shows a computational example where the Runge-Kutta-Fehlberg method is clearly superior to the Euler-Cromer scheme in long time simulations, but the comparison is not really fair because the Runge-Kutta-Fehlberg method applies about twice as many time steps in this computation and performs much more work per time step. It is quite a complicated task to compare two so different methods in a fair way so that the computational work versus accuracy is scientifically well reported.

4.3.7 The 4th-Order Runge-Kutta Method

The 4th-order Runge-Kutta method (RK4) is clearly the most widely used method to solve ODEs. Its power comes from high accuracy even with not so small time steps.

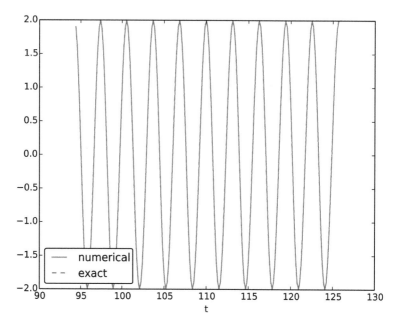

Fig. 4.24 The last 10 of 40 periods of oscillations by the 4th-order Runge-Kutta method

The algorithm We first just state the four-stage algorithm:

$$u^{n+1} = u^n + \frac{\Delta t}{6} \left(f^n + 2\hat{f}^{n+\frac{1}{2}} + 2\tilde{f}^{n+\frac{1}{2}} + \bar{f}^{n+1} \right), \tag{4.59}$$

where

$$\hat{f}^{n+\frac{1}{2}} = f \left(u^n + \frac{1}{2}\Delta t\, f^n, t_{n+\frac{1}{2}} \right), \tag{4.60}$$

$$\tilde{f}^{n+\frac{1}{2}} = f \left(u^n + \frac{1}{2}\Delta t\, \hat{f}^{n+\frac{1}{2}}, t_{n+\frac{1}{2}} \right), \tag{4.61}$$

$$\bar{f}^{n+1} = f \left(u^n + \Delta t\, \tilde{f}^{n+\frac{1}{2}}, t_{n+1} \right). \tag{4.62}$$

Application We can run the same simulation as in Figs. 4.16, 4.18, and 4.21, for 40 periods. The 10 last periods are shown in Fig. 4.24. The results look as impressive as those of the Euler-Cromer method.

Implementation The stages in the 4th-order Runge-Kutta method can easily be implemented as a modification of the `osc_Heun.py` code. Alternatively, one can use the `osc_odespy.py` code by just providing the argument `odespy_methods=` `[odespy.RK4]` to the `compare` function.

Derivation The derivation of the 4th-order Runge-Kutta method can be presented in a pedagogical way that brings many fundamental elements of numerical discretization techniques together and that illustrates many aspects of "numerical thinking" when constructing approximate solution methods.

We start with integrating the general ODE $u' = f(u, t)$ over a time step, from t_n to t_{n+1},

$$u(t_{n+1}) - u(t_n) = \int_{t_n}^{t_{n+1}} f(u(t), t) dt \,.$$

The goal of the computation is $u(t_{n+1})$ (u^{n+1}), while $u(t_n)$ (u^n) is the most recently known value of u. The challenge with the integral is that the integrand involves the unknown u between t_n and t_{n+1}.

The integral can be approximated by the famous Simpson's rule[6]:

$$\int_{t_n}^{t_{n+1}} f(u(t), t) dt \approx \frac{\Delta t}{6} \left(f^n + 4 f^{n+\frac{1}{2}} + f^{n+1} \right) \,.$$

The problem with this formula is that we do not know $f^{n+\frac{1}{2}} = f(u^{n+\frac{1}{2}}, t_{n+\frac{1}{2}})$ and $f^{n+1} = (u^{n+1}, t_{n+1})$ as only u^n is available and only f^n can then readily be computed.

To proceed, the idea is to use various approximations for $f^{n+\frac{1}{2}}$ and f^{n+1} based on using well-known schemes for the ODE in the intervals $[t_n, t_{n+\frac{1}{2}}]$ and $[t_n, t_{n+1}]$. Let us split the integral into four terms:

$$\int_{t_n}^{t_{n+1}} f(u(t), t) dt \approx \frac{\Delta t}{6} \left(f^n + 2 \hat{f}^{n+\frac{1}{2}} + 2 \tilde{f}^{n+\frac{1}{2}} + \bar{f}^{n+1} \right),$$

where $\hat{f}^{n+\frac{1}{2}}$, $\tilde{f}^{n+\frac{1}{2}}$, and $\bar{f}^{n+1}$ are approximations to $f^{n+\frac{1}{2}}$ and f^{n+1} that can utilize already computed quantities. For $\hat{f}^{n+\frac{1}{2}}$ we can simply apply an approximation to $u^{n+\frac{1}{2}}$ based on a Forward Euler step of size $\frac{1}{2}\Delta t$:

$$\hat{f}^{n+\frac{1}{2}} = f \left(u^n + \frac{1}{2} \Delta t f^n, t_{n+\frac{1}{2}} \right) \tag{4.63}$$

This formula provides a prediction of $f^{n+\frac{1}{2}}$, so we can for $\tilde{f}^{n+\frac{1}{2}}$ try a Backward Euler method to approximate $u^{n+\frac{1}{2}}$:

$$\tilde{f}^{n+\frac{1}{2}} = f \left(u^n + \frac{1}{2} \Delta t \hat{f}^{n+\frac{1}{2}}, t_{n+\frac{1}{2}} \right) \,. \tag{4.64}$$

With $\tilde{f}^{n+\frac{1}{2}}$ as an approximation to $f^{n+\frac{1}{2}}$, we can for the final term $\bar{f}^{n+1}$ use a midpoint method (or central difference, also called a Crank-Nicolson method) to approximate u^{n+1}:

$$\bar{f}^{n+1} = f(u^n + \Delta t \hat{f}^{n+\frac{1}{2}}, t_{n+1}) \,. \tag{4.65}$$

We have now used the Forward and Backward Euler methods as well as the centered difference approximation in the context of Simpson's rule. The hope is that

---

[6] http://en.wikipedia.org/wiki/Simpson's_rule

the combination of these methods yields an overall time-stepping scheme from t_n to t_n+1 that is much more accurate than the individual steps which have errors proportional to Δt and Δt^2. This is indeed true: the numerical error goes in fact like $C\Delta t^4$ for a constant C, which means that the error approaches zero very quickly as we reduce the time step size, compared to the Forward Euler method (error $\sim \Delta t$), the Euler-Cromer method (error $\sim \Delta t$) or the 2nd-order Runge-Kutta, or Heun's, method (error $\sim \Delta t^2$).

Note that the 4th-order Runge-Kutta method is fully explicit so there is never any need to solve linear or nonlinear algebraic equations, regardless of what f looks like. However, the stability is conditional and depends on f. There is a large family of *implicit* Runge-Kutta methods that are unconditionally stable, but require solution of algebraic equations involving f at each time step. The Odespy package has support for a lot of sophisticated *explicit* Runge-Kutta methods, but not yet implicit Runge-Kutta methods.

4.3.8   More Effects: Damping, Nonlinearity, and External Forces

Our model problem $u'' + \omega^2 u = 0$ is the simplest possible mathematical model for oscillating systems. Nevertheless, this model makes strong demands to numerical methods, as we have seen, and is very useful as a benchmark for evaluating the performance of numerical methods.

Real-life applications involve more physical effects, which lead to a differential equation with more terms and also more complicated terms. Typically, one has a damping force $f(u')$ and a spring force $s(u)$. Both these forces may depend nonlinearly on their argument, u' or u. In addition, environmental forces $F(t)$ may act on the system. For example, the classical pendulum has a nonlinear "spring" or restoring force $s(u) \sim \sin(u)$, and air resistance on the pendulum leads to a damping force $f(u') \sim |u'|u'$. Examples on environmental forces include shaking of the ground (e.g., due to an earthquake) as well as forces from waves and wind.

With three types of forces on the system: F, f, and s, the sum of forces is written $F(t) - f(u') - s(u)$. Note the minus sign in front of f and s, which indicates that these functions are defined such that they represent forces acting *against* the motion. For example, springs attached to the wheels in a car are combined with effective dampers, each providing a damping force $f(u') = bu'$ that acts against the spring velocity u'. The corresponding physical force is then $-f$: $-bu'$, which points downwards when the spring is being stretched (and u' points upwards), while $-f$ acts upwards when the spring is being compressed (and u' points downwards).

Figure 4.25 shows an example of a mass m attached to a potentially nonlinear spring and dashpot, and subject to an environmental force $F(t)$. Nevertheless, our general model can equally well be a pendulum as in Fig. 4.26 with $s(u) = mg \sin \theta$ and $f(\dot{u}) = \frac{1}{2}C_D A\varrho\dot{\theta}|\dot{\theta}|$ (where $C_D = 0.4$, A is the cross sectional area of the body, and ϱ is the density of air).

Newton's second law for the system can be written with the mass times acceleration on the left-hand side and the forces on the right-hand side:

$$mu'' = F(t) - f(u') - s(u).$$

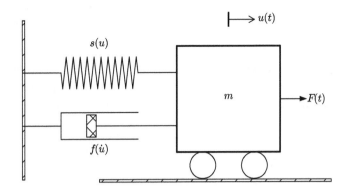

Fig. 4.25 General oscillating system

Fig. 4.26 A pendulum with forces

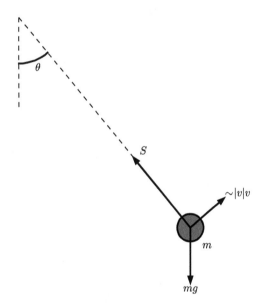

This equation is, however, more commonly reordered to

$$mu'' + f(u') + s(u) = F(t). \tag{4.66}$$

Because the differential equation is of second order, due to the term u'', we need two initial conditions:

$$u(0) = U_0, \quad u'(0) = V_0. \tag{4.67}$$

Note that with the choices $f(u') = 0$, $s(u) = ku$, and $F(t) = 0$ we recover the original ODE $u'' + \omega^2 u = 0$ with $\omega = \sqrt{k/m}$.

How can we solve (4.66)? As for the simple ODE $u'' + \omega^2 u = 0$, we start by rewriting the second-order ODE as a system of two first-order ODEs:

$$v' = \frac{1}{m} \left(F(t) - s(u) - f(v) \right), \tag{4.68}$$

$$u' = v. \tag{4.69}$$

The initial conditions become $u(0) = U_0$ and $v(0) = V_0$.

Any method for a system of first-order ODEs can be used to solve for $u(t)$ and $v(t)$.

The Euler-Cromer scheme An attractive choice from an implementational, accuracy, and efficiency point of view is the Euler-Cromer scheme where we take a forward difference in (4.68) and a backward difference in (4.69):

$$\frac{v^{n+1} - v^n}{\Delta t} = \frac{1}{m}\left(F(t_n) - s(u^n) - f(v^n)\right), \tag{4.70}$$

$$\frac{u^{n+1} - u^n}{\Delta t} = v^{n+1}, \tag{4.71}$$

We can easily solve for the new unknowns v^{n+1} and u^{n+1}:

$$v^{n+1} = v^n + \frac{\Delta t}{m}\left(F(t_n) - s(u^n) - f(v^n)\right), \tag{4.72}$$

$$u^{n+1} = u^n + \Delta t\, v^{n+1}. \tag{4.73}$$

Remark on the ordering of the ODEs

The ordering of the ODEs in the ODE system is important for the extended model (4.68)–(4.69). Imagine that we write the equation for u' first and then the one for v'. The Euler-Cromer method would then first use a forward difference for u^{n+1} and then a backward difference for v^{n+1}. The latter would lead to a *nonlinear* algebraic equation for v^{n+1},

$$v^{n+1} + \frac{\Delta t}{m} f(v^{n+1}) = v^n + \frac{\Delta t}{m}\left(F(t_{n+1}) - s(u^{n+1})\right),$$

if $f(v)$ is a nonlinear function of v. This would require a numerical method for nonlinear algebraic equations to find v^{n+1}, while updating v^{n+1} through a forward difference gives an equation for v^{n+1} that is linear and trivial to solve by hand.

The file `osc_EC_general.py` has a function `EulerCromer` that implements this method:

```python
def EulerCromer(f, s, F, m, T, U_0, V_0, dt):
    from numpy import zeros, linspace
    N_t = int(round(T/dt))
    print 'N_t:', N_t
    t = linspace(0, N_t*dt, N_t+1)

    u = zeros(N_t+1)
    v = zeros(N_t+1)

    # Initial condition
    u[0] = U_0
    v[0] = V_0
```

```
# Step equations forward in time
for n in range(N_t):
    v[n+1] = v[n] + dt*(1./m)*(F(t[n]) - f(v[n]) - s(u[n]))
    u[n+1] = u[n] + dt*v[n+1]
return u, v, t
```

The 4-th order Runge-Kutta method The RK4 method just evaluates the right-hand side of the ODE system,

$$\left(\frac{1}{m}\left(F(t) - s(u) - f(v)\right), v\right)$$

for known values of u, v, and t, so the method is very simple to use regardless of how the functions $s(u)$ and $f(v)$ are chosen.

4.3.9 Illustration of Linear Damping

We consider an engineering system with a linear spring, $s(u) = kx$, and a viscous damper, where the damping force is proportional to u', $f(u') = bu'$, for some constant $b > 0$. This choice may model the vertical spring system in a car (but engineers often like to illustrate such a system by a horizontal moving mass like the one depicted in Fig. 4.25). We may choose simple values for the constants to illustrate basic effects of damping (and later excitations). Choosing the oscillations to be the simple $u(t) = \cos t$ function in the undamped case, we may set $m = 1$, $k = 1$, $b = 0.3$, $U_0 = 1$, $V_0 = 0$. The following function implements this case:

```
def linear_damping():
    b = 0.3
    f = lambda v: b*v
    s = lambda u: k*u
    F = lambda t: 0

    m = 1
    k = 1
    U_0 = 1
    V_0 = 0

    T = 12*pi
    dt = T/5000.

    u, v, t = EulerCromer(f=f, s=s, F=F, m=m, T=T,
                          U_0=U_0, V_0=V_0, dt=dt)
    plot_u(u, t)
```

The `plot_u` function is a collection of plot statements for plotting $u(t)$, or a part of it. Figure 4.27 shows the effect of the bu' term: we have oscillations with (an approximate) period 2π, as expected, but the amplitude is efficiently damped.

Remark about working with a scaled problem

Instead of setting $b = 0.3$ and $m = k = U_0 = 1$ as fairly "unlikely" physical values, it would be better to *scale* the equation $mu'' + bu' + ku = 0$. This means

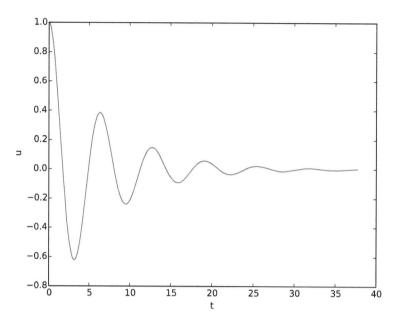

Fig. 4.27 Effect of linear damping

that we introduce dimensionless independent and dependent variables:

$$\bar{t} = \frac{t}{t_c}, \quad \bar{u} = \frac{u}{u_c},$$

where t_c and u_c are characteristic sizes of time and displacement, respectively, such that $\bar{t}$ and $\bar{u}$ have their typical size around unity. In the present problem, we can choose $u_c = U_0$ and $t_c = \sqrt{m/k}$. This gives the following scaled (or dimensionless) problem for the dimensionless quantity $\bar{u}(\bar{t})$:

$$\frac{d^2\bar{u}}{d\bar{t}^2} + \beta\frac{d\bar{u}}{d\bar{t}} + \bar{u} = 0, \quad \bar{u}(0) = 1, \bar{u}'(0) = 0, \quad \beta = \frac{b}{\sqrt{mk}}.$$

The striking fact is that there is only *one* physical parameter in this problem: the dimensionless number β. Solving this problem corresponds to solving the original problem (with dimensions) with the parameters $m = k = U_0 = 1$ and $b = \beta$. However, solving the dimensionless problem is more general: if we have a solution $\bar{u}(\bar{t}; \beta)$, we can find the physical solution of a range of problems since

$$u(t) = U_0\bar{u}\left(t\sqrt{k/m}; \beta\right).$$

As long as β is fixed, we can find u for any U_0, k, and m from the above formula! In this way, a time consuming simulation can be done only once, but still provide many solutions. This demonstrates the power of working with scaled or dimensionless problems.

4.3.10 Illustration of Linear Damping with Sinusoidal Excitation

We now extend the previous example to also involve some external oscillating force on the system: $F(t) = A \sin(wt)$. Driving a car on a road with sinusoidal bumps might give such an external excitation on the spring system in the car (w is related to the velocity of the car).

With $A = 0.5$ and $w = 3$,

```
from math import pi, sin
w = 3
A = 0.5
F = lambda t: A*sin(w*t)
```

we get the graph in Fig. 4.28. The striking difference from Fig. 4.27 is that the oscillations start out as a damped $\cos t$ signal without much influence of the external force, but then the free oscillations of the undamped system ($\cos t$) $u'' + u = 0$ die out and the external force $0.5 \sin(3t)$ induces oscillations with a shorter period $2\pi/3$. You are encouraged to play around with a larger A and switch from a sine to a cosine in F and observe the effects. If you look this up in a physics book, you can find exact analytical solutions to the differential equation problem in these cases.

A particularly interesting case arises when the excitation force has the same frequency as the free oscillations of the undamped system, i.e., $F(t) = A \sin t$. With the same amplitude $A = 0.5$, but a smaller damping $b = 0.1$, the oscillations in Fig. 4.28 becomes qualitatively very different as the amplitude grows significantly larger over some periods. This phenomenon is called *resonance* and is exemplified in Fig. 4.29. Removing the damping results in an amplitude that grows linearly in time.

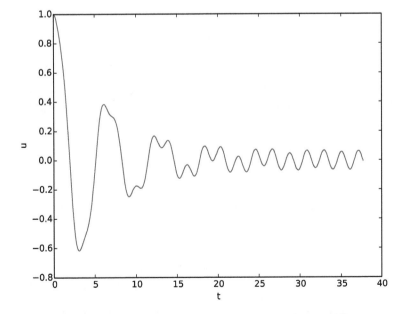

Fig. 4.28 Effect of linear damping in combination with a sinusoidal external force

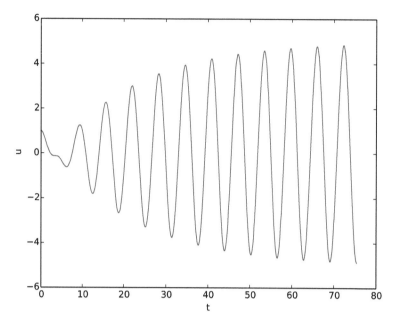

Fig. 4.29 Excitation force that causes resonance

4.3.11 Spring-Mass System with Sliding Friction

A body with mass m is attached to a spring with stiffness k while sliding on a plane
surface. The body is also subject to a friction force $f(u')$ due to the contact between
the body and the plane. Figure 4.30 depicts the situation. The friction force $f(u')$
can be modeled by Coulomb friction:

$$f(u') = \begin{cases} -\mu mg, & u' < 0, \\ \mu mg, & u' > 0, \\ 0, & u' = 0 \end{cases}$$

where μ is the friction coefficient, and mg is the normal force on the surface where
the body slides. This formula can also be written as $f(u') = \mu mg \, \text{sign}(u')$, pro-

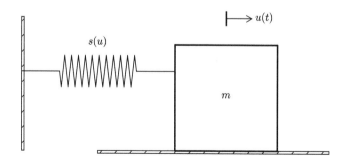

Fig. 4.30 Sketch of a one-dimensional, oscillating dynamic system subject to sliding friction and
a spring force

vided the signum function sign(x) is defined to be zero for $x = 0$ (numpy.sign has this property). To check that the signs in the definition of f are right, recall that the actual physical force is $-f$ and this is positive (i.e., $f < 0$) when it works against the body moving with velocity $u' < 0$.

The nonlinear spring force is taken as

$$s(u) = -k\alpha^{-1}\tanh(\alpha u),$$

which is approximately $-ku$ for small u, but stabilizes at $\pm k/\alpha$ for large $\pm\alpha u$. Here is a plot with $k = 1000$ and $u \in [-0.1, 0.1]$ for three α values:

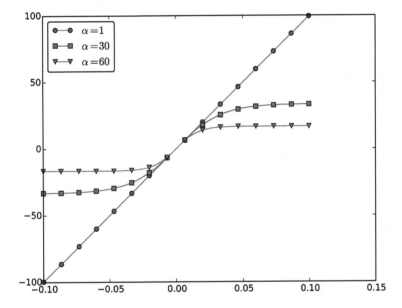

If there is no external excitation force acting on the body, we have the equation of motion

$$mu'' + \mu mg\,\text{sign}(u') + k\alpha^{-1}\tanh(\alpha u) = 0.$$

Let us simulate a situation where a body of mass 1 kg slides on a surface with $\mu = 0.4$, while attached to a spring with stiffness $k = 1000\,\text{kg/s}^2$. The initial displacement of the body is 10 cm, and the α parameter in $s(u)$ is set to 60 1/m. Using the EulerCromer function from the osc_EC_general code, we can write a function sliding_friction for solving this problem:

```
def sliding_friction():
    from numpy import tanh, sign

    f = lambda v: mu*m*g*sign(v)
    alpha = 60.0
    s = lambda u: k/alpha*tanh(alpha*u)
    F = lambda t: 0

    g = 9.81
    mu = 0.4
    m = 1
    k = 1000
```

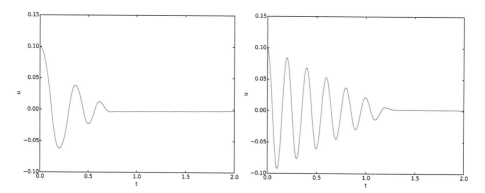

Fig. 4.31 Effect of nonlinear (*left*) and linear (*right*) spring on sliding friction

```
U_0 = 0.1
V_0 = 0

T = 2
dt = T/5000.

u, v, t = EulerCromer(f=f, s=s, F=F, m=m, T=T,
                      U_0=U_0, V_0=V_0, dt=dt)
plot_u(u, t)
```

Running the `sliding_friction` function gives us the results in Fig. 4.31 with $s(u) = k\alpha^{-1}\tanh(\alpha u)$ (left) and the linearized version $s(u) = ku$ (right).

4.3.12 A finite Difference Method; Undamped, Linear Case

We shall now address numerical methods for the second-order ODE

$$u'' + \omega^2 u = 0, \quad u(0) = U_0, \ u'(0) = 0, \ t \in (0, T],$$

without rewriting the ODE as a system of first-order ODEs. The primary motivation for "yet another solution method" is that the discretization principles result in a very good scheme, and more importantly, the thinking around the discretization can be reused when solving partial differential equations.

The main idea of this numerical method is to approximate the second-order derivative u'' by a finite difference. While there are several choices of difference approximations to first-order derivatives, there is one dominating formula for the second-order derivative:

$$u''(t_n) \approx \frac{u^{n+1} - 2u^n + u^{n-1}}{\Delta t^2}. \tag{4.74}$$

The error in this approximation is proportional to Δt^2. Letting the ODE be valid at some arbitrary time point t_n,

$$u''(t_n) + \omega^2 u(t_n) = 0,$$

we just insert the approximation (4.74) to get

$$\frac{u^{n+1} - 2u^n + u^{n-1}}{\Delta t^2} = -\omega^2 u^n . \tag{4.75}$$

We now assume that u^{n-1} and u^n are already computed and that u^{n+1} is the new unknown. Solving with respect to u^{n+1} gives

$$u^{n+1} = 2u^n - u^{n-1} - \Delta t^2 \omega^2 u^n . \tag{4.76}$$

A major problem arises when we want to start the scheme. We know that $u^0 = U_0$, but applying (4.76) for $n = 0$ to compute u^1 leads to

$$u^1 = 2u^0 - u^{-1} - \Delta t^2 \omega^2 u^0, \tag{4.77}$$

where we do not know u^{-1}. The initial condition $u'(0) = 0$ can help us to eliminate u^{-1} - and this condition must anyway be incorporated in some way. To this end, we discretize $u'(0) = 0$ by a *centered difference*,

$$u'(0) \approx \frac{u^1 - u^{-1}}{2\Delta t} = 0 .$$

It follows that $u^{-1} = u^1$, and we can use this relation to eliminate u^{-1} in (4.77):

$$u^1 = u^0 - \frac{1}{2}\Delta t^2 \omega^2 u^0 . \tag{4.78}$$

With $u^0 = U_0$ and u^1 computed from (4.78), we can compute u^2, u^3, and so forth from (4.76). Exercise 4.19 asks you to explore how the steps above are modified in case we have a nonzero initial condition $u'(0) = V_0$.

Remark on a simpler method for computing u^1

We could approximate the initial condition $u'(0)$ by a forward difference:

$$u'(0) \approx \frac{u^1 - u^0}{\Delta t} = 0,$$

leading to $u^1 = u^0$. Then we can use (4.76) for the coming time steps. However, this forward difference has an error proportional to Δt, while the centered difference we used has an error proportional to Δt^2, which is compatible with the accuracy (error goes like Δt^2) used in the discretization of the differential equation.

The method for the second-order ODE described above goes under the name Störmer's method or Verlet integration[7]. It turns out that this method is mathematically equivalent with the Euler-Cromer scheme (!). Or more precisely, the general formula (4.76) is equivalent with the Euler-Cromer formula, but the scheme for the

---

[7] http://en.wikipedia.org/wiki/Verlet_integration

first time level (4.78) implements the initial condition $u'(0)$ slightly more accurately than what is naturally done in the Euler-Cromer scheme. The latter will do

$$v^1 = v^0 - \Delta t \omega^2 u^0, \quad u^1 = u^0 + \Delta t v^1 = u^0 - \Delta t^2 \omega^2 u^0,$$

which differs from u^1 in (4.78) by an amount $\frac{1}{2} \Delta t^2 \omega^2 u^0$.

Because of the equivalence of (4.76) with the Euler-Cromer scheme, the numerical results will have the same nice properties such as a constant amplitude. There will be a phase error as in the Euler-Cromer scheme, but this error is effectively reduced by reducing Δt, as already demonstrated.

The implementation of (4.78) and (4.76) is straightforward in a function (file osc_2nd_order.py):

```python
from numpy import zeros, linspace

def osc_2nd_order(U_0, omega, dt, T):
    """
    Solve u'' + omega**2*u = 0 for t in (0,T], u(0)=U_0 and u'(0)=0,
    by a central finite difference method with time step dt.
    """
    dt = float(dt)
    Nt = int(round(T/dt))
    u = zeros(Nt+1)
    t = linspace(0, Nt*dt, Nt+1)

    u[0] = U_0
    u[1] = u[0] - 0.5*dt**2*omega**2*u[0]
    for n in range(1, Nt):
        u[n+1] = 2*u[n] - u[n-1] - dt**2*omega**2*u[n]
    return u, t
```

4.3.13   A Finite Difference Method; Linear Damping

A key issue is how to generalize the scheme from Sect. 4.3.12 to a differential equation with more terms. We start with the case of a linear damping term $f(u') = bu'$, a possibly nonlinear spring force $s(u)$, and an excitation force $F(t)$:

$$mu'' + bu' + s(u) = F(t), \quad u(0) = U_0, \, u'(0) = 0, \, t \in (0, T]. \quad (4.79)$$

We need to find the appropriate difference approximation to u' in the bu' term. A good choice is the *centered difference*

$$u'(t_n) \approx \frac{u^{n+1} - u^{n-1}}{2\Delta t}. \quad (4.80)$$

Sampling the equation at a time point t_n,

$$mu''(t_n) + bu'(t_n) + s(u^n) = F(t_n),$$

and inserting the finite difference approximations to u'' and u' results in

$$m\frac{u^{n+1} - 2u^n + u^{n-1}}{\Delta t^2} + b\frac{u^{n+1} - u^{n-1}}{2\Delta t} + s(u^n) = F^n, \qquad (4.81)$$

where F^n is a short notation for $F(t_n)$. Equation (4.81) is linear in the unknown u^{n+1}, so we can easily solve for this quantity:

$$u^{n+1} = \left(2mu^n + \left(\frac{b}{2}\Delta t - m\right)u^{n-1} + \Delta t^2(F^n - s(u^n))\right)\left(m + \frac{b}{2}\Delta t\right)^{-1}. \qquad (4.82)$$

As in the case without damping, we need to derive a special formula for u^1. The initial condition $u'(0) = 0$ implies also now that $u^{-1} = u^1$, and with (4.82) for $n = 0$, we get

$$u^1 = u^0 + \frac{\Delta t^2}{2m}(F^0 - s(u^0)). \qquad (4.83)$$

In the more general case with a nonlinear damping term $f(u')$,

$$mu'' + f(u') + s(u) = F(t),$$

we get

$$m\frac{u^{n+1} - 2u^n + u^{n-1}}{\Delta t^2} + f\left(\frac{u^{n+1} - u^{n-1}}{2\Delta t}\right) + s(u^n) = F^n,$$

which is a *nonlinear algebraic equation* for u^{n+1} that must be solved by numerical methods. A much more convenient scheme arises from using a backward difference for u',

$$u'(t_n) \approx \frac{u^n - u^{n-1}}{\Delta t},$$

because the damping term will then be known, involving only u^n and u^{n-1}, and we can easily solve for u^{n+1}.

The downside of the backward difference compared to the centered difference (4.80) is that it reduces the order of the accuracy in the overall scheme from Δt^2 to Δt. In fact, the Euler-Cromer scheme evaluates a nonlinear damping term as $f(v^n)$ when computing v^{n+1}, and this is equivalent to using the backward difference above. Consequently, the convenience of the Euler-Cromer scheme for nonlinear damping comes at a cost of lowering the overall accuracy of the scheme from second to first order in Δt. Using the same trick in the finite difference scheme for the second-order differential equation, i.e., using the backward difference in $f(u')$, makes this scheme equally convenient and accurate as the Euler-Cromer scheme in the general nonlinear case $mu'' + f(u') + s(u) = F$.

4.4 Exercises

Exercise 4.1: Geometric construction of the Forward Euler method
Section 4.1.4 describes a geometric interpretation of the Forward Euler method. This exercise will demonstrate the geometric construction of the solution in detail. Consider the differential equation $u' = u$ with $u(0) = 1$. We use time steps $\Delta t = 1$.

a) Start at $t = 0$ and draw a straight line with slope $u'(0) = u(0) = 1$. Go one time step forward to $t = \Delta t$ and mark the solution point on the line.
b) Draw a straight line through the solution point $(\Delta t, u^1)$ with slope $u'(\Delta t) = u^1$. Go one time step forward to $t = 2\Delta t$ and mark the solution point on the line.
c) Draw a straight line through the solution point $(2\Delta t, u^2)$ with slope $u'(2\Delta t) = u^2$. Go one time step forward to $t = 3\Delta t$ and mark the solution point on the line.
d) Set up the Forward Euler scheme for the problem $u' = u$. Calculate u^1, u^2, and u^3. Check that the numbers are the same as obtained in a)-c).

Filename: `ForwardEuler_geometric_solution.py`.

Exercise 4.2: Make test functions for the Forward Euler method
The purpose of this exercise is to make a file `test_ode_FE.py` that makes use of the `ode_FE` function in the file `ode_FE.py` and automatically verifies the implementation of `ode_FE`.

a) The solution computed by hand in Exercise 4.1 can be used as a reference solution. Make a function `test_ode_FE_1()` that calls `ode_FE` to compute three time steps in the problem $u' = u$, $u(0) = 1$, and compare the three values u^1, u^2, and u^3 with the values obtained in Exercise 4.1.
b) The test in a) can be made more general using the fact that if f is linear in u and does not depend on t, i.e., we have $u' = ru$, for some constant r, the Forward Euler method has a closed form solution as outlined in Sect. 4.1.1: $u^n = U_0(1 + r\Delta t)^n$. Use this result to construct a test function `test_ode_FE_2()` that runs a number of steps in `ode_FE` and compares the computed solution with the listed formula for u^n.

Filename: `test_ode_FE.py`.

Exercise 4.3: Implement and evaluate Heun's method

a) A 2nd-order Runge-Kutta method, also known has Heun's method, is derived in Sect. 4.3.5. Make a function `ode_Heun(f, U_0, dt, T)` (as a counterpart to `ode_FE(f, U_0, dt, T)` in `ode_FE.py`) for solving a scalar ODE problem $u' = f(u, t)$, $u(0) = U_0$, $t \in (0, T]$, with this method using a time step size Δt.
b) Solve the simple ODE problem $u' = u$, $u(0) = 1$, by the `ode_Heun` and the `ode_FE` function. Make a plot that compares Heun's method and the Forward Euler method with the exact solution $u(t) = e^t$ for $t \in [0, 6]$. Use a time step $\Delta t = 0.5$.

c) For the case in b), find through experimentation the largest value of Δt where the exact solution and the numerical solution by Heun's method cannot be distinguished visually. It is of interest to see how far off the curve the Forward Euler method is when Heun's method can be regarded as "exact" (for visual purposes).

Filename: `ode_Heun.py`.

Exercise 4.4: Find an appropriate time step; logistic model

Compute the numerical solution of the logistic equation for a set of repeatedly halved time steps: $\Delta t_k = 2^{-k} \Delta t$, $k = 0, 1, \ldots$. Plot the solutions corresponding to the last two time steps Δt_k and Δt_{k-1} in the same plot. Continue doing this until you cannot visually distinguish the two curves in the plot. Then one has found a sufficiently small time step.

Hint Extend the `logistic.py` file. Introduce a loop over k, write out Δt_k, and ask the user if the loop is to be continued.
Filename: `logistic_dt.py`.

Exercise 4.5: Find an appropriate time step; SIR model

Repeat Exercise 4.4 for the SIR model.

Hint Import the `ode_FE` function from the `ode_system_FE` module and make a modified `demo_SIR` function that has a loop over repeatedly halved time steps. Plot S, I, and R versus time for the two last time step sizes in the same plot.
Filename: `SIR_dt.py`.

Exercise 4.6: Model an adaptive vaccination campaign

In the SIRV model with time-dependent vaccination from Sect. 4.2.9, we want to test the effect of an adaptive vaccination campaign where vaccination is offered as long as half of the population is not vaccinated. The campaign starts after Δ days. That is, $p = p_0$ if $V < \frac{1}{2}(S^0 + I^0)$ and $t > \Delta$ days, otherwise $p = 0$.

Demonstrate the effect of this vaccination policy: choose β, γ, and ν as in Sect. 4.2.9, set $p = 0.001$, $\Delta = 10$ days, and simulate for 200 days.

Hint This discontinuous $p(t)$ function is easiest implemented as a Python function containing the indicated `if` test. You may use the file `SIRV1.py` as starting point, but note that it implements a time-dependent $p(t)$ via an array.
Filename: `SIRV_p_adapt.py`.

Exercise 4.7: Make a SIRV model with time-limited effect of vaccination

We consider the SIRV model from Sect. 4.2.8, but now the effect of vaccination is time-limited. After a characteristic period of time, π, the vaccination is no more effective and individuals are consequently moved from the V to the S category and can be infected again. Mathematically, this can be modeled as an average leakage $-\pi^{-1}V$ from the V category to the S category (i.e., a gain $\pi^{-1}V$ in the latter).

Write up the complete model, implement it, and rerun the case from Sect. 4.2.8 with various choices of parameters to illustrate various effects.
Filename: `SIRV1_V2S.py`.

Exercise 4.8: Refactor a flat program

Consider the file `osc_FE.py` implementing the Forward Euler method for the oscillating system model (4.43)–(4.44). The `osc_FE.py` is what we often refer to as a flat program, meaning that it is just one main program with no functions. To easily reuse the numerical computations in other contexts, place the part that produces the numerical solution (allocation of arrays, initializing the arrays at time zero, and the time loop) in a function `osc_FE(X_0, omega, dt, T)`, which returns `u`, `v`, `t`. Place the particular computational example in `osc_FE.py` in a function `demo()`.

Construct the file `osc_FE_func.py` such that the `osc_FE` function can easily be reused in other programs. In Python, this means that `osc_FE_func.py` is a module that can be imported in other programs. The requirement of a module is that there should be no main program, except in the test block. You must therefore call `demo` from a test block (i.e., the block after `if __name__ == '__main__'`).
Filename: `osc_FE_func.py`.

Exercise 4.9: Simulate oscillations by a general ODE solver

Solve the system (4.43)–(4.44) using the general solver `ode_FE` in the file `ode_system_FE.py` described in Sect. 4.2.6. Program the ODE system and the call to the `ode_FE` function in a separate file `osc_ode_FE.py`.

Equip this file with a test function that reads a file with correct u values and compares these with those computed by the `ode_FE` function. To find correct u values, modify the program `osc_FE.py` to dump the u array to file, run `osc_FE.py`, and let the test function read the reference results from that file.
Filename: `osc_ode_FE.py`.

Exercise 4.10: Compute the energy in oscillations

a) Make a function `osc_energy(u, v, omega)` for returning the potential and kinetic energy of an oscillating system described by (4.43)–(4.44). The potential energy is taken as $\frac{1}{2}\omega^2 u^2$ while the kinetic energy is $\frac{1}{2}v^2$. (Note that these expressions are not exactly the *physical* potential and kinetic energy, since these would be $\frac{1}{2}mv^2$ and $\frac{1}{2}ku^2$ for a model $mx'' + kx = 0$.)
   Place the `osc_energy` in a separate file `osc_energy.py` such that the function can be called from other functions.

b) Add a call to `osc_energy` in the programs `osc_FE.py` and `osc_EC.py` and plot the *sum* of the kinetic and potential energy. How does the total energy develop for the Forward Euler and the Euler-Cromer schemes?

Filenames: `osc_energy.py`, `osc_FE_energy.py`, `osc_EC_energy.py`.

Exercise 4.11: Use a Backward Euler scheme for population growth

We consider the ODE problem $N'(t) = rN(t)$, $N(0) = N_0$. At some time, $t_n = n\Delta t$, we can approximate the derivative $N'(t_n)$ by a *backward difference*, see Fig. 4.19:

$$N'(t_n) \approx \frac{N(t_n) - N(t_n - \Delta t)}{\Delta t} = \frac{N^n - N^{n-1}}{\Delta t},$$

which leads to

$$\frac{N^n - N^{n-1}}{\Delta t} = rN^n,$$

called the *Backward Euler scheme*.

a) Find an expression for the N^n in terms of N^{n-1} and formulate an algorithm for computing N^n, $n = 1, 2, \ldots, N_t$.
b) Implement the algorithm in a) in a function `growth_BE(N_0, dt, T)` for solving $N' = rN$, $N(0) = N_0$, $t \in (0, T]$, with time step Δt (dt).
c) Implement the Forward Euler scheme in a function `growth_FE(N_0, dt, T)` as described in b).
d) Compare visually the solution produced by the Forward and Backward Euler schemes with the exact solution when $r = 1$ and $T = 6$. Make two plots, one with $\Delta t = 0.5$ and one with $\Delta t = 0.05$.

Filename: `growth_BE.py`.

Exercise 4.12: Use a Crank-Nicolson scheme for population growth

It is recommended to do Exercise 4.11 prior to the present one. Here we look at the same population growth model $N'(t) = rN(t)$, $N(0) = N_0$. The time derivative $N'(t)$ can be approximated by various types of finite differences. Exercise 4.11 considers a backward difference (Fig. 4.19), while Sect. 4.1.2 explained the forward difference (Fig. 4.2). A *centered difference* is more accurate than a backward or forward difference:

$$N'\left(t_n + \frac{1}{2}\Delta t\right) \approx \frac{N(t_n + \Delta t) - N(t_n)}{\Delta t} = \frac{N^{n+1} - N^n}{\Delta t}.$$

This type of difference, applied at the point $t_{n+\frac{1}{2}} = t_n + \frac{1}{2}\Delta t$, is illustrated geometrically in Fig. 4.20.

a) Insert the finite difference approximation in the ODE $N' = rN$ and solve for the unknown N^{n+1}, assuming N^n is already computed and hence known. The resulting computational scheme is often referred to as a *Crank-Nicolson* scheme.
b) Implement the algorithm in a) in a function `growth_CN(N_0, dt, T)` for solving $N' = rN$, $N(0) = N_0$, $t \in (0, T]$, with time step Δt (dt).

c) Make plots for comparing the Crank-Nicolson scheme with the Forward and Backward Euler schemes in the same test problem as in Exercise 4.11.

Filename: growth_CN.py.

Exercise 4.13: Understand finite differences via Taylor series
The Taylor series around a point $x = a$ can for a function $f(x)$ be written

$$
f(x) = f(a) + \frac{d}{dx}f(a)(x - a) + \frac{1}{2!}\frac{d^2}{dx^2}f(a)(x - a)^2
$$
$$
+ \frac{1}{3!}\frac{d^3}{dx^3}f(a)(x - a)^3 + \ldots
$$
$$
= \sum_{i=0}^{\infty} \frac{1}{i!}\frac{d^i}{dx^i}f(a)(x - a)^i \,.
$$

For a function of time, as addressed in our ODE problems, we would use u instead of f, t instead of x, and a time point t_n instead of a:

$$
u(t) = u(t_n) + \frac{d}{dt}u(t_n)(t - t_n) + \frac{1}{2!}\frac{d^2}{dt^2}u(t_n)(t - t_n)^2
$$
$$
+ \frac{1}{3!}\frac{d^3}{dt^3}u(t_n)(t - t_n)^3 + \ldots
$$
$$
= \sum_{i=0}^{\infty} \frac{1}{i!}\frac{d^i}{dt^i}u(t_n)(t - t_n)^i \,.
$$

a) A forward finite difference approximation to the derivative $f'(a)$ reads

$$
u'(t_n) \approx \frac{u(t_n + \Delta t) - u(t_n)}{\Delta t} \,.
$$

We can justify this formula mathematically through Taylor series. Write up the Taylor series for $u(t_n + \Delta t)$ (around $t = t_n$, as given above), and then solve the expression with respect to $u'(t_n)$. Identify, on the right-hand side, the finite difference approximation *and* an infinite series. This series is then the error in the finite difference approximation. If Δt is assumed small (i.e. $\Delta t \ll 1$), Δt will be much larger than Δt^2, which will be much larger than Δt^3, and so on. The *leading order term* in the series for the error, i.e., the error with the least power of Δt is a good approximation of the error. Identify this term.

b) Repeat a) for a backward difference:

$$
u'(t_n) \approx \frac{u(t_n) - u(t_n - \Delta t)}{\Delta t} \,.
$$

This time, write up the Taylor series for $u(t_n - \Delta t)$ around t_n. Solve with respect to $u'(t_n)$, and identify the leading order term in the error. How is the error compared to the forward difference?

c) A centered difference approximation to the derivative, as explored in Exercise 4.12, can be written

$$u'(t_n + \frac{1}{2}\Delta t) \approx \frac{u(t_n + \Delta t) - u(t_n)}{\Delta t}.$$

Write up the Taylor series for $u(t_n)$ around $t_n + \frac{1}{2}\Delta t$ and the Taylor series for $u(t_n + \Delta t)$ around $t_n + \frac{1}{2}\Delta t$. Subtract the two series, solve with respect to $u'(t_n + \frac{1}{2}\Delta t)$, identify the finite difference approximation and the error terms on the right-hand side, and write up the leading order error term. How is this term compared to the ones for the forward and backward differences?

d) Can you use the leading order error terms in a)-c) to explain the visual observations in the numerical experiment in Exercise 4.12?

e) Find the leading order error term in the following standard finite difference approximation to the second-order derivative:

$$u''(t_n) \approx \frac{u(t_n + \Delta t) - 2u(t_n) + u(t_n - \Delta t)}{\Delta t}.$$

Hint Express $u(t_n \pm \Delta t)$ via Taylor series and insert them in the difference formula.
Filename: `Taylor_differences.pdf`.

Exercise 4.14: Use a Backward Euler scheme for oscillations

Consider (4.43)–(4.44) modeling an oscillating engineering system. This 2×2 ODE system can be solved by the *Backward Euler scheme*, which is based on discretizing derivatives by collecting information backward in time. More specifically, $u'(t)$ is approximated as

$$u'(t) \approx \frac{u(t) - u(t - \Delta t)}{\Delta t}.$$

A general vector ODE $u' = f(u, t)$, where u and f are vectors, can use this approximation as follows:

$$\frac{u^n - u^{n-1}}{\Delta t} = f(u^n, t_n),$$

which leads to an equation for the new value u^n:

$$u^n - \Delta t f(u^n, t_n) = u^{n-1}.$$

For a general f, this is a system of *nonlinear algebraic equations*.

However, the ODE (4.43)–(4.44) is *linear*, so a Backward Euler scheme leads to a system of two algebraic equations for two unknowns:

$$u^n - \Delta t v^n = u^{n-1}, \tag{4.84}$$

$$v^n + \Delta t \omega^2 u^n = v^{n-1}. \tag{4.85}$$

a) Solve the system for u^n and v^n.

b) Implement the found formulas for u^n and v^n in a program for computing the entire numerical solution of (4.43)–(4.44).

c) Run the program with a Δt corresponding to 20 time steps per period of the oscillations (see Sect. 4.3.3 for how to find such a Δt). What do you observe? Increase to 2000 time steps per period. How much does this improve the solution?

Filename: osc_BE.py.

Remarks While the Forward Euler method applied to oscillation problems $u'' + \omega^2 u = 0$ gives growing amplitudes, the Backward Euler method leads to significantly damped amplitudes.

Exercise 4.15: Use Heun's method for the SIR model

Make a program that computes the solution of the SIR model from Sect. 4.2.1 both by the Forward Euler method and by Heun's method (or equivalently: the 2nd-order Runge-Kutta method) from Sect. 4.3.5. Compare the two methods in the simulation case from Sect. 4.2.3. Make two comparison plots, one for a large and one for a small time step. Experiment to find what "large" and "small" should be: the large one gives significant differences, while the small one lead to very similar curves.
Filename: SIR_Heun.py.

Exercise 4.16: Use Odespy to solve a simple ODE

Solve

$$u' = -au + b, \quad u(0) = U_0, \quad t \in (0, T]$$

by the Odespy software. Let the problem parameters a and b be arguments to the right-hand side function that specifies the ODE to be solved. Plot the solution for the case when $a = 2$, $b = 1$, $T = 6/a$, and we use 100 time intervals in $[0, T]$.
Filename: odespy_demo.py.

Exercise 4.17: Set up a Backward Euler scheme for oscillations

Write the ODE $u'' + \omega^2 u = 0$ as a system of two first-order ODEs and discretize these with backward differences as illustrated in Fig. 4.19. The resulting method is referred to as a Backward Euler scheme. Identify the matrix and right-hand side of the linear system that has to be solved at each time level. Implement the method, either from scratch yourself or using Odespy (the name is odespy.BackwardEuler). Demonstrate that contrary to a Forward Euler scheme, the Backward Euler scheme leads to significant non-physical damping. The figure below shows that even with 60 time steps per period, the results after a few periods are useless:

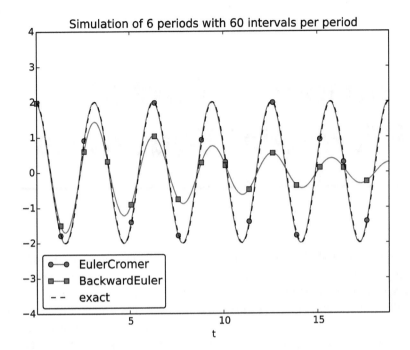

Filename: `osc_BE.py`.

Exercise 4.18: Set up a Forward Euler scheme for nonlinear and damped oscillations

Derive a Forward Euler method for the ODE system (4.68)–(4.69). Compare the method with the Euler-Cromer scheme for the sliding friction problem from Sect. 4.3.11:

1. Does the Forward Euler scheme give growing amplitudes?
2. Is the period of oscillation accurate?
3. What is the required time step size for the two methods to have visually coinciding curves?

Filename: `osc_FE_general.py`.

Exercise 4.19: Discretize an initial condition

Assume that the initial condition on u' is nonzero in the finite difference method from Sect. 4.3.12: $u'(0) = V_0$. Derive the special formula for u^1 in this case.
Filename: `ic_with_V_0.pdf`.

5

Solutions to Partial Differential Equations

The subject of partial differential equations (PDEs) is enormous. At the same time, it is very important, since so many phenomena in nature and technology find their mathematical formulation through such equations. Knowing how to solve at least some PDEs is therefore of great importance to engineers. In an introductory book like this, nowhere near full justice to the subject can be made. However, we still find it valuable to give the reader a glimpse of the topic by presenting a few basic and general methods that we will apply to a very common type of PDE.

We shall focus on one of the most widely encountered partial differential equations: the diffusion equation, which in one dimension looks like

$$\frac{\partial u}{\partial t} = \beta \frac{\partial^2 u}{\partial x^2} + g \, .$$

The multi-dimensional counterpart is often written as

$$\frac{\partial u}{\partial t} = \beta \nabla^2 u + g \, .$$

We shall restrict the attention here to the one-dimensional case.

The unknown in the diffusion equation is a function $u(x, t)$ of space and time. The physical significance of u depends on what type of process that is described by the diffusion equation. For example, u is the concentration of a substance if the diffusion equation models transport of this substance by *diffusion*. Diffusion processes are of particular relevance at the microscopic level in biology, e.g., diffusive transport of certain ion types in a cell caused by molecular collisions. There is also diffusion of atoms in a solid, for instance, and diffusion of ink in a glass of water.

One very popular application of the diffusion equation is for heat transport in solid bodies. Then u is the temperature, and the equation predicts how the temperature evolves in space and time within the solid body. For such applications, the equation is known as the *heat equation*. We remark that the temperature in a fluid is influenced not only by diffusion, but also by the flow of the liquid. If present, the latter effect requires an extra term in the equation (known as an advection or convection term).

The term g is known as the *source term* and represents generation, or loss, of heat (by some mechanism) within the body. For diffusive transport, g models injection or extraction of the substance.

We should also mention that the diffusion equation may appear after simplifying more complicated partial differential equations. For example, flow of a viscous fluid between two flat and parallel plates is described by a one-dimensional diffusion equation, where u then is the fluid velocity.

A partial differential equation is solved in some *domain* Ω in space and for a time interval $[0, T]$. The solution of the equation is not unique unless we also prescribe *initial and boundary conditions*. The type and number of such conditions depend on the type of equation. For the diffusion equation, we need one initial condition, $u(x, 0)$, stating what u is when the process starts. In addition, the diffusion equation needs one boundary condition at each point of the boundary $\partial\Omega$ of Ω. This condition can either be that u is known or that we know the normal derivative, $\nabla u \cdot \boldsymbol{n} = \partial u / \partial n$ ($\boldsymbol{n}$ denotes an outward unit normal to $\partial\Omega$).

Let us look at a specific application and how the diffusion equation with initial and boundary conditions then appears. We consider the evolution of temperature in a one-dimensional medium, more precisely a long rod, where the surface of the rod is covered by an insulating material. The heat can then not escape from the surface, which means that the temperature distribution will only depend on a coordinate along the rod, x, and time t. At one end of the rod, $x = L$, we also assume that the surface is insulated, but at the other end, $x = 0$, we assume that we have some device for controlling the temperature of the medium. Here, a function $s(t)$ tells what the temperature is in time. We therefore have a boundary condition $u(0, t) = s(t)$. At the other insulated end, $x = L$, heat cannot escape, which is expressed by the boundary condition $\partial u(L, t) / \partial x = 0$. The surface along the rod is also insulated and hence subject to the same boundary condition (here generalized to $\partial u / \partial n = 0$ at the curved surface). However, since we have reduced the problem to one dimension, we do not need this physical boundary condition in our mathematical model. In one dimension, we can set $\Omega = [0, L]$.

To summarize, the partial differential equation with initial and boundary conditions reads

$$\frac{\partial u(x, t)}{\partial t} = \beta \frac{\partial^2 u(x, t)}{\partial x^2} + g(x, t), \qquad x \in (0, L), t \in (0, T], \qquad (5.1)$$

$$u(0, t) = s(t), \qquad t \in (0, T], \qquad (5.2)$$

$$\frac{\partial}{\partial x} u(L, t) = 0, \qquad t \in (0, T], \qquad (5.3)$$

$$u(x, 0) = I(x), \qquad x \in [0, L]. \qquad (5.4)$$

Mathematically, we assume that at $t = 0$, the initial condition (5.4) holds and that the partial differential equation (5.1) comes into play for $t > 0$. Similarly, at the end points, the boundary conditions (5.2) and (5.3) govern u and the equation therefore is valid for $x \in (0, L)$.

Boundary and initial conditions are needed!

The initial and boundary conditions are extremely important. Without them, the solution is not unique, and no numerical method will work. Unfortunately, many physical applications have one or more initial or boundary conditions as unknowns. Such situations can be dealt with if we have measurements of u, but the mathematical framework is much more complicated.

What about the source term g in our example with temperature distribution in a rod? $g(x,t)$ models heat generation inside the rod. One could think of chemical reactions at a microscopic level in some materials as a reason to include g. However, in most applications with temperature evolution, g is zero and heat generation usually takes place at the boundary (as in our example with $u(0,t) = s(t)$).

Before continuing, we may consider an example of how the temperature distribution evolves in the rod. At time $t = 0$, we assume that the temperature is $10°$ C. Then we suddenly apply a device at $x = 0$ that keeps the temperature at $50°$ C at this end. What happens inside the rod? Intuitively, you think that the heat generation at the end will warm up the material in the vicinity of $x = 0$, and as time goes by, more and more of the rod will be heated, before the entire rod has a temperature of $50°$ C (recall that no heat escapes from the surface of the rod).

Mathematically, (with the temperature in Kelvin) this example has $I(x) = 283$ K, except at the end point: $I(0) = 323$ K, $s(t) = 323$ K, and $g = 0$. The figure below shows snapshots from four different times in the evolution of the temperature.

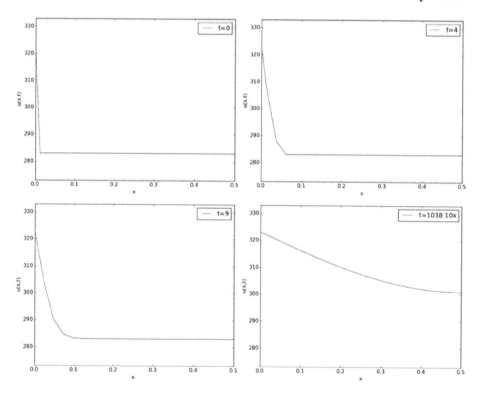

5.1 Finite Difference Methods

We shall now construct a numerical method for the diffusion equation. We know how to solve ordinary differential equations, so in a way we are able to deal with the time derivative. Very often in mathematics, a new problem can be solved by reducing it to a series of problems we know how to solve. In the present case, it means that we must do something with the spatial derivative $\partial^2/\partial x^2$ in order to reduce the partial differential equation to ordinary differential equations. One important technique for achieving this, is based on finite difference discretization of spatial derivatives.

5.1.1 Reduction of a PDE to a System of ODEs

Introduce a spatial mesh in Ω with *mesh points*

$$x_0 = 0 < x_1 < x_2 < \cdots < x_N = L.$$

The space between two mesh points x_i and x_{i+1}, i.e. the interval $[x_i, x_{i+1}]$, is call a *cell*. We shall here, for simplicity, assume that each cell has the same length $\Delta x = x_{i+1} - x_i$, $i = 0, \ldots, N-1$.

The partial differential equation is valid at all spatial points $x \in \Omega$, but we may relax this condition and demand that it is fulfilled at the internal mesh points only, $x_1, \ldots, x_{N-1}$:

$$\frac{\partial u(x_i, t)}{\partial t} = \beta \frac{\partial^2 u(x_i, t)}{\partial x^2} + g(x_i, t), \quad i = 1, \ldots, N-1. \tag{5.5}$$

Now, at any point x_i we can approximate the second-order derivative by a *finite difference*:

$$\frac{\partial^2 u(x_i, t)}{\partial x^2} \approx \frac{u(x_{i+1}, t) - 2u(x_i, t) + u(x_{i-1}, t)}{\Delta x^2}. \tag{5.6}$$

It is common to introduce a short notation $u_i(t)$ for $u(x_i, t)$, i.e., u approximated at some mesh point x_i in space. With this new notation we can, after inserting (5.6) in (5.5), write an approximation to the partial differential equation at mesh point (x_i, t) as

$$\frac{du_i(t)}{dt} = \beta \frac{u_{i+1}(t) - 2u_i(t) + u_{i-1}(t)}{\Delta x^2} + g_i(t), \quad i = 1, \ldots, N-1. \tag{5.7}$$

Note that we have adopted the notation $g_i(t)$ for $g(x_i, t)$ too.

What is (5.7)? This is nothing but a *system of ordinary differential equations* in $N-1$ unknowns $u_1(t), \ldots, u_{N-1}(t)$! In other words, with aid of the finite difference approximation (5.6), we have reduced the single partial differential equation to a system of ODEs, which we know how to solve. In the literature, this strategy is called the *method of lines*.

We need to look into the initial and boundary conditions as well. The initial condition $u(x, 0) = I(x)$ translates to an initial condition for every unknown function $u_i(t)$: $u_i(0) = I(x_i)$, $i = 0, \ldots, N$. At the boundary $x = 0$ we need an ODE in our ODE system, which must come from the boundary condition at this point. The boundary condition reads $u(0, t) = s(t)$. We can derive an ODE from this equation by differentiating both sides: $u_0'(t) = s'(t)$. The ODE system above cannot be used for u_0' since that equation involves some quantity u_{-1}' outside the domain. Instead, we use the equation $u_0'(t) = s'(t)$ derived from the boundary condition. For this particular equation we also need to make sure the initial condition is $u_0(0) = s(0)$ (otherwise nothing will happen: we get $u = 283$ K forever).

We remark that a separate ODE for the (known) boundary condition $u_0 = s(t)$ is not strictly needed. We can just work with the ODE system for $u_1, \ldots, u_N$, and in the ODE for u_0, replace $u_0(t)$ by $s(t)$. However, these authors prefer to have an ODE for every point value u_i, $i = 0, \ldots, N$, which requires formulating the known boundary at $x = 0$ as an ODE. The reason for including the boundary values in the ODE system is that the solution of the system is then the complete solution at *all* mesh points, which is convenient, since special treatment of the boundary values is then avoided.

The condition $\partial u / \partial x = 0$ at $x = L$ is a bit more complicated, but we can approximate the spatial derivative by a centered finite difference:

$$\frac{\partial u}{\partial x}\Big|_{i=N} \approx \frac{u_{N+1} - u_{N-1}}{2\Delta x} = 0.$$

This approximation involves a fictitious point x_{N+1} outside the domain. A common trick is to use (5.7) for $i = N$ and eliminate u_{N+1} by use of the discrete boundary condition ($u_{N+1} = u_{N-1}$):

$$\frac{du_N(t)}{dt} = \beta \frac{2u_{N-1}(t) - 2u_N(t)}{\Delta x^2} + g_N(t). \tag{5.8}$$

That is, we have a special version of (5.7) at the boundary $i = N$.

What about simpler finite differences at the boundary?

Some reader may think that a smarter trick is to approximate the boundary condition $\partial u / \partial x$ at $x = L$ by a one-sided difference:

$$\frac{\partial u}{\partial x}\Big|_{i=N} \approx \frac{u_N - u_{N-1}}{\Delta x} = 0.$$

This gives a simple equation $u_N = u_{N-1}$ for the boundary value, and a corresponding ODE $u'_N = u'_{N-1}$. However, this approximation has an error of order Δx, while the centered approximation we used above has an error of order Δx^2. The finite difference approximation we used for the second-order derivative in the diffusion equation also has an error of order Δx^2. Thus, if we use the simpler one-sided difference above, it turns out that we reduce the overall accuracy of the method.

We are now in a position to summarize how we can approximate the partial differential equation problem (5.1)–(5.4) by a system of ordinary differential equations:

$$\frac{du_0}{dt} = s'(t), \tag{5.9}$$

$$\frac{du_i}{dt} = \frac{\beta}{\Delta x^2}(u_{i+1}(t) - 2u_i(t) + u_{i-1}(t)) + g_i(t), \quad i = 1, \ldots, N-1, \tag{5.10}$$

$$\frac{du_N}{dt} = \frac{2\beta}{\Delta x^2}(u_{N-1}(t) - u_N(t)) + g_N(t). \tag{5.11}$$

The initial conditions are

$$u_0(0) = s(0), \tag{5.12}$$

$$u_i(0) = I(x_i), \quad i = 1, \ldots, N. \tag{5.13}$$

We can apply any method for systems of ODEs to solve (5.9)–(5.11).

5.1.2 Construction of a Test Problem with Known Discrete Solution

At this point, it is tempting to implement a real physical case and run it. However, partial differential equations constitute a non-trivial topic where mathematical and programming mistakes come easy. A better start is therefore to address a carefully designed test example where we can check that the method works. The most attractive examples for testing implementations are those without approximation errors, because we know exactly what numbers the program should produce. It turns out that solutions $u(x, t)$ that are linear in time and in space can be exactly reproduced by most numerical methods for partial differential equations. A candidate solution might be

$$u(x, t) = (3t + 2)(x - L).$$

Inserting this u in the governing equation gives

$$3(x - L) = 0 + g(x, t) \quad \Rightarrow \quad g(x, t) = 3(x - L).$$

What about the boundary conditions? We realize that $\partial u / \partial x = 3t + 2$ for $x = L$, which breaks the assumption of $\partial u / \partial x = 0$ at $x = L$ in the formulation of the numerical method above. Moreover, $u(0, t) = -L(3t + 2)$, so we must set $s(t) = -L(3t+2)$ and $s'(t) = -3L$. Finally, the initial condition dictates $I(x) = 2(x-L)$, but recall that we must have $u_0 = s(0)$, and $u_i = I(x_i)$, $i = 1, \ldots, N$: it is important that u_0 starts out at the right value dictated by $s(t)$ in case $I(0)$ is not equal this value.

First we need to generalize our method to handle $\partial u / \partial x = \gamma \neq 0$ at $x = L$. We then have

$$\frac{u_{N+1}(t) - u_{N-1}(t)}{2\Delta x} = \gamma \quad \Rightarrow \quad u_{N+1} = u_{N-1} + 2\gamma\Delta x,$$

which inserted in (5.7) gives

$$\frac{du_N(t)}{dt} = \beta \frac{2u_{N-1}(t) + 2\gamma\Delta x - 2u_N(t)}{\Delta x^2} + g_N(t). \tag{5.14}$$

5.1.3 Implementation: Forward Euler Method

In particular, we may use the Forward Euler method as implemented in the general function ode_FE in the module ode_system_FE from Sect. 4.2.6. The ode_FE function needs a specification of the right-hand side of the ODE system.

This is a matter of translating (5.9), (5.10), and (5.14) to Python code (in file `test_diffusion_pde_exact_linear.py`):

```
def rhs(u, t):
    N = len(u) - 1
    rhs = zeros(N+1)
    rhs[0] = dsdt(t)
    for i in range(1, N):
        rhs[i] = (beta/dx**2)*(u[i+1] - 2*u[i] + u[i-1]) + \
                 g(x[i], t)
    rhs[N] = (beta/dx**2)*(2*u[N-1] + 2*dx*dudx(t) -
                           2*u[N]) + g(x[N], t)
    return rhs

def u_exact(x, t):
    return (3*t + 2)*(x - L)

def dudx(t):
    return (3*t + 2)

def s(t):
    return u_exact(0, t)

def dsdt(t):
    return 3*(-L)

def g(x, t):
    return 3*(x-L)
```

Note that `dudx(t)` is the function representing the γ parameter in (5.14). Also note that the `rhs` function relies on access to global variables `beta`, `dx`, `L`, and `x`, and global functions `dsdt`, `g`, and `dudx`.

We expect the solution to be correct regardless of N and Δt, so we can choose a small N, $N = 4$, and $\Delta t = 0.1$. A test function with $N = 4$ goes like

```
def test_diffusion_exact_linear():
    global beta, dx, L, x   # needed in rhs
    L = 1.5
    beta = 0.5
    N = 4
    x = linspace(0, L, N+1)
    dx = x[1] - x[0]
    u = zeros(N+1)

    U_0 = zeros(N+1)
    U_0[0] = s(0)
    U_0[1:] = u_exact(x[1:], 0)
    dt = 0.1
    print dt

    u, t = ode_FE(rhs, U_0, dt, T=1.2)
```

```
tol = 1E-12
for i in range(0, u.shape[0]):
    diff = abs(u_exact(x, t[i]) - u[i,:]).max()
    assert diff < tol, 'diff=%.16g' % diff
    print 'diff=%g at t=%g' % (diff, t[i])
```

With $N = 4$ we reproduce the linear solution exactly. This brings confidence to the implementation, which is just what we need for attacking a real physical problem next.

Problems with reusing the rhs function

The rhs function *must* take u and t as arguments, because that is required by the ode_FE function. What about the variables beta, dx, L, x, dsdt, g, and dudx that the rhs function needs? These are global in the solution we have presented so far. Unfortunately, this has an undesired side effect: we cannot import the rhs function in a new file, define dudx and dsdt in this new file and get the imported rhs to use these functions. The imported rhs will use the global variables, including functions, in its own module.

How can we find solutions to this problem? Technically, we must pack the extra data beta, dx, L, x, dsdt, g, and dudx with the rhs function, which requires more advanced programming considered beyond the scope of this text.

A class is the simplest construction for packing a function together with data, see the beginning of Chapter 7 in [13] for a detailed example on how classes can be used in such a context. Another solution in Python, and especially in computer languages supporting *functional programming*, is so called *closures*. They are also covered in Chapter 7 in the mentioned reference and behave in a magic way. The third solution is to allow an arbitrary set of arguments for rhs in a list to be transferred to ode_FE and then back to rhs. Appendix H.4 in [13] explains the technical details.

5.1.4 Application: Heat Conduction in a Rod

Let us return to the case with heat conduction in a rod (5.1)–(5.4). Assume that the rod is 50 cm long and made of aluminum alloy 6082. The β parameter equals $\kappa/(\varrho c)$, where κ is the heat conduction coefficient, ϱ is the density, and c is the heat capacity. We can find proper values for these physical quantities in the case of aluminum alloy 6082: $\varrho = 2.7 \cdot 10^3$ kg/m^3, $\kappa = 200 \frac{W}{mK}$, $c = 900 \frac{J}{Kkg}$. This results in $\beta = \kappa/(\varrho c) = 8.2 \cdot 10^{-5}$ m^2/s. Preliminary simulations show that we are close to a constant steady state temperature after 1 h, i.e., $T = 3600$ s.

The rhs function from the previous section can be reused, only the functions s, dsdt, g, and dudx must be changed (see file rod_FE.py):

```
def dudx(t):
    return 0

def s(t):
    return 323
```

```
def dsdt(t):
    return 0

def g(x, t):
    return 0
```

Parameters can be set as

```
L = 0.5
beta = 8.2E-5
N = 40
x = linspace(0, L, N+1)
dx = x[1] - x[0]
u = zeros(N+1)


U_0 = zeros(N+1)
U_0[0] = s(0)
U_0[1:] = 283
```

Let us use $\Delta t = 0.00034375$. We can now call `ode_FE` and then make an animation on the screen to see how $u(x, t)$ develops in time:

```
t0 = time.clock()
from ode_system_FE import ode_FE
u, t = ode_FE(rhs, U_0, dt, T=1*60*60)
t1 = time.clock()
print 'CPU time: %.1fs' % (t1 - t0)

# Make movie
import os
os.system('rm tmp_*.png')
import matplotlib.pyplot as plt
plt.ion()
y = u[0,:]
lines = plt.plot(x, y)
plt.axis([x[0], x[-1], 273, s(0)+10])
plt.xlabel('x')
plt.ylabel('u(x,t)')
counter = 0
# Plot each of the first 100 frames, then increase speed by 10x
change_speed = 100
for i in range(0, u.shape[0]):
    print t[i]
    plot = True if i <= change_speed else i % 10 == 0
    lines[0].set_ydata(u[i,:])
    if i > change_speed:
        plt.legend(['t=%.0f 10x' % t[i]])
    else:
        plt.legend(['t=%.0f' % t[i]])
    plt.draw()
    if plot:
        plt.savefig('tmp_%04d.png' % counter)
        counter += 1
    #time.sleep(0.2)
```

The plotting statements update the $u(x,t)$ curve on the screen. In addition, we save a fraction of the plots to files `tmp_0000.png`, `tmp_0001.png`, `tmp_0002.png`, and so on. These plots can be combined to ordinary video files. A common tool is `ffmpeg` or its sister `avconv`.

These programs take the same type of command-line options. To make a Flash video `movie.flv`, run

```
Terminal
Terminal> ffmpeg -i tmp_%04d.png -r 4 -vcodec flv movie.flv
```

The `-i` option specifies the naming of the plot files in printf syntax, and `-r` specifies the number of frames per second in the movie. On Mac, run `ffmpeg` instead of `avconv` with the same options. Other video formats, such as MP4, WebM, and Ogg can also be produced:

```
Terminal
Terminal> ffmpeg -i tmp_%04d.png -r 4 -vcodec libx264   movie.mp4
Terminal> ffmpeg -i tmp_%04d.png -r 4 -vcodec libvpx    movie.webm
Terminal> ffmpeg -i tmp_%04d.png -r 4 -vcodec libtheora movie.ogg
```

The results of a simulation start out as in Figs. 5.1 and 5.2. We see that the solution definitely looks wrong. The temperature is expected to be smooth, not having such a saw-tooth shape. Also, after some time (Fig. 5.2), the temperature starts to increase much more than expected. We say that this solution is *unstable*, meaning that it does not display the same characteristics as the true, physical solution. Even though we tested the code carefully in the previous section, it does not seem to work for a physical application! How can that be?

The problem is that Δt is too large, making the solution *unstable*. It turns out that the Forward Euler time integration method puts a restriction on the size of Δt. For the heat equation and the way we have discretized it, this restriction can be shown to be [15]

$$\Delta t \le \frac{\Delta x^2}{2\beta} . \tag{5.15}$$

This is called a *stability criterion*. With the chosen parameters, (5.15) tells us that the upper limit is $\Delta t = 0.0003125$, which is smaller than our choice above. Re-running the case with a Δt equal to $\Delta x^2/(2\beta)$, indeed shows a smooth evolution of $u(x,t)$. Find the program `rod_FE.py` and run it to see an animation of the $u(x,t)$ function on the screen.

Scaling and dimensionless quantities

Our setting of parameters required finding three physical properties of a certain material. The time interval for simulation and the time step depend crucially on the values for β and L, which can vary significantly from case to case. Often, we are more interested in how the shape of $u(x,t)$ develops, than in the actual u, x, and t values for a specific material. We can then simplify the setting of physical parameters by *scaling* the problem.

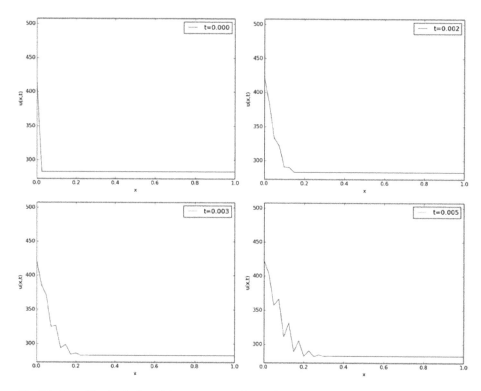

Fig. 5.1 Unstable simulation of the temperature in a rod

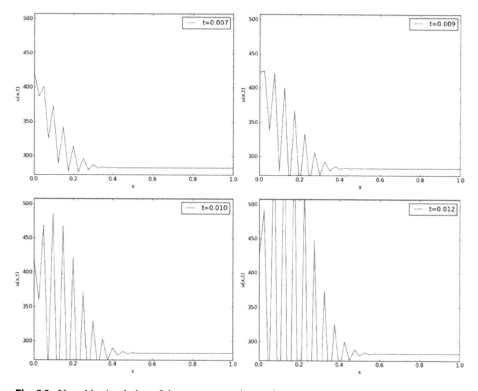

Fig. 5.2 Unstable simulation of the temperature in a rod

Scaling means that we introduce dimensionless independent and dependent variables, here denoted by a bar:

$$\bar{u} = \frac{u - u^*}{u_c - u^*}, \quad \bar{x} = \frac{x}{x_c}, \quad \bar{t} = \frac{t}{t_c},$$

where u_c is a characteristic size of the temperature, u^* is some reference temperature, while x_c and t_c are characteristic time and space scales. Here, it is natural to choose u^* as the initial condition, and set u_c to the stationary (end) temperature. Then $\bar{u} \in [0, 1]$, starting at 0 and ending at 1 as $t \to \infty$. The length L is x_c, while choosing t_c is more challenging, but one can argue for $t_c = L^2/\beta$. The resulting equation for $\bar{u}$ reads

$$\frac{\partial \bar{u}}{\partial \bar{t}} = \frac{\partial^2 \bar{u}}{\partial \bar{x}^2}, \quad \bar{x} \in (0, 1).$$

Note that in this equation, there are *no physical parameters*! In other words, we have found a model that is independent of the length of the rod and the material it is made of (!).

We can easily solve this equation with our program by setting $\beta = 1$, $L = 1$, $I(x) = 0$, and $s(t) = 1$. It turns out that the total simulation time (to "infinity") can be taken as 1.2. When we have the solution $\bar{u}(\bar{x}, \bar{t})$, the solution with dimension Kelvin, reflecting the true temperature in our medium, is given by

$$u(x, t) = u^* + (u_c - u^*)\bar{u}(x/L, t\beta/L^2).$$

Through this formula we can quickly generate the solutions for a rod made of aluminum, wood, or rubber - it is just a matter of plugging in the right β value.

Figure 5.3 shows four snapshots of the scaled (dimensionless) solution $(\bar{x}, \bar{t})$.

The power of scaling is to reduce the number of physical parameters in a problem, and in the present case, we found one single problem that is independent of the material (β) and the geometry (L).

5.1.5 Vectorization

Occasionally in this book, we show how to speed up code by replacing loops over arrays by vectorized expressions. The present problem involves a loop for computing the right-hand side:

```
for i in range(1, N):
    rhs[i] = (beta/dx**2)*(u[i+1] - 2*u[i] + u[i-1]) + g(x[i], t)
```

This loop can be replaced by a vectorized expression with the following reasoning. We want to set all the inner points at once: rhs[1:N-1] (this goes from index 1 up to, but not including, N). As the loop index i runs from 1 to N-1, the u[i+1] term will cover all the inner u values displaced one index to the right (compared to 1:N-1), i.e., u[2:N]. Similarly, u[i-1] corresponds to all inner u values displaced one index to the left: u[0:N-2]. Finally, u[i] has the same indices as rhs: u[1:N-1]. The vectorized loop can therefore be written in terms of slices:

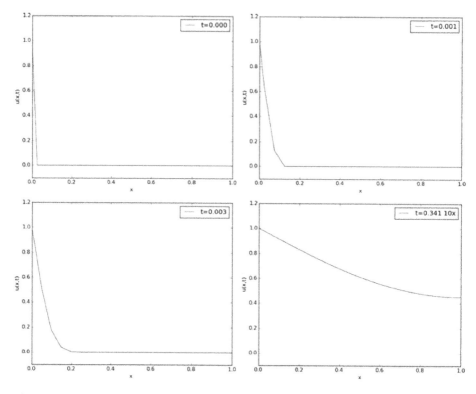

Fig. 5.3 Snapshots of the dimensionless solution of a scaled problem

```
rhs[1:N-1] = (beta/dx**2)*(u[2:N+1] - 2*u[1:N] + u[0:N-1]) +
             g(x[1:N], t)
```

This rewrite speeds up the code by about a factor of 10. A complete code is found in the file rod_FE_vec.py.

5.1.6   Using Odespy to Solve the System of ODEs

Let us now show how to apply a general ODE package like Odespy (see Sect. 4.3.6) to solve our diffusion problem. As long as we have defined a right-hand side function rhs this is very straightforward:

```
import odespy
solver = odespy.RKFehlberg(rhs)
solver.set_initial_condition(U_0)
T = 1.2
N_t = int(round(T/float(dt)))
time_points = linspace(0, T, N_t+1)
u, t = solver.solve(time_points)
```

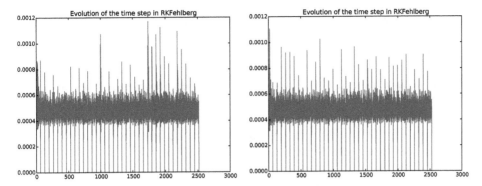

Fig. 5.4 Time steps used by the Runge-Kutta-Fehlberg method: error tolerance 10^{-3} (*left*) and 10^{-6} (*right*)

```
# Check how many time steps are required by adaptive vs
# fixed-step methods
if hasattr(solver, 't_all'):
    print '# time steps:', len(solver.t_all)
else:
    print '# time steps:', len(t)
```

The very nice thing is that we can now easily experiment with many different integration methods. Trying out some simple ones first, like RK2 and RK4, quickly reveals that the time step limitation of the Forward Euler scheme also applies to these more sophisticated Runge-Kutta methods, but their accuracy is better. However, the Odespy package offers also adaptive methods. We can then specify a much larger time step in `time_points`, and the solver will figure out the appropriate step. Above we indicated how to use the adaptive Runge-Kutta-Fehlberg 4–5 solver. While the Δt corresponding to the Forward Euler method requires over 8000 steps for a simulation, we started the `RKFehlberg` method with 100 times this time step and in the end it required just slightly more than 2500 steps, using the default tolerance parameters. Lowering the tolerance did not save any significant amount of computational work. Figure 5.4 shows a comparison of the length of all the time steps for two values of the tolerance. We see that the influence of the tolerance is minor in this computational example, so it seems that the blow-up due to instability is what governs the time step size. The nice feature of this adaptive method is that we can just specify when we want the solution to be computed, and the method figures out on its own what time step that has to be used because of stability restrictions.

We have seen how easy it is to apply sophisticated methods for ODEs to this PDE example. We shall take the use of Odespy one step further in the next section.

5.1.7 Implicit Methods

A major problem with the stability criterion (5.15) is that the time step becomes very small if Δx is small. For example, halving Δx requires four times as many time steps and eight times the work. Now, with $N = 40$, which is a reasonable resolution for the test problem above, the computations are very fast. What takes time, is the visualization on the screen, but for that purpose one can visualize only a subset of the time steps. However, there are occasions when you need to take larger time steps with the diffusion equation, especially if interest is in the long-term behavior as $t \to \infty$. You must then turn to *implicit methods* for ODEs. These methods require the solutions of *linear systems*, if the underlying PDE is linear, and systems of *nonlinear algebraic equations* if the underlying PDE is non-linear.

The simplest implicit method is the Backward Euler scheme, which puts no restrictions on Δt for stability, but obviously, a large Δt leads to inaccurate results. The Backward Euler scheme for a scalar ODE $u' = f(u, t)$ reads

$$\frac{u^{n+1} - u^n}{\Delta t} = f(u^{n+1}, t_{n+1}).$$

This equation is to be solved for u^{n+1}. If f is linear in u, it is a linear equation, but if f is nonlinear in u, one needs approximate methods for nonlinear equations (Chap. 6).

In our case, we have a system of linear ODEs (5.9)–(5.11). The Backward Euler scheme applied to each equation leads to

$$\frac{u_0^{n+1} - u_0^n}{\Delta t} = s'(t_{n+1}), \tag{5.16}$$

$$\frac{u_i^{n+1} - u_i^n}{\Delta t} = \frac{\beta}{\Delta x^2}(u_{i+1}^{n+1} - 2u_i^{n+1} + u_{i-1}^{n+1}) + g_i(t_{n+1}), \tag{5.17}$$

$$i = 1, \ldots, N - 1,$$

$$\frac{u_N^{n+1} - u_N^n}{\Delta t} = \frac{2\beta}{\Delta x^2}(u_{N-1}^{n+1} - u_N^{n+1}) + g_i(t_{n+1}). \tag{5.18}$$

This is a system of linear equations in the unknowns u_i^{n+1}, $i = 0, \ldots, N$, which is easy to realize by writing out the equations for the case $N = 3$, collecting all the unknown terms on the left-hand side and all the known terms on the right-hand side:

$$u_0^{n+1} = u_0^n + \Delta t\, s'(t_{n+1}), \tag{5.19}$$

$$u_1^{n+1} - \Delta t \frac{\beta}{\Delta x^2}(u_2^{n+1} - 2u_1^{n+1} + u_0^{n+1}) = u_1^n + \Delta t\, g_1(t_{n+1}), \tag{5.20}$$

$$u_2^{n+1} - \Delta t \frac{2\beta}{\Delta x^2}(u_1^{n+1} - u_2^{n+1}) = u_2^n + \Delta t\, g_2(t_{n+1}). \tag{5.21}$$

A system of linear equations like this, is usually written on matrix form $Au = b$, where A is a coefficient matrix, $u = (u_0^{n+1}, \ldots, n_N^{n+1})$ is the vector of unknowns, and b is a vector of known values. The coefficient matrix for the case (5.19)–(5.21) becomes

$$A = \begin{pmatrix} 1 & 0 & 0 \\ -\Delta t \frac{\beta}{\Delta x^2} & 1 + 2\Delta t \frac{\beta}{\Delta x^2} & -\Delta t \frac{\beta}{\Delta x^2} \\ 0 & -\Delta t \frac{2\beta}{\Delta x^2} & 1 + \Delta t \frac{2\beta}{\Delta x^2} \end{pmatrix}$$

In the general case (5.16)–(5.18), the coefficient matrix is an $(N + 1) \times (N + 1)$ matrix with zero entries, except for

$$A_{1,1} = 1 \qquad (5.22)$$

$$A_{i,i-1} = -\Delta t \frac{\beta}{\Delta x^2}, \quad i = 2, \ldots, N - 1 \qquad (5.23)$$

$$A_{i,i+1} = -\Delta t \frac{\beta}{\Delta x^2}, \quad i = 2, \ldots, N - 1 \qquad (5.24)$$

$$A_{i,i} = 1 + 2\Delta t \frac{\beta}{\Delta x^2}, \quad i = 2, \ldots, N - 1 \qquad (5.25)$$

$$A_{N,N-1} = -\Delta t \frac{2\beta}{\Delta x^2} \qquad (5.26)$$

$$A_{N,N} = 1 + \Delta t \frac{2\beta}{\Delta x^2} \qquad (5.27)$$

If we want to apply general methods for systems of ODEs on the form $u' = f(u, t)$, we can assume a linear $f(u, t) = Ku$. The coefficient matrix K is found from the right-hand side of (5.16)–(5.18) to be

$$K_{1,1} = 0 \qquad (5.28)$$

$$K_{i,i-1} = \frac{\beta}{\Delta x^2}, \quad i = 2, \ldots, N - 1 \qquad (5.29)$$

$$K_{i,i+1} = \frac{\beta}{\Delta x^2}, \quad i = 2, \ldots, N - 1 \qquad (5.30)$$

$$K_{i,i} = -\frac{2\beta}{\Delta x^2}, \quad i = 2, \ldots, N - 1 \qquad (5.31)$$

$$K_{N,N-1} = \frac{2\beta}{\Delta x^2} \qquad (5.32)$$

$$K_{N,N} = -\frac{2\beta}{\Delta x^2} \qquad (5.33)$$

We see that $A = I - \Delta t\, K$.

To implement the Backward Euler scheme, we can either fill a matrix and call a linear solver, or we can apply Odespy. We follow the latter strategy. Implicit methods in Odespy need the K matrix above, given as an argument jac (Jacobian of f) in the call to odespy.BackwardEuler. Here is the Python code for the right-hand side of the ODE system (rhs) and the K matrix (K) as well as statements for initializing and running the Odespy solver BackwardEuler (in the file rod_BE.py):

```
def rhs(u, t):
    N = len(u) - 1
    rhs = zeros(N+1)
    rhs[0] = dsdt(t)
    for i in range(1, N):
        rhs[i] = (beta/dx**2)*(u[i+1] - 2*u[i] + u[i-1]) + \
                 g(x[i], t)
    rhs[N] = (beta/dx**2)*(2*u[i-1] + 2*dx*dudx(t) -
                            2*u[i]) + g(x[N], t)

    return rhs
```

```
def K(u, t):
    N = len(u) - 1
    K = zeros((N+1,N+1))
    K[0,0] = 0
    for i in range(1, N):
        K[i,i-1] = beta/dx**2
        K[i,i] = -2*beta/dx**2
        K[i,i+1] = beta/dx**2
    K[N,N-1] = (beta/dx**2)*2
    K[N,N] = (beta/dx**2)*(-2)
    return K
```

```
import odespy
solver = odespy.BackwardEuler(rhs, f_is_linear=True, jac=K)
solver = odespy.ThetaRule(rhs, f_is_linear=True, jac=K, theta=0.5)
solver.set_initial_condition(U_0)
T = 1*60*60
N_t = int(round(T/float(dt)))
time_points = linspace(0, T, N_t+1)
u, t = solver.solve(time_points)
```

The file `rod_BE.py` has all the details and shows a movie of the solution. We can run it with any Δt we want, its size just impacts the accuracy of the first steps.

Odespy solvers apply dense matrices!

Looking at the entries of the K matrix, we realize that there are at maximum three entries different from zero in each row. Therefore, most of the entries are zeroes. The Odespy solvers expect dense square matrices as input, here with $(N + 1) \times (N + 1)$ elements. When solving the linear systems, a lot of storage and work are spent on the zero entries in the matrix. It would be much more efficient to store the matrix as a *tridiagonal* matrix and apply a specialized Gaussian elimination solver for tridiagonal systems. Actually, this reduces the work from the order N^3 to the order N.

In one-dimensional diffusion problems, the savings of using a tridiagonal matrix are modest in practice, since the matrices are very small anyway. In two- and three-dimensional PDE problems, however, one cannot afford dense square matrices. Rather, one *must* resort to more efficient storage formats and algorithms tailored to such formats, but this is beyond the scope of the present text.

5.2 Exercises

Exercise 5.1: Simulate a diffusion equation by hand

Consider the problem given by (5.9), (5.10) and (5.14). Set $N = 2$ and compute u_i^0, u_i^1 and u_i^2 by hand for $i = 0, 1, 2$. Use these values to construct a test function for checking that the implementation is correct. Copy useful functions from `test_diffusion_pde_exact_linear.py` and make a new test function `test_diffusion_hand_calculation`.

Filename: `test_rod_hand_calculations.py`.

Exercise 5.2: Compute temperature variations in the ground

The surface temperature at the ground shows daily and seasonal oscillations. When the temperature rises at the surface, heat is propagated into the ground, and the coefficient β in the diffusion equation determines how fast this propagation is. It takes some time before the temperature rises down in the ground. At the surface, the temperature has then fallen. We are interested in how the temperature varies down in the ground because of temperature oscillations on the surface.

Assuming homogeneous horizontal properties of the ground, at least locally, and no variations of the temperature at the surface at a fixed point of time, we can neglect the horizontal variations of the temperature. Then a one-dimensional diffusion equation governs the heat propagation along a vertical axis called x. The surface corresponds to $x = 0$ and the x axis point downwards into the ground. There is no source term in the equation (actually, if rocks in the ground are radioactive, they emit heat and that can be modeled by a source term, but this effect is neglected here).

At some depth $x = L$ we assume that the heat changes in x vanish, so $\partial u / \partial x = 0$ is an appropriate boundary condition at $x = L$. We assume a simple sinusoidal temperature variation at the surface:

$$u(0, t) = T_0 + T_a \sin\left(\frac{2\pi}{P} t\right),$$

where P is the period, taken here as 24 hours ($24 \cdot 60 \cdot 60$ s). The β coefficient may be set to $10^{-6} \, \mathrm{m}^2/\mathrm{s}$. Time is then measured in seconds. Set appropriate values for T_0 and T_a.

a) Show that the present problem has an analytical solution of the form

$$u(x, t) = A + Be^{-rx} \sin(\omega t - rx),$$

for appropriate values of A, B, r, and ω.

b) Solve this heat propagation problem numerically for some days and animate the temperature. You may use the Forward Euler method in time. Plot both the numerical and analytical solution. As initial condition for the numerical solution, use the exact solution during program development, and when the curves coincide in the animation for all times, your implementation works, and you can then switch to a constant initial condition: $u(x, 0) = T_0$. For this latter initial condition, how many periods of oscillations are necessary before there is a good (visual) match between the numerical and exact solution (despite differences at $t = 0$)?

Filename: `ground_temp.py`.

Exercise 5.3: Compare implicit methods

An equally stable, but more accurate method than the Backward Euler scheme, is the so-called 2-step backward scheme, which for an ODE $u' = f(u, t)$ can be expressed by

$$\frac{3u^{n+1} - 4u^n + u^{n-1}}{2\Delta t} = f(u^{n+1}, t_{n+1}).$$

The Odespy package offers this method as odespy.Backward2Step. The purpose of this exercise is to compare three methods and animate the three solutions:

1. The Backward Euler method with $\Delta t = 0.001$
2. The backward 2-step method with $\Delta t = 0.001$
3. The backward 2-step method with $\Delta t = 0.01$

Choose the model problem from Sect. 5.1.4.
Filename: rod_BE_vs_B2Step.py.

Exercise 5.4: Explore adaptive and implicit methods
We consider the same problem as in Exercise 5.2. Now we want to explore the use of adaptive and implicit methods from Odespy to see if they are more efficient than the Forward Euler method. Assume that you want the accuracy provided by the Forward Euler method with its maximum Δt value. Since there exists an analytical solution, you can compute an error measure that summarizes the error in space and time over the whole simulation:

$$E = \sqrt{\Delta x \Delta t \sum_i \sum_n (U_i^n - u_i^n)^2}.$$

Here, U_i^n is the exact solution. Use the Odespy package to run the following implicit and adaptive solvers:

1. BackwardEuler
2. Backward2Step
3. RKFehlberg

Experiment to see if you can use larger time steps than what is required by the Forward Euler method and get solutions with the same order of accuracy.

Hint To avoid oscillations in the solutions when using the RKFehlberg method, the rtol and atol parameters to RKFFehlberg must be set no larger than 0.001 and 0.0001, respectively. You can print out solver_RKF.t_all to see all the time steps used by the RKFehlberg solver (if solver is the RKFehlberg object). You can then compare the number of time steps with what is required by the other methods.
Filename: ground_temp_adaptive.py.

Exercise 5.5: Investigate the θ rule

a) The Crank-Nicolson method for ODEs is very popular when combined with diffusion equations. For a linear ODE $u' = au$ it reads

$$\frac{u^{n+1} - u^n}{\Delta t} = \frac{1}{2}(au^n + au^{n+1}).$$

   Apply the Crank-Nicolson method in time to the ODE system for a one-dimensional diffusion equation. Identify the linear system to be solved.

b) The Backward Euler, Forward Euler, and Crank-Nicolson methods can be given a unified implementation. For a linear ODE $u' = au$ this formulation is known as the θ rule:

$$\frac{u^{n+1} - u^n}{\Delta t} = (1 - \theta)au^n + \theta au^{n+1}.$$

For $\theta = 0$ we recover the Forward Euler method, $\theta = 1$ gives the Backward Euler scheme, and $\theta = 1/2$ corresponds to the Crank-Nicolson method. The approximation error in the θ rule is proportional to Δt, except for $\theta = 1/2$ where it is proportional to Δt^2. For $\theta \geq 1/2$ the method is stable for all Δt. Apply the θ rule to the ODE system for a one-dimensional diffusion equation. Identify the linear system to be solved.

c) Implement the θ rule with aid of the Odespy package. The relevant object name is ThetaRule:

```
solver = odespy.ThetaRule(rhs, f_is_linear=True, jac=K, theta=0.5)
```

d) Consider the physical application from Sect. 5.1.4. Run this case with the θ rule and $\theta = 1/2$ for the following values of Δt: $0.001, 0.01, 0.05$. Report what you see.

Filename: rod_ThetaRule.py.

Remarks Despite the fact that the Crank-Nicolson method, or the θ rule with $\theta = 1/2$, is theoretically more accurate than the Backward Euler and Forward Euler schemes, it may exhibit non-physical oscillations as in the present example if the solution is very steep. The oscillations are damped in time, and decreases with decreasing Δt. To avoid oscillations one must have Δt at maximum twice the stability limit of the Forward Euler method. This is one reason why the Backward Euler method (or a 2-step backward scheme, see Exercise 5.3) are popular for diffusion equations with abrupt initial conditions.

Exercise 5.6: Compute the diffusion of a Gaussian peak
Solve the following diffusion problem:

$$\frac{\partial u}{\partial t} = \beta \frac{\partial^2 u}{\partial x^2}, \qquad\qquad x \in (-1, 1), \ t \in (0, T] \qquad (5.34)$$

$$u(x, 0) = \frac{1}{\sqrt{2\pi}\sigma} \exp\left(-\frac{x^2}{2\sigma^2}\right), \qquad\qquad x \in [-1, 1], \qquad (5.35)$$

$$\frac{\partial}{\partial x}u(-1, t) = 0 \qquad\qquad t \in (0, T], \qquad (5.36)$$

$$\frac{\partial}{\partial x}u(1, t) = 0 \qquad\qquad t \in (0, T]. \qquad (5.37)$$

The initial condition is the famous and widely used *Gaussian function* with standard deviation (or "width") σ, which is here taken to be small, $\sigma = 0.01$, such that the initial condition is a peak. This peak will then diffuse and become lower and wider. Compute $u(x, t)$ until u becomes approximately constant over the domain.
Filename: gaussian_diffusion.py.

Remarks Running the simulation with $\sigma = 0.2$ results in a constant solution $u \approx 1$ as $t \rightarrow \infty$, while one might expect from "physics of diffusion" that the solution should approach zero. The reason is that we apply Neumann conditions as boundary conditions. One can then easily show that the area under the u curve remains constant. Integrating the PDE gives

$$\int_{-1}^{1} \frac{\partial u}{\partial t} dx = \beta \int_{-1}^{1} \frac{\partial d^2 u}{\partial x^2} dx .$$

Using the Gauss divergence theorem on the integral on the right-hand and moving the time-derivative outside the integral on the left-hand side results in

$$\frac{\partial}{\partial t} \int_{-1}^{1} u(x,t) dx = \beta \left[\frac{\partial d u}{\partial x} \right]_{-1}^{1} = 0.$$

(Recall that $\partial u/\partial x = 0$ at the end points.) The result means that $\int_{-1}^{1} u dx$ remains constant during the simulation. Giving the PDE an interpretation in terms of heat conduction can easily explain the result: with Neumann conditions no heat can escape from the domain so the initial heat will just be evenly distributed, but not leak out, so the temperature cannot go to zero (or the scaled and translated temperature u, to be precise). The area under the initial condition is 1, so with a sufficiently fine mesh, $u \rightarrow 1$, regardless of σ.

Exercise 5.7: Vectorize a function for computing the area of a polygon
Vectorize the implementation of the function for computing the area of a polygon in Exercise 2.5. Make a test function that compares the scalar implementation in Exercise 2.5 and the new vectorized implementation for the test cases used in Exercise 2.5.

Hint Notice that the formula $x_1 y_2 + x_2 y_3 + \cdots + x_{n-1} y_n = \sum_{i=0}^{n-1} x_i y_{i+1}$ is the dot product of two vectors, `x[:-1]` and `y[1:]`, which can be computed as `numpy.dot(x[:-1], y[1:])`, or more explicitly as `numpy.sum(x[:-1]*y[1:])`. Filename: `polyarea_vec.py`.

Exercise 5.8: Explore symmetry
One can observe (and also mathematically prove) that the solution $u(x,t)$ of the problem in Exercise 5.6 is symmetric around $x = 0$: $u(-x,t) = u(x,t)$. In such a case, we can split the domain in two and compute u in only one half, $[-1,0]$ or $[0,1]$. At the symmetry line $x = 0$ we have the symmetry boundary condition $\partial u/\partial x = 0$. Reformulate the problem in Exercise 5.6 such that we compute only for $x \in [0,1]$. Display the solution and observe that it equals the right part of the solution in Exercise 5.6.
Filename: `symmetric_gaussian_diffusion.py`.

Remarks In 2D and 3D problems, where the CPU time to compute a solution of PDE can be hours and days, it is very important to utilize symmetry as we do above to reduce the size of the problem.

Also note the remarks in Exercise 5.6 about the constant area under the $u(x,t)$ curve: here, the area is 0.5 and $u \to 0.5$ as $t \to 0.5$ (if the mesh is sufficiently fine - one will get convergence to smaller values for small σ if the mesh is not fine enough to properly resolve a thin-shaped initial condition).

Exercise 5.9: Compute solutions as $t \to \infty$

Many diffusion problems reach a stationary time-independent solution as $t \to \infty$. The model problem from Sect. 5.1.4 is one example where $u(x,t) = s(t) = \text{const}$ for $t \to \infty$. When u does not depend on time, the diffusion equation reduces to

$$-\beta u''(x) = f(x),$$

in one dimension, and

$$-\beta \nabla^2 u = f(x),$$

in 2D and 3D. This is the famous *Poisson* equation, or if $f = 0$, it is known as the *Laplace* equation. In this limit $t \to \infty$, there is no need for an initial condition, but the boundary conditions are the same as for the diffusion equation.

We now consider a one-dimensional problem

$$-u''(x) = 0, \ x \in (0, L), \quad u(0) = C, \ u'(L) = 0, \tag{5.38}$$

which is known as a *two-point boundary value problem*. This is nothing but the stationary limit of the diffusion problem in Sect. 5.1.4. How can we solve such a stationary problem (5.38)? The simplest strategy, when we already have a solver for the corresponding time-dependent problem, is to use that solver and simulate until $t \to \infty$, which in practice means that $u(x,t)$ no longer changes in time (within some tolerance).

A nice feature of implicit methods like the Backward Euler scheme is that one can take *one very long time step* to "infinity" and produce the solution of (5.38).

a) Let (5.38) be valid at mesh points x_i in space, discretize u'' by a finite difference, and set up a system of equations for the point values $u_i, i = 0, \ldots, N$, where u_i is the approximation at mesh point x_i.
b) Show that if $\Delta t \to \infty$ in (5.16) - (5.18), it leads to the same equations as in a).
c) Demonstrate, by running a program, that you can take one large time step with the Backward Euler scheme and compute the solution of (5.38). The solution is very boring since it is constant: $u(x) = C$.

Filename: `rod_stationary.py`.

Remarks If the interest is in the stationary limit of a diffusion equation, one can either solve the associated Laplace or Poisson equation directly, or use a Backward Euler scheme for the time-dependent diffusion equation with a very long time step. Using a Forward Euler scheme with small time steps is typically inappropriate in such situations because the solution changes more and more slowly, but the time step must still be kept small, and it takes "forever" to approach the stationary state. This is yet another example why one needs implicit methods like the Backward Euler scheme.

Exercise 5.10: Solve a two-point boundary value problem
Solve the following two-point boundary-value problem

$$u''(x) = 2, \; x \in (0, 1), \quad u(0) = 0, \, u(1) = 1.$$

Hint Do Exercise 5.9. Modify the boundary condition in the code so it incorporates a known value for $u(1)$.
Filename: 2ptBVP.py.

6

Solutions to Nonlinear Algebraic Equations

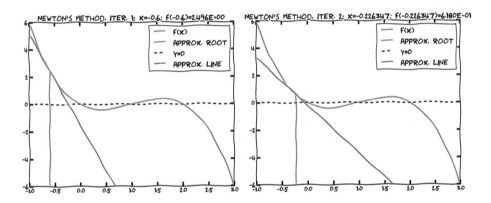

As a reader of this book you are probably well into mathematics and often "accused" of being particularly good at "solving equations" (a typical comment at family dinners!). However, is it *really* true that you, with pen and paper, can solve *many* types of equations? Restricting our attention to *algebraic equations in one unknown x*, you can certainly do linear equations: $ax + b = 0$, and quadratic ones: $ax^2 + bx + c = 0$. You may also know that there are formulas for the roots of cubic and quartic equations too. Maybe you can do the special trigonometric equation $\sin x + \cos x = 1$ as well, but there it (probably) stops. Equations that are not reducible to one of the mentioned cannot be solved by general analytical techniques, which means that most algebraic equations arising in applications cannot be treated with pen and paper!

If we exchange the traditional idea of finding *exact* solutions to equations with the idea of rather finding *approximate* solutions, a whole new world of possibilities opens up. With such an approach, we can in principle solve *any* algebraic equation.

Let us start by introducing a common generic form for any algebraic equation:

$$f(x) = 0 .$$

Here, $f(x)$ is some prescribed formula involving x. For example, the equation

$$e^{-x} \sin x = \cos x$$

has

$$f(x) = e^{-x} \sin x - \cos x \, .$$

Just move all terms to the left-hand side and then the formula to the left of the equality sign is $f(x)$.

So, when do we really need to solve algebraic equations beyond the simplest types we can treat with pen and paper? There are two major application areas. One is when using *implicit* numerical methods for ordinary differential equations. These give rise to one or a system of algebraic equations. The other major application type is optimization, i.e., finding the maxima or minima of a function. These maxima and minima are normally found by solving the algebraic equation $F'(x) = 0$ if $F(x)$ is the function to be optimized. Differential equations are very much used throughout science and engineering, and actually most engineering problems are optimization problems in the end, because one wants a design that maximizes performance and minimizes cost.

We first consider one algebraic equation in one variable, with our usual emphasis on how to program the algorithms. *Systems* of nonlinear algebraic equations with *many variables* arise from implicit methods for ordinary and partial differential equations as well as in multivariate optimization. Our attention will be restricted to Newton's method for such systems of nonlinear algebraic equations.

Terminology
When solving algebraic equations $f(x) = 0$, we often say that the solution x is a *root* of the equation. The solution process itself is thus often called *root finding*.

6.1 Brute Force Methods

The representation of a mathematical function $f(x)$ on a computer takes two forms. One is a Python function returning the function value given the argument, while the other is a collection of points $(x, f(x))$ along the function curve. The latter is the representation we use for plotting, together with an assumption of linear variation between the points.

This representation is also very suited for equation solving and optimization: we simply go through all points and see if the function crosses the x axis, or for optimization, test for a local maximum or minimum point. Be-cause there is a lot of work to examine a huge number of points, and also because the idea is extremely simple, such approaches are often referred to as *brute force* methods. However, we are not embarrassed of explaining the methods in detail and implementing them.

6.1.1 Brute Force Root Finding

Assume that we have a set of points along the curve of a function $f(x)$:

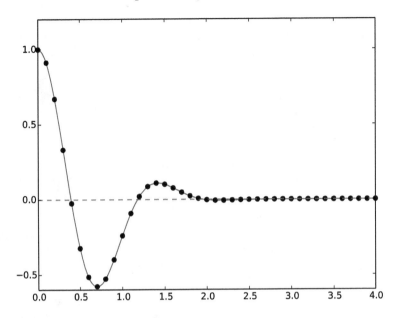

We want to solve $f(x) = 0$, i.e., find the points x where f crosses the x axis. A brute force algorithm is to run through all points on the curve and check if one point is below the x axis and if the next point is above the x axis, or the other way around. If this is found to be the case, we know that f must be zero in between these two x points.

Numerical algorithm More precisely, we have a set of $n + 1$ points (x_i, y_i), $y_i = f(x_i)$, $i = 0, \ldots, n$, where $x_0 < \ldots < x_n$. We check if $y_i < 0$ and $y_{i+1} > 0$ (or the other way around). A compact expression for this check is to perform the test $y_i y_{i+1} < 0$. If so, the root of $f(x) = 0$ is in $[x_i, x_{i+1}]$. Assuming a linear variation of f between x_i and x_{i+1}, we have the approximation

$$f(x) \approx \frac{f(x_{i+1}) - f(x_i)}{x_{i+1} - x_i}(x - x_i) + f(x_i) = \frac{y_{i+1} - y_i}{x_{i+1} - x_i}(x - x_i) + y_i,$$

which, when set equal to zero, gives the root

$$x = x_i - \frac{x_{i+1} - x_i}{y_{i+1} - y_i} y_i .$$

Implementation Given some Python implementation $f(x)$ of our mathematical function, a straightforward implementation of the above numerical algorithm looks like

```
x = linspace(0, 4, 10001)
y = f(x)

root = None  # Initialization
for i in range(len(x)-1):
    if y[i]*y[i+1] < 0:
        root = x[i] - (x[i+1] - x[i])/(y[i+1] - y[i])*y[i]
        break  # Jump out of loop

if root is None:
    print 'Could not find any root in [%g, %g]' % (x[0], x[-1])
else:
    print 'Find (the first) root as x=%g' % root
```

(See the file `brute_force_root_finder_flat.py`.)

Note the nice use of setting `root` to None: we can simply test `if root is None` to see if we found a root and overwrote the None value, or if we did not find any root among the tested points.

Running this program with some function, say $f(x) = e^{-x^2} \cos(4x)$ (which has a solution at $x = \frac{\pi}{8}$), gives the root 0.392701, which has an error of $1.9 \cdot 10^{-6}$. Increasing the number of points with a factor of ten gives a root with an error of $2.4 \cdot 10^{-8}$.

After such a quick "flat" implementation of an algorithm, we should always try to offer the algorithm as a Python function, applicable to as wide a problem domain as possible. The function should take f and an associated interval $[a, b]$ as input, as well as a number of points (n), and return a list of all the roots in $[a, b]$. Here is our candidate for a good implementation of the brute force rooting finding algorithm:

```
def brute_force_root_finder(f, a, b, n):
    from numpy import linspace
    x = linspace(a, b, n)
    y = f(x)
    roots = []
    for i in range(n-1):
        if y[i]*y[i+1] < 0:
            root = x[i] - (x[i+1] - x[i])/(y[i+1] - y[i])*y[i]
            roots.append(root)
    return roots
```

(See the file `brute_force_root_finder_function.py`.)

This time we use another elegant technique to indicate if roots were found or not: `roots` is an empty list if the root finding was unsuccessful, otherwise it contains all the roots. Application of the function to the previous example can be coded as

```
def demo():
    from numpy import exp, cos
    roots = brute_force_root_finder(
        lambda x: exp(-x**2)*cos(4*x), 0, 4, 1001)
    if roots:
        print roots
    else:
        print 'Could not find any roots'
```

Note that if `roots` evaluates to True if `roots` is non-empty. This is a general test in Python: if X evaluates to True if X is non-empty or has a nonzero value.

6.1.2   Brute Force Optimization

Numerical algorithm We realize that x_i corresponds to a maximum point if $y_{i-1} < y_i > y_{i+1}$. Similarly, x_i corresponds to a minimum if $y_{i-1} > y_i < y_{i+1}$. We can do this test for all "inner" points $i = 1, \ldots, n-1$ to find all local minima and maxima. In addition, we need to add an end point, $i = 0$ or $i = n$, if the corresponding y_i is a global maximum or minimum.

Implementation The algorithm above can be translated to the following Python function (file `brute_force_optimizer.py`):

```
def brute_force_optimizer(f, a, b, n):
    from numpy import linspace
    x = linspace(a, b, n)
    y = f(x)
    # Let maxima and minima hold the indices corresponding
    # to (local) maxima and minima points
    minima = []
    maxima = []
    for i in range(n-1):
        if y[i-1] < y[i] > y[i+1]:
            maxima.append(i)
        if y[i-1] > y[i] < y[i+1]:
            minima.append(i)

    # What about the end points?
    y_max_inner = max([y[i] for i in maxima])
    y_min_inner = min([y[i] for i in minima])
    if y[0] > y_max_inner:
        maxima.append(0)
    if y[len(x)-1] > y_max_inner:
        maxima.append(len(x)-1)
    if y[0] < y_min_inner:
        minima.append(0)
    if y[len(x)-1] < y_min_inner:
        minima.append(len(x)-1)

    # Return x and y values
    return [(x[i], y[i]) for i in minima], \
           [(x[i], y[i]) for i in maxima]
```

The `max` and `min` functions are standard Python functions for finding the maximum and minimum element of a list or an object that one can iterate over with a for loop.

An application to $f(x) = e^{-x^2} \cos(4x)$ looks like

```
def demo():
    from numpy import exp, cos
    minima, maxima = brute_force_optimizer(
        lambda x: exp(-x**2)*cos(4*x), 0, 4, 1001)
    print 'Minima:', minima
    print 'Maxima:', maxima
```

6.1.3   Model Problem for Algebraic Equations

We shall consider the very simple problem of finding the square root of 9, which is the positive solution of $x^2 = 9$. The nice feature of solving an equation whose solution is known beforehand is that we can easily investigate how the numerical method and the implementation perform in the search for the solution. The $f(x)$ function corresponding to the equation $x^2 = 9$ is

$$f(x) = x^2 - 9.$$

Our interval of interest for solutions will be $[0, 1000]$ (the upper limit here is chosen somewhat arbitrarily).

In the following, we will present several efficient and accurate methods for solving nonlinear algebraic equations, both single equation and systems of equations. The methods all have in common that they search for *approximate* solutions. The methods differ, however, in the way they perform the search for solutions. The idea for the search influences the efficiency of the search and the reliability of actually finding a solution. For example, Newton's method is very fast, but not reliable, while the bisection method is the slowest, but absolutely reliable. No method is best at all problems, so we need different methods for different problems.

What is the difference between linear and nonlinear equations?

You know how to solve linear equations $ax + b = 0$: $x = -b/a$. All other types of equations $f(x) = 0$, i.e., when $f(x)$ is not a linear function of x, are called nonlinear. A typical way of recognizing a nonlinear equation is to observe that x is "not alone" as in ax, but involved in a product with itself, such as in $x^3 + 2x^2 - 9 = 0$. We say that x^3 and $2x^2$ are nonlinear terms. An equation like $\sin x + e^x \cos x = 0$ is also nonlinear although x is not explicitly multiplied by itself, but the Taylor series of $\sin x$, e^x, and $\cos x$ all involve polynomials of x where x is multiplied by itself.

6.2   Newton's Method

Newton's method, also known as *Newton-Raphson's method*, is a very famous and widely used method for solving nonlinear algebraic equations. Compared to the other methods we will consider, it is generally the fastest one (usually by far). It does not guarantee that an existing solution will be found, however.

A fundamental idea of numerical methods for nonlinear equations is to construct a series of linear equations (since we know how to solve linear equations) and hope that the solutions of these linear equations bring us closer and closer to the solution of the nonlinear equation. The idea will be clearer when we present Newton's method and the secant method.

6.2.1 Deriving and Implementing Newton's Method

Figure 6.1 shows the $f(x)$ function in our model equation $x^2 - 9 = 0$. Numerical methods for algebraic equations require us to guess at a solution first. Here, this guess is called x_0. The fundamental idea of Newton's method is to approximate the original function $f(x)$ by a straight line, i.e., a linear function, since it is straightforward to solve linear equations. There are infinitely many choices of how to approximate $f(x)$ by a straight line. Newton's method applies the tangent of $f(x)$ at x_0, see the rightmost tangent in Fig. 6.1. This linear tangent function crosses the x axis at a point we call x_1. This is (hopefully) a better approximation to the solution of $f(x) = 0$ than x_0. The next fundamental idea is to repeat this process. We find the tangent of f at x_1, compute where it crosses the x axis, at a point called x_2, and repeat the process again. Figure 6.1 shows that the process brings us closer and closer to the left. It remains, however, to see if we hit $x = 3$ or come sufficiently close to this solution.

How do we compute the tangent of a function $f(x)$ at a point x_0? The tangent function, here called $\tilde{f}(x)$, is linear and has two properties:

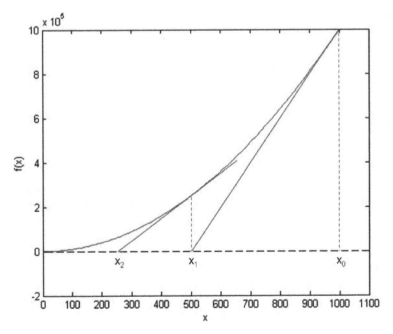

Fig. 6.1 Illustrates the idea of Newton's method with $f(x) = x^2 - 9$, repeatedly solving for crossing of tangent lines with the x axis

1. the slope equals to $f'(x_0)$
2. the tangent touches the $f(x)$ curve at x_0

So, if we write the tangent function as $\tilde{f}(x) = ax + b$, we must require $\tilde{f}'(x_0) = f'(x_0)$ and $\tilde{f}(x_0) = f(x_0)$, resulting in

$$\tilde{f}(x) = f(x_0) + f'(x_0)(x - x_0).$$

The key step in Newton's method is to find where the tangent crosses the x axis, which means solving $\tilde{f}(x) = 0$:

$$\tilde{f}(x) = 0 \quad \Rightarrow \quad x = x_0 - \frac{f(x_0)}{f'(x_0)}.$$

This is our new candidate point, which we call x_1:

$$x_1 = x_0 - \frac{f(x_0)}{f'(x_0)}.$$

With $x_0 = 1000$, we get $x_1 \approx 500$, which is in accordance with the graph in Fig. 6.1. Repeating the process, we get

$$x_2 = x_1 - \frac{f(x_1)}{f'(x_1)} \approx 250.$$

The general scheme of Newton's method may be written as

$$x_{n+1} = x_n - \frac{f(x_n)}{f'(x_n)}, \quad n = 0, 1, 2, \ldots \tag{6.1}$$

The computation in (6.1) is repeated until $f(x_n)$ is close enough to zero. More precisely, we test if $|f(x_n)| < \epsilon$, with ϵ being a small number.

We moved from 1000 to 250 in two iterations, so it is exciting to see how fast we can approach the solution $x = 3$. A computer program can automate the calculations. Our first try at implementing Newton's method is in a function `naive_Newton`:

```python
def naive_Newton(f, dfdx, x, eps):
    while abs(f(x)) > eps:
        x = x - float(f(x))/dfdx(x)
    return x
```

The argument x is the starting value, called x_0 in our previous mathematical description. We use `float(f(x))` to ensure that an integer division does not happen by accident if `f(x)` and `dfdx(x)` both are integers for some x.

To solve the problem $x^2 = 9$ we also need to implement

```python
def f(x):
    return x**2 - 9

def dfdx(x):
    return 2*x

print naive_Newton(f, dfdx, 1000, 0.001)
```

Newton's method is normally formulated with an *iteration index n*,

$$x_{n+1} = x_n - \frac{f(x_n)}{f'(x_n)}.$$

Seeing such an index, many would implement this as

```
x[n+1] = x[n] - f(x[n])/dfdx(x[n])
```

Such an array is fine, but requires storage of all the approximations. In large industrial applications, where Newton's method solves millions of equations at once, one cannot afford to store all the intermediate approximations in memory, so then it is important to understand that the algorithm in Newton's method has no more need for x_n when x_{n+1} is computed. Therefore, we can work with one variable x and overwrite the previous value:

```
x = x - f(x)/dfdx(x)
```

Running `naive_Newton(f, dfdx, 1000, eps=0.001)` results in the approximate solution 3.000027639. A smaller value of eps will produce a more accurate solution. Unfortunately, the plain `naive_Newton` function does not return how many iterations it used, nor does it print out all the approximations $x_0, x_1, x_2, \ldots$, which would indeed be a nice feature. If we insert such a printout, a rerun results in

```
500.0045
250.011249919
125.02362415
62.5478052723
31.3458476066
15.816483488
8.1927550496
4.64564330569
3.2914711388
3.01290538807
3.00002763928
```

We clearly see that the iterations approach the solution quickly. This speed of the search for the solution is the primary strength of Newton's method compared to other methods.

6.2.2   Making a More Efficient and Robust Implementation

The `naive_Newton` function works fine for the example we are considering here. However, for more general use, there are some pitfalls that should be fixed in an improved version of the code. An example may illustrate what the problem is: let us solve $\tanh(x) = 0$, which has solution $x = 0$. With $|x_0| \leq 1.08$ everything works fine. For example, x_0 leads to six iterations if $\epsilon = 0.001$:

```
-1.05895313436
0.989404207298
-0.784566773086
0.36399816111
-0.0330146961372
2.3995252668e-05
```

Adjusting x_0 slightly to 1.09 gives division by zero! The approximations computed by Newton's method become

```
-1.09331618202
1.10490354324
-1.14615550788
1.30303261823
-2.06492300238
13.4731428006
-1.26055913647e+11
```

The division by zero is caused by $x_7 = -1.26055913647 \cdot 10^{11}$, because $\tanh(x_7)$ is 1.0 to machine precision, and then $f'(x) = 1 - \tanh(x)^2$ becomes zero in the denominator in Newton's method.

The underlying problem, leading to the division by zero in the above example, is that Newton's method *diverges*: the approximations move further and further away from $x = 0$. If it had not been for the division by zero, the condition in the while loop would always be true and the loop would run forever. Divergence of Newton's method occasionally happens, and the remedy is to abort the method when a maximum number of iterations is reached.

Another disadvantage of the naive_Newton function is that it calls the $f(x)$ function twice as many times as necessary. This extra work is of no concern when $f(x)$ is fast to evaluate, but in large-scale industrial software, one call to $f(x)$ might take hours or days, and then removing unnecessary calls is important. The solution in our function is to store the call f(x) in a variable (f_value) and reuse the value instead of making a new call f(x).

To summarize, we want to write an improved function for implementing Newton's method where we

- avoid division by zero
- allow a maximum number of iterations
- avoid the extra evaluation of $f(x)$

A more robust and efficient version of the function, inserted in a complete program Newtons_method.py for solving $x^2 - 9 = 0$, is listed below.

```
def Newton(f, dfdx, x, eps):
    f_value = f(x)
    iteration_counter = 0
    while abs(f_value) > eps and iteration_counter < 100:
        try:
            x = x - float(f_value)/dfdx(x)
```

```
        except ZeroDivisionError:
            print "Error! - derivative zero for x = ", x
            sys.exit(1)     # Abort with error

        f_value = f(x)
        iteration_counter += 1

    # Here, either a solution is found, or too many iterations
    if abs(f_value) > eps:
        iteration_counter = -1
    return x, iteration_counter

def f(x):
    return x**2 - 9

def dfdx(x):
    return 2*x

solution, no_iterations = Newton(f, dfdx, x=1000, eps=1.0e-6)

if no_iterations > 0:    # Solution found
    print "Number of function calls: %d" % (1 + 2*no_iterations)
    print "A solution is: %f" % (solution)
else:
    print "Solution not found!"
```

Handling of the potential division by zero is done by a try-except construction. Python *tries* to run the code in the try block. If anything goes wrong here, or more precisely, if Python raises an *exception* caused by a problem (such as division by zero, array index out of bounds, use of undefined variable, etc.), the execution jumps immediately to the except block. Here, the programmer can take appropriate actions. In the present case, we simply stop the program. (Professional programmers would avoid calling sys.exit inside a function. Instead, they would raise a new exception with an informative error message, and let the calling code have another try-except construction to stop the program.)

The division by zero will always be detected and the program will be stopped. The main purpose of our way of treating the division by zero is to give the user a more informative error message and stop the program in a gentler way.

Calling sys.exit with an argument different from zero (here 1) signifies that the program stopped because of an error. It is a good habit to supply the value 1, because tools in the operating system can then be used by other programs to detect that our program failed.

To prevent an infinite loop because of divergent iterations, we have introduced the integer variable iteration_counter to count the number of iterations in Newton's method. With iteration_counter we can easily extend the condition in the while such that no more iterations take place when the number of iterations reaches 100. We could easily let this limit be an argument to the function rather than a fixed constant.

The Newton function returns the approximate solution and the number of iterations. The latter equals -1 if the convergence criterion $|f(x)| < \epsilon$ was not reached within the maximum number of iterations. In the calling code, we print out the solution and the number of function calls. The main cost of a method for solving $f(x) = 0$ equations is usually the evaluation of $f(x)$ and $f'(x)$, so the total number of calls to these functions is an interesting measure of the computational work. Note that in function Newton there is an initial call to $f(x)$ and then one call to f and one to f' in each iteration.

Running Newtons_method.py, we get the following printout on the screen:

```
Number of function calls: 25
A solution is: 3.000000
```

As we did with the integration methods in Chapter 3, we will collect our solvers for nonlinear algebraic equations in a separate file named nonlinear_solvers.py for easy import and use. The first function placed in this file is then Newton.

The Newton scheme will work better if the starting value is close to the solution. A good starting value may often make the difference as to whether the code actually *finds* a solution or not. Because of its speed, Newton's method is often the method of first choice for solving nonlinear algebraic equations, even if the scheme is not guaranteed to work. In cases where the initial guess may be far from the solution, a good strategy is to run a few iterations with the bisection method (see Chapter 6.4) to narrow down the region where f is close to zero and then switch to Newton's method for fast convergence to the solution.

Newton's method requires the analytical expression for the derivative $f'(x)$. Derivation of $f'(x)$ is not always a reliable process by hand if $f(x)$ is a complicated function. However, Python has the symbolic package SymPy, which we may use to create the required dfdx function. In our sample problem, the recipe goes as follows:

```
from sympy import *
x = symbols('x')              # define x as a mathematical symbol
f_expr = x**2 - 9             # symbolic expression for f(x)
dfdx_expr = diff(f_expr, x)   # compute f'(x) symbolically
# Turn f_expr and dfdx_expr into plain Python functions
f = lambdify([x],      # argument to f
             f_expr)   # symbolic expression to be evaluated
dfdx = lambdify([x], dfdx_expr)
print dfdx(5)          # will print 10
```

The nice feature of this code snippet is that dfdx_expr is the exact analytical expression for the derivative, 2*x, if you print it out. This is a symbolic expression so we cannot do numerical computing with it, but the lambdify constructions turn symbolic expressions into callable Python functions.

The next method is the secant method, which is usually slower than Newton's method, but it does not require an expression for $f'(x)$, and it has only one function call per iteration.

6.3 The Secant Method

When finding the derivative $f'(x)$ in Newton's method is problematic, or when function evaluations take too long; we may adjust the method slightly. Instead of using tangent lines to the graph we may use secants[1]. The approach is referred to as the *secant method*, and the idea is illustrated graphically in Fig. 6.2 for our example problem $x^2 - 9 = 0$.

The idea of the secant method is to think as in Newton's method, but instead of using $f'(x_n)$, we approximate this derivative by a finite difference or the *secant*, i.e., the slope of the straight line that goes through the points $(x_n, f(x_n))$ and $(x_{n-1}, f(x_{n-1}))$ on the graph, given by the two most recent approximations x_n and x_{n-1}. This slope reads

$$\frac{f(x_n) - f(x_{n-1})}{x_n - x_{n-1}}. \tag{6.2}$$

Inserting this expression for $f'(x_n)$ in Newton's method simply gives us the secant method:

$$x_{n+1} = x_n - \frac{f(x_n)}{\frac{f(x_n)-f(x_{n-1})}{x_n-x_{n-1}}},$$

or

$$x_{n+1} = x_n - f(x_n)\frac{x_n - x_{n-1}}{f(x_n) - f(x_{n-1})}. \tag{6.3}$$

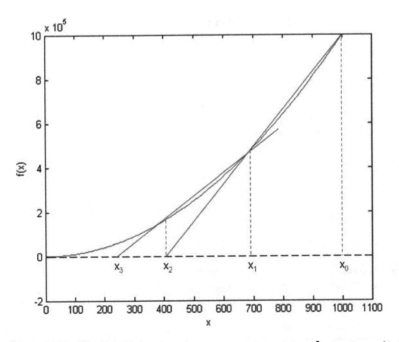

Fig. 6.2 Illustrates the use of secants in the secant method when solving $x^2 - 9 = 0$, $x \in [0, 1000]$. From two chosen starting values, $x_0 = 1000$ and $x_1 = 700$ the crossing x_2 of the corresponding secant with the x axis is computed, followed by a similar computation of x_3 from x_1 and x_2

---

[1] https://en.wikipedia.org/wiki/Secant_line

Comparing (6.3) to the graph in Fig. 6.2, we see how *two* chosen starting points ($x_0 = 1000$, $x_1 = 700$, and corresponding function values) are used to compute x_2. Once we have x_2, we similarly use x_1 and x_2 to compute x_3. As with Newton's method, the procedure is repeated until $f(x_n)$ is below some chosen limit value, or some limit on the number of iterations has been reached. We use an iteration counter here too, based on the same thinking as in the implementation of Newton's method.

We can store the approximations x_n in an array, but as in Newton's method, we notice that the computation of x_{n+1} only needs knowledge of x_n and x_{n-1}, not "older" approximations. Therefore, we can make use of only three variables: x for x_{n+1}, x1 for x_n, and x0 for x_{n-1}. Note that x0 and x1 must be given (guessed) for the algorithm to start.

A program secant_method.py that solves our example problem may be written as:

```
def secant(f, x0, x1, eps):
    f_x0 = f(x0)
    f_x1 = f(x1)
    iteration_counter = 0
    while abs(f_x1) > eps and iteration_counter < 100:
        try:
            denominator = float(f_x1 - f_x0)/(x1 - x0)
            x = x1 - float(f_x1)/denominator
        except ZeroDivisionError:
            print "Error! - denominator zero for x = ", x
            sys.exit(1)        # Abort with error
        x0 = x1
        x1 = x
        f_x0 = f_x1
        f_x1 = f(x1)
        iteration_counter += 1
    # Here, either a solution is found, or too many iterations
    if abs(f_x1) > eps:
        iteration_counter = -1
    return x, iteration_counter

def f(x):
    return x**2 - 9

x0 = 1000;    x1 = x0 - 1

solution, no_iterations = secant(f, x0, x1, eps=1.0e-6)

if no_iterations > 0:    # Solution found
    print "Number of function calls: %d" % (2 + no_iterations)
    print "A solution is: %f" % (solution)
else:
    print "Solution not found!"
```

The number of function calls is now related to no_iterations, i.e., the number of iterations, as 2 + no_iterations, since we need two function calls before entering the while loop, and then one function call per loop iteration. Note that, even though we need two points on the graph to compute each updated estimate, only a *single* function call (`f(x1)`) is required in each iteration since `f(x0)` becomes the "old" `f(x1)` and may simply be copied as `f_x0 = f_x1` (the exception is the very first iteration where two function evaluations are needed).

Running `secant_method.py`, gives the following printout on the screen:

```
Number of function calls: 19
A solution is: 3.000000
```

As with the function `Newton`, we place `secant` in the file `nonlinear_solvers.py` for easy import and use later.

6.4   The Bisection Method

Neither Newton's method nor the secant method can guarantee that an existing solution will be found (see Exercises 6.1 and 6.2). The bisection method, however, does that. However, if there are several solutions present, it finds only one of them, just as Newton's method and the secant method. The bisection method is slower than the other two methods, so reliability comes with a cost of speed.

To solve $x^2 - 9 = 0$, $x \in [0, 1000]$, with the bisection method, we reason as follows. The first key idea is that if $f(x) = x^2 - 9$ is *continuous* on the interval and the function values for the interval endpoints ($x_L = 0$, $x_R = 1000$) have *opposite signs*, $f(x)$ *must* cross the x axis at least once on the interval. That is, we know there is at least one solution.

The second key idea comes from dividing the interval in two equal parts, one to the left and one to the right of the midpoint $x_M = 500$. By evaluating the sign of $f(x_M)$, we will immediately know whether a solution must exist to the left or right of x_M. This is so, since if $f(x_M) \geq 0$, we know that $f(x)$ has to cross the x axis between x_L and x_M at least once (using the same argument as for the original interval). Likewise, if instead $f(x_M) \leq 0$, we know that $f(x)$ has to cross the x axis between x_M and x_R at least once.

In any case, we may proceed with half the interval only. The exception is if $f(x_M) \approx 0$, in which case a solution is found. Such interval halving can be continued until a solution is found. A "solution" in this case, is when $|f(x_M)|$ is sufficiently close to zero, more precisely (as before): $|f(x_M)| < \epsilon$, where ϵ is a small number specified by the user.

The sketched strategy seems reasonable, so let us write a reusable function that can solve a general algebraic equation $f(x) = 0$ (`bisection_method.py`):

```
def bisection(f, x_L, x_R, eps, return_x_list=False):
    f_L = f(x_L)
    if f_L*f(x_R) > 0:
        print "Error! Function does not have opposite \
                signs at interval endpoints!"
        sys.exit(1)
    x_M = float(x_L + x_R)/2.0
    f_M = f(x_M)
    iteration_counter = 1
```

```
    if return_x_list:
        x_list = []

    while abs(f_M) > eps:
        if f_L*f_M > 0:    # i.e. same sign
            x_L = x_M
            f_L = f_M
        else:
            x_R = x_M
        x_M = float(x_L + x_R)/2
        f_M = f(x_M)
        iteration_counter += 1
        if return_x_list:
            x_list.append(x_M)
    if return_x_list:
        return x_list, iteration_counter
    else:
        return x_M, iteration_counter

def f(x):
    return x**2 - 9

a = 0;   b = 1000

solution, no_iterations = bisection(f, a, b, eps=1.0e-6)

print "Number of function calls: %d" % (1 + 2*no_iterations)
print "A solution is: %f" % (solution)
```

Note that we first check if f changes sign in $[a, b]$, because that is a requirement for the algorithm to work. The algorithm also relies on a continuous $f(x)$ function, but this is very challenging for a computer code to check.

We get the following printout to the screen when `bisection_method.py` is run:

```
Number of function calls: 61
A solution is: 3.000000
```

We notice that the number of function calls is much higher than with the previous methods.

Required work in the bisection method

If the starting interval of the bisection method is bounded by a and b, and the solution at step n is taken to be the middle value, the error is bounded as

$$\frac{|b - a|}{2^n},\tag{6.4}$$

because the initial interval has been halved n times. Therefore, to meet a tolerance ϵ, we need n iterations such that the length of the current interval equals ϵ:

$$\frac{|b - a|}{2^n} = \epsilon \quad \Rightarrow \quad n = \frac{\ln((b - a)/\epsilon)}{\ln 2}.$$

This is a great advantage of the bisection method: we know beforehand how many iterations n it takes to meet a certain accuracy ϵ in the solution.

As with the two previous methods, the function `bisection` is placed in the file `nonlinear_solvers.py` for easy import and use.

6.5 Rate of Convergence

With the methods above, we noticed that the number of iterations or function calls could differ quite substantially. The number of iterations needed to find a solution is closely related to the *rate of convergence*, which dictates the speed of error reduction as we approach the root. More precisely, we introduce the error in iteration n as $e_n = |x - x_n|$, and define the *convergence rate q* as

$$e_{n+1} = Ce_n^q, \tag{6.5}$$

where C is a constant. The exponent q measures how fast the error is reduced from one iteration to the next. The larger q is, the faster the error goes to zero, and the fewer iterations we need to meet the stopping criterion $|f(x)| < \epsilon$.

A single q in (6.5) is defined in the limit $n \to \infty$. For finite n, and especially smaller n, q will vary with n. To estimate q, we can compute all the errors e_n and set up (6.5) for three consecutive experiments $n - 1, n$, and $n + 1$:

$$e_n = Ce_{n-1}^q,$$
$$e_{n+1} = Ce_n^q.$$

Dividing these two equations by each other and solving with respect to q gives

$$q = \frac{\ln(e_{n+1}/e_n)}{\ln(e_n/e_{n-1})}.$$

Since this q will vary somewhat with n, we call it q_n. As n grows, we expect q_n to approach a limit ($q_n \to q$). To compute all the q_n values, we need all the x_n approximations. However, our previous implementations of Newton's method, the secant method, and the bisection method returned just the final approximation.

Therefore, we have extended the implementations in the module file `nonlinear_solvers.py` such that the user can choose whether the final value or the whole history of solutions is to be returned. Each of the extended implementations now takes an extra parameter `return_x_list`. This parameter is a boolean, set to `True` if the function is supposed to return all the root approximations, or `False`, if the function should only return the final approximation. As an example, let us take a closer look at `Newton`:

```
def Newton(f, dfdx, x, eps, return_x_list=False):
    f_value = f(x)
    iteration_counter = 0
    if return_x_list:
        x_list = []
```

```
while abs(f_value) > eps and iteration_counter < 100:
    try:
        x = x - float(f_value)/dfdx(x)
    except ZeroDivisionError:
        print "Error! - derivative zero for x = ", x
        sys.exit(1)        # Abort with error

    f_value = f(x)
    iteration_counter += 1
    if return_x_list:
        x_list.append(x)

# Here, either a solution is found, or too many iterations
if abs(f_value) > eps:
    iteration_counter = -1  # i.e., lack of convergence

if return_x_list:
    return x_list, iteration_counter
else:
    return x, iteration_counter
```

The function is found in the file `nonlinear_solvers.py`.
We can now make a call

```
x, iter = Newton(f, dfdx, x=1000, eps=1e-6, return_x_list=True)
```

and get a list x returned. With knowledge of the exact solution x of $f(x) = 0$ we can compute all the errors e_n and all the associated q_n values with the compact function

```
def rate(x, x_exact):
    e = [abs(x_ - x_exact) for x_ in x]
    q = [log(e[n+1]/e[n])/log(e[n]/e[n-1])
         for n in range(1, len(e)-1, 1)]
    return q
```

The error model (6.5) works well for Newton's method and the secant method. For the bisection method, however, it works well in the beginning, but not when the solution is approached.

We can compute the rates q_n and print them nicely,

```
def print_rates(method, x, x_exact):
    q = ['%.2f' % q_ for q_ in rate(x, x_exact)]
    print method + ':'
    for q_ in q:
        print q_,
    print
```

The result for `print_rates('Newton', x, 3)` is

```
Newton:
1.01 1.02 1.03 1.07 1.14 1.27 1.51 1.80 1.97 2.00
```

indicating that $q = 2$ is the rate for Newton's method. A similar computation using the secant method, gives the rates

```
secant:
1.26 0.93 1.05 1.01 1.04 1.05 1.08 1.13 1.20 1.30 1.43
1.54 1.60 1.62 1.62
```

Here it seems that $q \approx 1.6$ is the limit.

Remark If we in the bisection method think of the length of the current interval containing the solution as the error e_n, then (6.5) works perfectly since $e_{n+1} = \frac{1}{2}e_n$, i.e., $q = 1$ and $C = \frac{1}{2}$, but if e_n is the true error $|x - x_n|$, it is easily seen from a sketch that this error can oscillate between the current interval length and a potentially very small value as we approach the exact solution. The corresponding rates q_n fluctuate widely and are of no interest.

6.6 Solving Multiple Nonlinear Algebraic Equations

So far in this chapter, we have considered a single nonlinear algebraic equation. However, *systems* of such equations arise in a number of applications, foremost nonlinear ordinary and partial differential equations. Of the previous algorithms, only Newton's method is suitable for extension to systems of nonlinear equations.

6.6.1 Abstract Notation

Suppose we have n nonlinear equations, written in the following abstract form:

$$F_0(x_0, x_1, \ldots, x_n) = 0, \tag{6.6}$$
$$F_1(x_0, x_1, \ldots, x_n) = 0, \tag{6.7}$$
$$\vdots = \vdots \tag{6.8}$$
$$F_n(x_0, x_1, \ldots, x_n) = 0. \tag{6.9}$$
$$\tag{6.10}$$

It will be convenient to introduce a *vector notation*

$$\boldsymbol{F} = (F_0, \ldots, F_1), \quad \boldsymbol{x} = (x_0, \ldots, x_n).$$

The system can now be written as $\boldsymbol{F}(\boldsymbol{x}) = \boldsymbol{0}$.

As a specific example on the notation above, the system

$$x^2 = y - x\cos(\pi x) \tag{6.11}$$
$$yx + e^{-y} = x^{-1} \tag{6.12}$$

can be written in our abstract form by introducing $x_0 = x$ and $x_1 = y$. Then

$$F_0(x_0, x_1) = x^2 - y + x\cos(\pi x) = 0,$$
$$F_1(x_0, x_1) = yx + e^{-y} - x^{-1} = 0.$$

6.6.2 Taylor Expansions for Multi-Variable Functions

We follow the ideas of Newton's method for one equation in one variable: approximate the nonlinear f by a linear function and find the root of that function. When n variables are involved, we need to approximate a *vector function* $F(x)$ by some linear function $\tilde{F} = Jx + c$, where J is an $n \times n$ matrix and c is some vector of length n.

The technique for approximating F by a linear function is to use the first two terms in a Taylor series expansion. Given the value of F and its partial derivatives with respect to x at some point x_i, we can approximate the value at some point x_{i+1} by the two first term in a Taylor series expansion around x_i:

$$F(x_{i+1}) \approx F(x_i) + \nabla F(x_i)(x_{i+1} - x_i).$$

The next terms in the expansions are omitted here and of size $||x_{i+1} - x_i||^2$, which are assumed to be small compared with the two terms above.

The expression ∇F is the matrix of all the partial derivatives of F. Component (i, j) in ∇F is

$$\frac{\partial F_i}{\partial x_j}.$$

For example, in our 2×2 system (6.11)-(6.12) we can use SymPy to compute the Jacobian:

```
>>> from sympy import *
>>> x0, x1 = symbols('x0 x1')
>>> F0 = x0**2 - x1 + x0*cos(pi*x0)
>>> F1 = x0*x1 + exp(-x1) - x0**(-1)
>>> diff(F0, x0)
-pi*x0*sin(pi*x0) + 2*x0 + cos(pi*x0)
>>> diff(F0, x1)
-1
>>> diff(F1, x0)
x1 + x0**(-2)
>>> diff(F1, x1)
x0 - exp(-x1)
```

We can then write

$$\nabla F = \begin{pmatrix} \frac{\partial F_0}{\partial x_0} & \frac{\partial F_0}{\partial x_1} \\ \frac{\partial F_1}{\partial x_0} & \frac{\partial F_1}{\partial x_1} \end{pmatrix} = \begin{pmatrix} 2x_0 + \cos(\pi x_0) - \pi x_0 \sin(\pi x_0) & -1 \\ x_1 + x_0^{-2} & x_0 - e^{-x_1} \end{pmatrix}$$

The matrix ∇F is called the *Jacobian* of F and often denoted by J.

6.6.3   Newton's Method

The idea of Newton's method is that we have some approximation x_i to the root and seek a new (and hopefully better) approximation x_{i+1} by approximating $F(x_{i+1})$ by a linear function and solve the corresponding linear system of algebraic equations. We approximate the nonlinear problem $F(x_{i+1}) = 0$ by the linear problem

$$F(x_i) + J(x_i)(x_{i+1} - x_i) = 0, \qquad (6.13)$$

where $J(x_i)$ is just another notation for $\nabla F(x_i)$. The equation (6.13) is a linear system with coefficient matrix J and right-hand side vector $F(x_i)$. We therefore write this system in the more familiar form

$$J(x_i)\delta = -F(x_i),$$

where we have introduce a symbol δ for the unknown vector $x_{i+1} - x_i$ that multiplies the Jacobian J.

The i-th iteration of Newton's method for systems of algebraic equations consists of two steps:

1. Solve the linear system $J(x_i)\delta = -F(x_i)$ with respect to δ.
2. Set $x_{i+1} = x_i + \delta$.

Solving systems of linear equations must make use of appropriate software. Gaussian elimination is the most common, and in general the most robust, method for this purpose. Python's numpy package has a module linalg that interfaces the well-known LAPACK package with high-quality and very well tested subroutines for linear algebra. The statement x = numpy.linalg.solve(A, b) solves a system $Ax = b$ with a LAPACK method based on Gaussian elimination.

When nonlinear systems of algebraic equations arise from discretization of partial differential equations, the Jacobian is very often sparse, i.e., most of its elements are zero. In such cases it is important to use algorithms that can take advantage of the many zeros. Gaussian elimination is then a slow method, and (much) faster methods are based on iterative techniques.

6.6.4   Implementation

Here is a very simple implementation of Newton's method for systems of nonlinear algebraic equations:

```
import numpy as np

def Newton_system(F, J, x, eps):
    """
    Solve nonlinear system F=0 by Newton's method.
    J is the Jacobian of F. Both F and J must be functions of x.
    At input, x holds the start value. The iteration continues
    until ||F|| < eps.
    """
```

```
    F_value = F(x)
    F_norm = np.linalg.norm(F_value, ord=2)   # 12 norm of vector
    iteration_counter = 0
    while abs(F_norm) > eps and iteration_counter < 100:
        delta = np.linalg.solve(J(x), -F_value)
        x = x + delta
        F_value = F(x)
        F_norm = np.linalg.norm(F_value, ord=2)
        iteration_counter += 1

    # Here, either a solution is found, or too many iterations
    if abs(F_norm) > eps:
        iteration_counter = -1
    return x, iteration_counter
```

We can test the function `Newton_system` with the 2×2 system (6.11)-(6.12):

```
def test_Newton_system1():
    from numpy import cos, sin, pi, exp

    def F(x):
        return np.array(
            [x[0]**2 - x[1] + x[0]*cos(pi*x[0]),
             x[0]*x[1] + exp(-x[1]) - x[0]**(-1)])

    def J(x):
        return np.array(
            [[2*x[0] + cos(pi*x[0]) - pi*x[0]*sin(pi*x[0]), -1],
             [x[1] + x[0]**(-2), x[0] - exp(-x[1])]])

    expected = np.array([1, 0])
    tol = 1e-4
    x, n = Newton_system(F, J, x=np.array([2, -1]), eps=0.0001)
    print n, x
    error_norm = np.linalg.norm(expected - x, ord=2)
    assert error_norm < tol, 'norm of error =%g' % error_norm
    print 'norm of error =%g' % error_norm
```

Here, the testing is based on the L2 norm of the error vector. Alternatively, we could test against the values of x that the algorithm finds, with appropriate tolerances. For example, as chosen for the error norm, if eps=0.0001, a tolerance of 10^{-4} can be used for x[0] and x[1].

6.7 Exercises

Exercise 6.1: Understand why Newton's method can fail

The purpose of this exercise is to understand when Newton's method works and fails. To this end, solve $\tanh x = 0$ by Newton's method and study the intermediate details of the algorithm. Start with $x_0 = 1.08$. Plot the tangent in each iteration of Newton's method. Then repeat the calculations and the plotting when $x_0 = 1.09$. Explain what you observe.

Filename: `Newton_failure.*`.

Exercise 6.2: See if the secant method fails

Does the secant method behave better than Newton's method in the problem described in Exercise 6.1? Try the initial guesses

1. $x_0 = 1.08$ and $x_1 = 1.09$
2. $x_0 = 1.09$ and $x_1 = 1.1$
3. $x_0 = 1$ and $x_1 = 2.3$
4. $x_0 = 1$ and $x_1 = 2.4$

Filename: `secant_failure.*`.

Exercise 6.3: Understand why the bisection method cannot fail

Solve the same problem as in Exercise 6.1, using the bisection method, but let the initial interval be $[-5, 3]$. Report how the interval containing the solution evolves during the iterations.
Filename: `bisection_nonfailure.*`.

Exercise 6.4: Combine the bisection method with Newton's method

An attractive idea is to combine the reliability of the bisection method with the speed of Newton's method. Such a combination is implemented by running the bisection method until we have a narrow interval, and then switch to Newton's method for speed.

Write a function that implements this idea. Start with an interval $[a, b]$ and switch to Newton's method when the current interval in the bisection method is a fraction s of the initial interval (i.e., when the interval has length $s(b - a)$). Potential divergence of Newton's method is still an issue, so if the approximate root jumps out of the narrowed interval (where the solution is known to lie), one can switch back to the bisection method. The value of s must be given as an argument to the function, but it may have a default value of 0.1.

Try the new method on $\tanh(x) = 0$ with an initial interval $[-10, 15]$.
Filename: `bisection_Newton.py`.

Exercise 6.5: Write a test function for Newton's method

The purpose of this function is to verify the implementation of Newton's method in the `Newton` function in the file `nonlinear_solvers.py`. Construct an algebraic equation and perform two iterations of Newton's method by hand or with the aid of SymPy. Find the corresponding size of $|f(x)|$ and use this as value for eps when calling `Newton`. The function should then also perform two iterations and return the same approximation to the root as you calculated manually. Implement this idea for a unit test as a test function `test_Newton()`.
Filename: `test_Newton.py`.

Exercise 6.6: Solve nonlinear equation for a vibrating beam

An important engineering problem that arises in a lot of applications is the vibrations of a clamped beam where the other end is free. This problem can be analyzed analytically, but the calculations boil down to solving the following nonlinear algebraic equation:

$$\cosh \beta \cos \beta = -1,$$

where β is related to important beam parameters through

$$\beta^4 = \omega^2 \frac{\varrho A}{EI},$$

where ϱ is the density of the beam, A is the area of the cross section, E is Young's modulus, and I is the moment of the inertia of the cross section. The most important parameter of interest is ω, which is the frequency of the beam. We want to compute the frequencies of a vibrating steel beam with a rectangular cross section having width $b = 25$ mm and height $h = 8$ mm. The density of steel is 7850 kg/m^3, and $E = 2 \cdot 10^{11}$ Pa. The moment of inertia of a rectangular cross section is $I = bh^3/12$.

a) Plot the equation to be solved so that one can inspect where the zero crossings occur.

Hint When writing the equation as $f(\beta) = 0$, the f function increases its amplitude dramatically with β. It is therefore wise to look at an equation with damped amplitude, $g(\beta) = e^{-\beta} f(\beta) = 0$. Plot g instead.

b) Compute the first three frequencies.

Filename: `beam_vib.py`.

A

Python Access

This appendix describes different technologies for either installing Python on your own computer or accessing Python in the cloud. Plain Python is very easy to install and use in cloud services, but for this book we need many add-on packages for doing scientific computations. Python together with these packages constitute a complex software eco system that is non-trivial to build, so we strongly recommend to use one of the techniques described next[1].

A.1 Required Software

The strictly required software packages for working with this book are

- Python[2] version 2.7 [25]
- Numerical Python[3] (NumPy) [19, 20] for array computing
- Matplotlib[4] [8, 9] for plotting

Desired add-on packages are

- IPython[5] [22, 23] for interactive computing
- SciTools[6] [14] for add-ons to NumPy
- ScientificPython[7] [7] for add-ons to NumPy
- pytest[8] or nose[9] for testing programs
- pip[10] for installing Python packages
- Cython[11] for compiling Python to C

---

[1] Some of the text is taken from the 4th edition of the book *A Primer on Scientifi Programming with Python*, by H. P. Langtangen.
[2] http://python.org
[3] http://www.numpy.org
[4] http://matplotlib.org
[5] http://ipython.org
[6] https://github.com/hplgit/scitools
[7] http://starship.python.net/crew/hinsen
[8] http://pytest.org/latest/
[9] https://nose.readthedocs.org
[10] http://www.pip-installer.org
[11] http://cython.org

- SymPy[12] [2] for symbolic mathematics
- SciPy[13] [10] for advanced scientific computing

Python 2 or 3?

Python comes in two versions, version 2 and 3, and these are not fully compatible. However, for the programs in this book, the differences are very small, the major one being `print`, which in Python 2 is a statement like

```
print 'a:', a, 'b:', b
```

while in Python 3 it is a function call

```
print( 'a:', a, 'b:', b)
```

The authors have written Python v2.7 code in this book in a way that makes porting to version 3.4 or later trivial: most programs will just need a fix of the `print` statement. This can be automatically done by running `2to3 prog.py` to transform a Python 2 program `prog.py` to its Python 3 counterpart. One can also use tools like `future` or `six` to easily write programs that run under both versions 2 and 3, or the `futurize` program can automatically do this for you based on v2.7 code.

Since many tools for doing scientific computing in Python are still only available for Python version 2, we use this version in the present book, but emphasize that it has to be v2.7 and not older versions.

There are different ways to get access to Python with the required packages:

1. Use a computer system at an institution where the software is installed. Such a system can also be used from your local laptop through remote login over a network.
2. Install the software on your own laptop.
3. Use a web service.

A system administrator can take the list of software packages and install the missing ones on a computer system. For the two other options, detailed descriptions are given below.

Using a web service is very straightforward, but has the disadvantage that you are constrained by the packages that are allowed to install on the service. There are services at the time of this writing that suffice for working with most of this book, but if you are going to solve more complicated mathematical problems, you will need more sophisticated mathematical Python packages, more storage and more computer resources, and then you will benefit greatly from having Python installed on your own computer.

---

[12] http://sympy.org
[13] http://scipy.org

A.2 Anaconda and Spyder

Anaconda[14] is a free Python distribution produced by Continuum Analytics and contains about 200 Python packages, as well as Python itself, for doing a wide range of scientific computations. Anaconda can be downloaded from http://continuum.io/downloads. Choose Python version 2.7.

The Integrated Development Environment (IDE) *Spyder* is included with Anaconda and is our recommended tool for writing and running Python programs on Mac and Windows, unless you have preference for a plain text editor for writing programs and a terminal window for running them.

A.2.1 Spyder on Mac

Spyder is started by typing `spyder` in a (new) Terminal application. If you get an error message *unknown locale*, you need to type the following line in the Terminal application, or preferably put the line in your $HOME/.bashrc Unix initialization file:

```
export LANG=en_US.UTF-8; export LC_ALL=en_US.UTF-8
```

A.2.2 Installation of Additional Packages

Anaconda installs the `pip` tool that is handy to install additional packages. In a Terminal application on Mac or in a PowerShell terminal on Windows, write

```
                              Terminal
pip install --user packagename
```

A.3 How to Write and Run a Python Program

You have basically three choices to develop and test a Python program:

1. use a text editor and a terminal window
2. use an Integrated Development Environment (IDE), like Spyder, which offers a window with a text editor and functionality to run programs and observe the output
3. use the IPython notebook

The IPython notebook is briefly descried in Sect. A.5, while the other two options are outlined below.

---

[14] https://store.continuum.io/cshop/anaconda/

A.3.1   The Need for a Text Editor

Since programs consist of plain text, we need to write this text with the help of another program that can store the text in a file. You have most likely extensive experience with writing text on a computer, but for writing your own programs you need special programs, called *editors*, which preserve exactly the characters you type. The widespread word processors, Microsoft Word being a primary example, are aimed at producing nice-looking reports. These programs *format* the text and are *not* acceptable tools for writing your own programs, even though they can save the document in a pure text format. Spaces are often important in Python programs, and *editors* for plain text give you complete control of the spaces and all other characters in the program file.

A.3.2   Text Editors

The most widely used editors for writing programs are Emacs and Vim, which are available on all major platforms. Some simpler alternatives for beginners are

- Linux: Gedit
- Mac OS X: TextWrangler
- Windows: Notepad++

We may mention that Python comes with an editor called Idle, which can be used to write programs on all three platforms, but running the program with command-line arguments is a bit complicated for beginners in Idle so Idle is not my favorite recommendation.

Gedit is a standard program on Linux platforms, but all other editors must be installed in your system. This is easy: just google the name, download the file, and follow the standard procedure for installation. All of the mentioned editors come with a graphical user interface that is intuitive to use, but the major popularity of Emacs and Vim is due to their rich set of short-keys so that you can avoid using the mouse and consequently edit at higher speed.

A.3.3   Terminal Windows

To run the Python program, you need a *terminal window*. This is a window where you can issue Unix commands in Linux and Mac OS X systems and DOS commands in Windows. On a Linux computer, gnome-terminal is my favorite, but other choices work equally well, such as xterm and konsole. On a Mac computer, launch the application *Utilities - Terminal*. On Windows, launch *PowerShell*.

You must first move to the right folder using the cd foldername command. Then running a python program prog.py is a matter of writing python prog.py. Whatever the program prints can be seen in the terminal window.

A.3.4 Using a Plain Text Editor and a Terminal Window

1. Create a folder where your Python programs can be located, say with name mytest under your home folder. This is most conveniently done in the terminal window since you need to use this window anyway to run the program. The command for creating a new folder is `mkdir mytest`.
2. Move to the new folder: `cd mytest`.
3. Start the editor of your choice.
4. Write a program in the editor, e.g., just the line `print 'Hello!'`. Save the program under the name `myprog1.py` in the `mytest` folder.
5. Move to the terminal window and write `python myprog1.py`. You should see the word `Hello!` being printed in the window.

A.3.5 Spyder

Spyder is a graphical application for developing and running Python programs, available on all major platforms. Spyder comes with Anaconda and some other pre-built environments for scientific computing with Python. On Ubuntu it is conveniently installed by `sudo apt-get install spyder`.

The left part of the Spyder window contains a plain text editor. Click in this window and write `print 'Hello!'` and return. Choose *Run* from the *Run* pull-down menu, and observe the output `Hello!` in the lower right window where the output from programs is visible.

You may continue with more advanced statements involving graphics:

```
import matplotlib.pyplot as plt
import numpy as np
x = np.linspace(0, 4, 101)
y = np.exp(-x)*np.sin(np.pi*x)
plt.plot(x,y)
plt.title('First test of Spyder')
plt.savefig('tmp.png')
plt.show()
```

Choosing *Run – Run* now leads to a separate window with a plot of the function $e^{-x}\sin(\pi x)$. Figure A.1 shows how the Spyder application may look like.

The plot file we generate in the above program, `tmp.png`, is by default found in the Spyder folder listed in the default text in the top of the program. You can choose *Run – Configure ...* to change this folder as desired. The program you write is written to a file `.temp.py` in the same default folder, but any name and folder can be specified in the standard *File – Save as...* menu.

A convenient feature of Spyder is that the upper right window continuously displays documentation of the statements you write in the editor to the left.

Fig. A.1 The Spyder Integrated Development Environment

A.4   The SageMathCloud and Wakari Web Services

You can avoid installing Python on your machine completely by using a web service that allows you to write and run Python programs. Computational science projects will normally require some kind of visualization and associated graphics packages, which is not possible unless the service offers IPython notebooks. There are two excellent web services with notebooks: *SageMathCloud* at https://cloud.sagemath. com/ and *Wakari* at https://www.wakari.io/wakari. At both sites you must create an account before you can write notebooks in the web browser and download them to your own computer.

A.4.1   Basic Intro to SageMathCloud

Sign in, click on *New Project*, give a title to your project and decide whether it should be private or public, click on the project when it appears in the browser, and click on *Create or Import a File, Worksheet, Terminal or Directory....* If your Python program needs graphics, you need to choose *IPython Notebook*, otherwise you can choose *File*. Write the name of the file above the row of buttons. Assuming we do not need any graphics, we create a plain Python file, say with name py1.py. By clicking *File* you are brought to a browser window with a text editor where you can write Python code. Write some code and click *Save*. To run the program, click on the plus icon (*New*), choose *Terminal*, and you have a plain Unix terminal window where you can write python py1.py to run the program. Tabs over the terminal (or editor) window make it easy to jump between the editor and the terminal. To download the file, click on *Files*, point on the relevant line with the file, and a download icon appears to the very right. The IPython notebook option works much in the same way, see Sect. A.5.

A.4.2 Basic Intro to Wakari

After having logged in at the `wakari.io` site, you automatically enter an IPython notebook with a short introduction to how the notebook can be used. Click on the *New Notebook* button to start a new notebook. Wakari enables creating and editing plain Python files too: click on the *Add file* icon in pane to the left, fill in the program name, and you enter an editor where you can write a program. Pressing *Execute* launches an IPython session in a terminal window, where you can run the program by run `prog.py` if `prog.py` is the name of the program. To download the file, select `test2.py` in the left pane and click on the *Download file* icon.

There is a pull-down menu where you can choose what type of terminal window you want: a plain Unix shell, an IPython shell, or an IPython shell with Matplotlib for plotting. Using the latter, you can run plain Python programs or commands with graphics. Just choose the type of terminal and click on +*Tab* to make a new terminal window of the chosen type.

A.4.3 Installing Your Own Python Packages

Both SageMathCloud and Wakari let you install your own Python packages. To install any package packagename available at PyPi[15], run

```
———————————————— Terminal ————————————————
pip install --user packagename
```

To install the SciTools package, which is useful when working with this book, run the command

```
———————————————— Terminal ————————————————
pip install --user -e \
    git+https://github.com/hplgit/scitools.git#egg=scitools
```

A.5 Writing IPython Notebooks

The IPython notebook is a splendid interactive tool for doing science, but it can also be used as a platform for developing Python code. You can either run it locally on your computer or in a web service like SageMathCloud or Wakari. Installation on your computer is trivial on Ubuntu, just `sudo apt-get install ipython-notebook`, and also on Windows and Mac[16] by using Anaconda or Enthought Canopy for the Python installation.

The interface to the notebook is a web browser: you write all the code and see all the results in the browser window. There are excellent YouTube videos on how to use the IPython notebook, so here we provide a very quick "step zero" to get anyone started.

---

[15] https://pypi.python.org/pypi
[16] http://ipython.org/install.html

A.5.1   A Simple Program in the Notebook

Start the IPython notebook locally by the command `ipython notebook` or go to SageMathCloud or Wakari as described above. The default input area is a *cell* for Python code. Type

```
g = 9.81
v0 = 5
t = 0.6
y = v0*t - 0.5*g*t**2
```

in a cell and *run the cell* by clicking on *Run Selected* (notebook running locally on your machine) or on the "play" button (notebook running in the cloud). This action will execute the Python code and initialize the variables g, v0, t, and y. You can then write `print y` in a new cell, execute that cell, and see the output of this statement in the browser. It is easy to go back to a cell, edit the code, and re-execute it.

To download the notebook to your computer, choose the *File – Download as* menu and select the type of file to be downloaded: the original notebook format (`.ipynb` file extension) or a plain Python program version of the notebook (`.py` file extension).

A.5.2   Mixing Text, Mathematics, Code, and Graphics

The real strength of IPython notebooks arises when you want to write a report to document how a problem can be explored and solved. As a teaser, open a new notebook, click in the first cell, and choose *Markdown* as format (notebook running locally) or switch from *Code* to *Markdown* in the pull-down menu (notebook in the cloud). The cell is now a text field where you can write text with Markdown[17] syntax. Mathematics can be entered as LaTeX code. Try some text with inline mathematics and an equation on a separate line:

```
Plot the curve $y=f(x)$, where

$$
f(x) = e^{-x}\sin (2\pi x),\quad x\in [0, 4]
$$
```

Execute the cell and you will see nicely typeset mathematics in the browser. In the new cell, add some code to plot $f(x)$:

```
import numpy as np
import matplotlib.pyplot as plt
%matplotlib inline  # make plots inline in the notebook

x = np.linspace(0, 4, 101)
y = np.exp(-x)*np.sin(2*pi*x)
plt.plot(x, y, 'b-')
plt.xlabel('x'); plt.ylabel('y')
```

---

[17] http://daringfireball.net/projects/markdown/syntax

Executing these statements results in a plot in the browser, see Fig. A.2. It was popular to start the notebook by `ipython notebook -pylab` to import everything from `numpy` and `matplotlib.pyplot` and make all plots inline, but the `-pylab` option is now officially discouraged[18]. If you want the notebook to behave more as MATLAB and not use the `np` and `plt` prefix, you can instead of the first three lines above write `%pylab`.

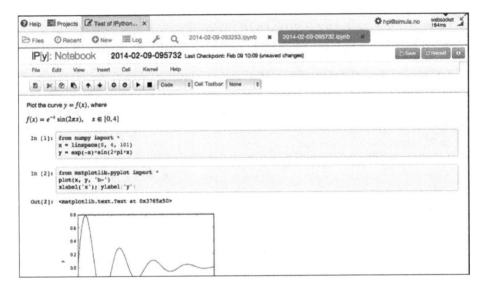

Fig. A.2 Example on an IPython notebook

---

[18] http://carreau.github.io/posts/10-No-PyLab-Thanks.ipynb.html

References

1. L. Baochuan. *Introduction to Numerical Methods*. 2015. http://en.wikibooks.org/wiki/Introduction_to_Numerical_Methods.

2. O. Certik et al. SymPy: Python library for symbolic mathematics. http://sympy.org/.

3. S. D. Conte and C. de Boor. *Elementary Numerical Analysis - An Algorithmic Approach*. McGraw-Hill, third edition, 1980.

4. I. Danaila, P. Joly, S. M. Kaber, and M. Postel. *An Introduction to Scientific Computing*. Springer, 2007.

5. C. Greif and U. M. Ascher. *A First Course in Numerical Methods*. Computational Science and Engineering. SIAM, 2011.

6. D. W. Harder and R. *Numerical Analysis for Engineering*. 2015. https://ece.uwaterloo.ca/~dwharder/NumericalAnalysis/.

7. ScientificPython software package. http://starship.python.net/crew/hinsen.

8. J. D. Hunter. Matplotlib: a 2D graphics environment. *Computing in Science & Engineering*, 9, 2007.

9. J. D. Hunter et al. Matplotlib: Software package for 2D graphics. http://matplotlib.org/.

10. E. Jones, T. E. Oliphant, P. Peterson, et al. SciPy scientific computing library for Python. http://scipy.org.

11. J. Kiusalaas. *Numerical Methods in Engineering with Python*. Cambridge, second edition, 2014.

12. H. P. Langtangen. DocOnce publishing platform. https://github.com/hplgit/doconce.

13. H. P. Langtangen. *A Primer on Scientific Programming with Python*. Texts in Computational Science and Engineering. Springer, fifth edition, 2016.

14. H. P. Langtangen and J. H. Ring. SciTools: Software tools for scientific computing. https://github.com/hplgit/scitools.

15. R. LeVeque. *Finite Difference Methods for Ordinary and Partial Differential Equations: Steady-State and Time-Dependent Problems*. SIAM, 2007.

16. T. Lyche and J.-L. Merrien. *Exercises in Computational Mathematics with MATLAB*. Springer, 2014.

17. C. Moler. *Numerical Computing with MATLAB*. SIAM, 2004. http://se.mathworks.com/moler/chapters.html.

18. S. Nakamura. *Numerical Analysis and Graphic Visualization with Matlab*. Prentice Hall, second edition, 2002.

19. T. E. Oliphant. Python for scientific computing. *Computing in Science & Engineering*, 9, 2007.

20. T. E. Oliphant et al. NumPy array processing package for Python. http://www.numpy.org.

21. S. Otto and J. P. Denier. *An Introduction to Programming and Numerical Methods in MATLAB*. Springer, 2005.

22. F. Perez and B. E. Granger. IPython: a system for interactive scientific computing. *Computing in Science & Engineering*, 9, 2007.

23. F. Perez, B. E. Granger, et al. IPython software package for interactive scientific computing. http://ipython.org/.

24. W. H. Press, S. A. Teukolsky, W. T. Vetterling, and B. P. Flannery. *Numerical Recipes*. Cambridge, 1992. http://www.nrbook.com/a/bookcpdf.php.

25. Python programming language. http://python.org.

26. G. Recktenwald. *Numerical Methods with MATLAB: Implementations and Applications.* Prentice-Hall, 2000. http://web.cecs.pdx.edu/~gerry/nmm/.

27. G. Sewell. *The Numerical Solution of Ordinary and Partial Differential Equations.* Wiley, 2005.

28. T. Siauw and A. Bayen. *An Introduction to MATLAB Programming and Numerical Methods for Engineers.* Academic Press, 2014. http://www.sciencedirect.com/science/book/9780124202283.

29. L. N. Trefethen. *Spectral Methods in MATLAB.* SIAM, 2000.

30. L. N. Trefethen. *Approximation Theory and Approximation Practice.* SIAM, 2012.

31. T. Young and M. J. Mohlenkamp. *Introduction to Numerical Methods and MATLAB Programming for Engineers.* 2015. https://www.math.ohiou.edu/courses/math3600/book.pdf.

Permissions

All chapters in this book were first published in PCP, by Springer by Svein Linge and Hans Petter Langtangen; hereby published with permission under the Creative Commons Attribution License or equivalent. Every chapter published in this book has been scrutinized by our experts. Their significance has been extensively debated. The topics covered herein carry significant information for a comprehensive understanding. They may even be implemented as practical applications or may be referred to as a beginning point for further studies.

We would like to thank the editorial team for lending their expertise to make the book truly unique. They have played a crucial role in the development of this book. Without their invaluable contributions this book wouldn't have been possible. They have made vital efforts to compile up to date information on the varied aspects of this subject to make this book a valuable addition to the collection of many professionals and students.

This book was conceptualized with the vision of imparting up-to-date and integrated information in this field. To ensure the same, a matchless editorial board was set up. Every individual on the board went through rigorous rounds of assessment to prove their worth. After which they invested a large part of their time researching and compiling the most relevant data for our readers.

The editorial board has been involved in producing this book since its inception. They have spent rigorous hours researching and exploring the diverse topics which have resulted in the successful publishing of this book. They have passed on their knowledge of decades through this book. To expedite this challenging task, the publisher supported the team at every step. A small team of assistant editors was also appointed to further simplify the editing procedure and attain best results for the readers.

Apart from the editorial board, the designing team has also invested a significant amount of their time in understanding the subject and creating the most relevant covers. They scrutinized every image to scout for the most suitable representation of the subject and create an appropriate cover for the book.

The publishing team has been an ardent support to the editorial, designing and production team. Their endless efforts to recruit the best for this project, has resulted in the accomplishment of this book. They are a veteran in the field of academics and their pool of knowledge is as vast as their experience in printing. Their expertise and guidance has proved useful at every step. Their uncompromising quality standards have made this book an exceptional effort. Their encouragement from time to time has been an inspiration for everyone.

The publisher and the editorial board hope that this book will prove to be a valuable piece of knowledge for students, practitioners and scholars across the globe.

Index